"This book is a rigorous, compelling, timely and highly readable contribution to the growing literature on migration and humanitarian governance. It helps fill a critical gap in our understanding of IOM as actor of ever-increasing significance in global, regional, national and local responses to displacement. It is essential reading for students, researchers, practitioners and policy-makers working these issues."

James Milner, Carleton University, Canada

"If you only read one book about IOM, read this. Bradley provides a thorough, balanced and engaging analysis of an organization which very few scholars have examined. The book explores IOM's evolution, expansion, and limitations. It is a must read for students and scholars interested in global migration governance."

Nina Hall, John Hopkins University, USA

"In this clear, insightful and accessible introduction, Bradley explores the evolution and workings of IOM, now the UN-affiliated migration agency. This book should be mandatory reading for all students of international organisations, humanitarianism and migration and refugee studies."

Cathryn Costello, Professor of Refugee and
Migration Law, University of Oxford, UK

THE INTERNATIONAL ORGANIZATION FOR MIGRATION

Since its establishment in 1951, the International Organization for Migration (IOM) has expanded from a small, regionally specific, logistically focused outfit into a major international organization involved in an almost dizzying array of activities related to human mobility. In 2016, IOM joined the UN system and has rebranded itself as the "UN migration agency." Despite its dramatic expansion and increasing influence, IOM remains understudied.

This book provides an accessible, incisive introduction to IOM, focusing on its humanitarian activities and responses to forced migration – work that now makes up the majority of the organization's budget, staff, and field presence. IOM's humanitarian work is often overlooked or dismissed as a veil for its involvement in other activities that serve states' interests in restricting migration. In contrast, Bradley argues that understanding IOM's involvement in humanitarian action and work with displaced persons is pivotal to comprehending its evolution and contemporary significance. Examining tensions and controversies surrounding the agency's activities, including in the complex cases of Haiti and Libya, the book considers how IOM's structure, culture, and internal and external power struggles have shaped its behavior. It demonstrates how IOM has grown by acting as an entrepreneur, cultivating autonomy and influence well beyond its formal mandate.

The International Organization for Migration is essential reading for students and scholars of migration, humanitarianism, and international organizations.

Megan Bradley is an associate professor of political science and international development studies at McGill University, where her research focuses on refugees and forced migration, human rights, humanitarianism, transitional justice, and disasters.

Routledge Global Institutions Series

Edited by Thomas G. Weiss
The CUNY Graduate Center, New York, USA

Rorden Wilkinson
University of Sussex, Brighton, UK

About the series

The "Global Institutions Series" provides cutting-edge books about many aspects of what we know as "global governance." It emerges from our shared frustrations with the state of available knowledge – electronic and print-wise – for research and teaching. The series is designed as a resource for those interested in exploring issues of international organization and global governance. And since the first volumes appeared in 2005, we have taken significant strides toward filling many conceptual gaps.

The series consists of two related "streams" distinguished by their blue and red covers. The blue volumes, comprising the majority of the books in the series, provide user-friendly and short (usually no more than 50,000 words) but authoritative guides to major global and regional organizations, as well as key issues in the global governance of security, the environment, human rights, poverty, and humanitarian action, among others. The books with red covers are designed to present original research and serve as extended and more specialized treatments of issues pertinent for advancing understanding about global governance.

The books in each of the streams are written by experts in the field, ranging from the most senior and respected authors to first-rate scholars at the beginning of their careers. In combination, the components of the series serve as key resources for faculty, students, and practitioners alike. The works in the blue stream have value as core and complementary readings in courses on, among other things, international organization, global governance, international law, international relations, and international political economy; the red volumes allow further reflection and investigation in these and related areas.

The books in the series also provide a segue to the foundation volume that offers the most comprehensive textbook treatment available dealing with all the major issues, approaches, institutions, and actors in contemporary global governance.

The second edition of our edited work *International Organization and Global Governance* (2018) contains essays by many of the authors in the series.

Understanding global governance – past, present, and future – is far from a finished journey. The books in this series nonetheless represent significant steps toward a better way of conceiving contemporary problems and issues as well as, hopefully, doing something to improve world order. We value the feedback from our readers and their role in helping shape the ongoing development of the series.

Moral Obligations and Sovereignty in International Relations (2019)
A Genealogy of Humanitarianism
Andrea Paras

Protecting the Internally Displaced (2019)
Rhetoric and Reality
Phil Orchard

Accessing and Implementing Human Rights and Justice (2019)
Kurt Mills and Melissa Labonte

The IMF, the WTO & the Politics of Economic Surveillance (2019)
Martin Edwards

Multinational Rapid Response Mechanisms (2019)
John Karlsrud and Yf Rykers

Towards a Global Consensus Against Corruption (2019)
International Agreements as Products of Diffusion and Signals of Commitment
Mathis Lohaus

Negotiating Trade in Uncertain Worlds (2019)
Misperception and Contestation in EU-West Africa Relations
Clara Weinhardt

Negotiations in the World Trade Organization (2019)
Design and Performance
Michal Parizek

The International Organization for Migration (2020)
Challenges, Commitments, Complexities
Megan Bradley

A complete list of titles can be viewed online here: www.routledge.com/ Global-Institutions/book-series/GI.

THE INTERNATIONAL ORGANIZATION FOR MIGRATION

Challenges, Commitments, Complexities

Megan Bradley

LONDON AND NEW YORK

First published 2020
by Routledge
2 Park Square, Milton Park, Abingdon, Oxon OX14 4RN

and by Routledge
52 Vanderbilt Avenue, New York, NY 10017

Routledge is an imprint of the Taylor & Francis Group, an informa business

© 2020 Megan Bradley

The right of Megan Bradley to be identified as author of this work has been asserted by her in accordance with sections 77 and 78 of the Copyright, Designs and Patents Act 1988.

All rights reserved. No part of this book may be reprinted or reproduced or utilised in any form or by any electronic, mechanical, or other means, now known or hereafter invented, including photocopying and recording, or in any information storage or retrieval system, without permission in writing from the publishers.

Trademark notice: Product or corporate names may be trademarks or registered trademarks, and are used only for identification and explanation without intent to infringe.

British Library Cataloguing-in-Publication Data
A catalogue record for this book is available from the British Library

Library of Congress Cataloging-in-Publication Data
Names: Bradley, Megan, 1980– author.
Title: The International Organization for Migration : challenges, commitments, complexities / Megan Bradley.
Description: Abingdon, Oxon ; New York, NY : Routledge, 2020. | Series: Global institutions | Includes bibliographical references and index.
Identifiers: LCCN 2019039375 | ISBN 9781138818934 (hardback) | ISBN 9781138818965 (paperback) | ISBN 9781315744896 (ebook)
Subjects: LCSH: International Organization for Migration. | Humanitarian assistance—International cooperation.
Classification: LCC JV6008 .B73 2020 | DDC 362.87/526—dc23
LC record available at https://lccn.loc.gov/2019039375

ISBN: 978-1-138-81893-4 (hbk)
ISBN: 978-1-138-81896-5 (pbk)
ISBN: 978-1-315-74489-6 (ebk)

Typeset in Times New Roman
by Apex CoVantage, LLC

Printed in the United Kingdom
by Henry Ling Limited

CONTENTS

List of tables	*x*
About the author	*xi*
Acknowledgements	*xii*
Abbreviations	*xiv*
Introduction	1
1 A servant of state masters? IOM's mandate, structure, and culture	17
2 An evolving humanitarian entrepreneur	47
3 IOM in action: contributions and controversies in Haiti and Libya	76
4 The UN migration agency? IOM–UN relations	99
5 Conclusion	126
Selected bibliography	*136*
Index	*138*

TABLES

1.1 Top donors to IOM: voluntary contributions to operational programs (member states and European Commission), 2007–2016   28

1.2 Geographic distribution of IOM offices, 2019   31

1.3 IOM directors general, 1951–2019   34

ABOUT THE AUTHOR

Megan Bradley is an associate professor of political science and international development studies at McGill University, where her research focuses on refugees and forced migration, human rights, humanitarianism, transitional justice, and disasters. She is the author of *Refugee Repatriation: Justice, Responsibility and Redress* (2013), editor of *Forced Migration, Reconciliation, and Justice* (2015) and co-editor of *Refugees' Roles in Resolving Displacement and Building Peace: Beyond Beneficiaries* (2019). From 2012 to 2014, she was a Fellow in the Foreign Policy Program at the Brookings Institution in Washington, D.C., where she worked with the Brookings Project on Internal Displacement. She has also worked with the Office of the United Nations High Commissioner for Refugees (UNHCR) and the International Development Research Centre (IDRC), and served as the Cadieux-Léger Fellow at Global Affairs Canada.

ACKNOWLEDGEMENTS

This book is part of a broader study on the International Organization for Migration (IOM) supported by the Social Sciences and Humanities Research Council of Canada (SSHRC). I would like to express my gratitude to SSHRC, and to the many people who have assisted me in this work. First and foremost, I would like to thank all those who shared their time and views with me in interviews I have been conducting on IOM since 2015. Without the candor and enthusiasm of the many IOM and UN officials, member state representatives, advocates, and other experts who shared their experiences, ideas, and insights, this project would not have been possible. I would also like to thank Sarah Rhodes and Joanna Soedring from the Bodleian Social Science Library at the University of Oxford, who provided valuable help in accessing material on IOM and its forerunners contained in the Refugee Studies Centre "grey literature" collection. The introduction to this book includes parts of the following article: Megan Bradley (2017) "The International Organization for Migration (IOM): Gaining Power in the Forced Migration Regime," *Refuge* 33(1): 91–106. I am grateful to *Refuge* for permission to reproduce this work here.

This book, and my wider project on IOM, have benefited enormously from the support of several exceptional research assistants, including Victoria Spiteri and Leyla Prezelin. I am especially indebted to Merve Erdilmen for her excellent work examining the evolution of IOM's institutional discourses, and to Isabelle Lemay for her careful and diligent research on IOM's funding, and activities in Haiti and Libya.

I am thankful for the many colleagues who have shaped my thoughts on IOM, including James Milner, Jeff Crisp, Beth Ferris, Martin Geiger, Nick Micinski, Phil Orchard, and Cathryn Costello. I am particularly grateful to Angela Sherwood, Nina Hall and Blair Peruniak for reading and sharing helpful feedback on the manuscript, and also to the peer reviewers who provided such perceptive and constructive suggestions. Additional thanks are due to Tom Weiss and Rorden

Wilkinson, editors of the Global Institutions series, for their timely comments, and to the team at Routledge for their support and patience. My friends and colleagues at McGill University have been a source of happiness and help over the long gestation of this project. It is a sign of my good fortune that I have too many people to name here. I have presented my work on IOM at conferences of the American Political Science Association, the International Studies Association, the International Association for the Study of Forced Migration, and the Canadian Association for Refugee and Forced Migration Studies, and at workshops and seminar series hosted by the University of Oxford, the University of Pennsylvania, and McGill University's Centre for International Peace and Security Studies. I am grateful to the many discussants and other colleagues who shared their views and questions at these events, which have in turn influenced this book.

And now, words fail me. My deepest thanks go to my family, especially Tim and Vivian. They are my greatest help and my greatest joy.

ABBREVIATIONS

AVR	Assisted voluntary return
CAR	Central African Republic
CCCM	Camp coordination and camp management
CEB	Chief Executives Board for Coordination
CERF	Central Emergency Response Fund
CMA	Camp management agency
CTBTO	Comprehensive Nuclear-Test-Ban Treaty Organization
DCIM	Directorate for Combatting Illegal Migration (Libya)
DESA	United Nations Department of Economic and Social Affairs
DMM	Department of Migration Management
DOE	Department of Operations and Emergencies
DRC	Democratic Republic of Congo
DRR	Disarmament, demobilization, and reintegration
DTM	Displacement Tracking Matrix
ECOSOC	United Nations Economic and Social Council
ERU	Emergency Response Unit
EU	European Union
GMDAC	Global Migration Data Analysis Centre
HLP	Housing, land, and property
HSI	Haiti Stabilization Initiative
HTI	Haiti Transition Initiative
IAEA	International Atomic Energy Agency
IASC	Inter-Agency Standing Committee
ICEM	Intergovernmental Committee for European Migration
ICM	Intergovernmental Committee for Migration
ICRC	International Committee of the Red Cross
IDP	Internally displaced person
ILO	International Labour Organization

IO	International organization
IR	International relations
IRO	International Refugee Organization
IOM	International Organization for Migration
MCOF	Migration Crisis Operational Framework
MICIC	Migrants in Countries in Crisis Initiative
MiGOF	Migration Governance Framework
NGO	Non-governmental organization
OCHA	Office for the Coordination of Humanitarian Affairs
OHCHR	Office of the United Nations High Commissioner for Human Rights
PICMME	Provisional Intergovernmental Committee for the Movement of Migrants from Europe
PREPEP	*Programme de Revitalisation et de Promotion de l'Entente et de la Paix*
UN	United Nations
UNDG	United Nations Development Group
UNHCR	Office of the United Nations High Commissioner for Refugees
UNRWA	UN Relief and Works Agency for Palestine Refugees in the Near East
UNSMIL	UN Support Mission in Libya
VHR	Voluntary humanitarian return
WFP	World Food Programme
WTO	World Trade Organization

INTRODUCTION

- *The tip of the iceberg: researching IOM*
- *IOM's expanding humanitarian engagement: background*
- *From the margins to the center: rethinking IOM through its humanitarian engagements*
- *Structure*

As aid agencies scramble to assist in humanitarian emergencies from massive earthquakes to civil wars, a sea of logos emerges on tarps and tents, shirts, and signs, representing the groups who pour in from around the world. Amidst the well-known emblems of UN agencies, the Red Cross, and major NGOs like Oxfam and Médecins Sans Frontières (Doctors Without Borders), a less familiar logo is now often seen: the blue and white insignia of the International Organization for Migration (IOM).

Since its establishment in 1951 as the Provisional Intergovernmental Committee for the Movement of Migrants from Europe (PICMME), IOM has expanded from a small, regionally specific, logistically focused outfit into a major international organization (IO) involved in an almost dizzying array of activities related to human mobility, including humanitarian responses to forced migration. IOM's humanitarian work, broadly construed, runs the gambit from typical aid efforts such as food and water distribution and shelter construction, to more specialized activities like emergency evacuations, data collection, camp management, disaster preparedness, and refugee resettlement. Recognized by its member states as the "leading inter-governmental organization in the field of migration," IOM was established outside the UN system but has long worked closely with UN agencies, including the Office of the UN High Commissioner for Refugees (UNHCR).[1] In September 2016, IOM joined the "UN family" as a related organization in the UN system, and has rebranded itself as the UN migration agency.[2]

2 Introduction

IOM's self-professed goal is to promote managed migration "for the benefit of all."[3] More specifically, the agency aims "to help ensure the orderly and humane management of migration, to promote international cooperation on migration issues, to assist in the search for practical solutions to migration problems and to provide humanitarian assistance to migrants in need, including refugees and internally displaced people."[4] Migration management serves as a broad umbrella under which IOM organizes its activities in four areas: (i) migration and development; (ii) facilitating migration; (iii) regulating migration; and (iv) responding to forced migration.[5] The agency's rapid growth, particularly since the 1990s, reflects states' keen interest in these issues: IOM's member state ranks swelled from 67 in 1998 to 173 in 2019, while its budget ballooned from US$242.2 million in 1998 to US$1.8 billion in 2018 – a sevenfold increase.[6] With more than 400 field locations and over 12,600 staff members, IOM is now among the largest inter-governmental organizations worldwide.[7]

Despite this dramatic expansion, IOM remains remarkably understudied.[8] To the limited extent that researchers have examined IOM, the focus has typically been on the contested notion of migration management, and IOM's involvement in controversial activities such as working with migrants in detention, and the purportedly voluntary return of failed asylum seekers and other migrants.[9] Although IOM now asserts a role for itself in protecting migrants' rights, it lacks a formal legal protection mandate, and some suggest that the agency has thrived first and foremost by serving as a compliant executor for states looking to have their migration dirty work done by a partner that won't talk back about principles.[10] In the limited literature on IOM, the agency's restrictive migration management activities are often portrayed as revealing its true institutional character, while its humanitarian work is overlooked, dismissed as window dressing, or critiqued as a veil for its efforts to constrain mobility in line with state interests.[11] Unsurprisingly, the story is more complex. Although it is often assumed that IOM's "bread-and-butter" is work with economic migrants, much of IOM's expansion is attributable to its increased involvement in humanitarian emergencies and "post-crisis" situations, activities that have had important effects – positive and negative, intended and unintended – on "beneficiaries," states, the humanitarian system, and IOM itself, and merits closer analysis as IOM continues to grow. This book provides a brief introduction to IOM, arguing that understanding IOM's involvement in humanitarian action and with displaced persons is pivotal to understanding the organization's evolution and influence. It examines the development and implications of IOM's work with forced migrants and in humanitarian operations, exploring the characteristics, tensions, and controversies surrounding the agency's activities, particularly over the last 30 years.[12]

This discussion is premised on the recognition that there is no clear line dividing forced and voluntary movement, or separating IOM's work in the humanitarian sector, development activities, and other aspects of migration management. Longstanding IOM staff insist that the agency is and has always been a humanitarian actor, even if it has sometimes undermined itself as such.[13] Others question this designation, arguing that the humanitarian label "effaces the coercive practices inherent" in IOM's "ordering of movement," and its involvement in activities such as migrant detention that are seen by many as incompatible with human rights and humanitarian values.[14] In considering IOM's evolution as a humanitarian actor, my intention is not to minimize such ethical concerns, but to accurately position IOM among the growing ranks of institutions with multiple "hats," mandates, and interests that engage in humanitarian work, generating new tensions, possibilities, and problems. I use the term "humanitarian" broadly to refer to efforts to respond to emergencies and their aftermath, recognizing the contested, risky nature of the crisis-talk that pervades the humanitarian world, especially in relation to migration. Crisis-talk can call attention to populations in urgent need of help, but can also fuel fear and restrictive reactions such as border closures and deportations.[15] Normatively, humanitarian responses to crisis situations are to focus on saving lives and reducing suffering. Humanitarianism and human rights protection are not identical endeavors, but humanitarianism is increasingly also understood to require a clear commitment to protecting rights.[16]

This introduction sets the stage for this discussion. First, I situate this study in relation to prior research on IOM. Second, I provide a brief overview of IOM's organizational development and engagement in humanitarian affairs. Third, I detail the central arguments advanced in this work, and the structure of the book.

The tip of the iceberg: researching IOM

IOM has produced several detailed accounts of its own organizational development and activities, and regularly publishes reports on its wide-ranging programs.[17] Independent research on IOM is, however, thin. In contrast to the numerous advocacy organizations that closely monitor and report on UNHCR, human rights NGOs rarely undertake focused analyses of IOM, despite suspicion in some quarters about the organization and its work.[18] Although scholarly interest in IOM is growing, the existing academic literature on IOM is "fragmented and heterogeneous."[19] Few studies concentrate squarely on IOM, but investigate the agency indirectly, through the lens of concepts such as migration management, or in terms of its involvement with issues such as trafficking or returns.[20] Although important studies have emerged in recent years on the organization's early history, issues such as IOM's member state politics, the varying approaches and influence of IOM's directors general, and the organization's culture and internal dynamics remain almost completely unexamined.[21]

Scholars are divided on the extent to which IOM has the power to meaningfully shape the governance and experience of migration. Skeptics such as Castles, de Haas, and Miller argue that IOM "lacks the capacity to bring about significant change," while Martin highlights the organization's maturation and increasing influence, contending that IOM has "the strongest capabilities to take on the range of activities needed if an international migration regime were to be adopted."[22] Given IOM's reputation for efficiency, logistical prowess, and flexibility, some characterize IOM as a quintessentially neoliberal agency, available to states looking to outsource complex, tedious, or unsavory work. Others

4 Introduction

elucidate the ways in which IOM, from local to global levels, shapes understandings and experiences of migration through its involvement in policy development, international dialogues and negotiations, data collection and research, trainings, information campaigns, and "borderwork."[23]

IOM embraces an astoundingly broad definition of a migrant as "any person who is moving or has moved across an international border or within a State away from his/her habitual place of residence, regardless of (1) the person's legal status; (2) whether the movement is voluntary or involuntary; (3) what the causes for the movement are; or (4) what the length of stay is."[24] This definition includes all those slotted into the fraught categories that structure policy, practice, and research in relation to people "on the move," including labor migrants, those pursuing family reunification, refugees, and internally displaced persons (IDPs). IOM is active globally, but most of its interventions unfold in the global South, where the lion's share of migrants remain. By IOM's own estimates, the vast majority of the migrants with whom it works directly are IDPs in conflict and disaster situations. For example, in 2014 IOM assisted almost 20 million migrants, and 19.6 million – some 98 percent – were IDPs or other migrants in crisis situations.[25] In contrast, in the same year, IOM resettled 121,000 refugees, trained 38,400 migrants, assisted 6,200 trafficked individuals, repatriated 13,800 refugees, and returned 43,700 other migrants, often from European states to their countries of origin.[26]

IOM is involved in myriad other activities that are not captured in such statistics, and the comparatively low number of individuals involved in IOM's return, anti-trafficking, and migrant training programs does not mean that these are not critical interventions to study. However, it is striking that while IOM's operations are by many measures overwhelmingly weighted towards work in the global South, particularly with IDPs, this is rarely reflected in how the organization presents itself, or in the evolving research base on IOM. Rather, most research concentrates on IOM's involvement in governing international migration, particularly in relation to Europe, concentrating on topics such as border control, information campaigns, returns, anti-trafficking, and migration policy development.[27] This distribution reveals as much about the political economies of knowledge production in the global North as it does about the activities of IOM writ large. In this sense, most research on IOM examines only the tip of the iceberg, overlooking the bulk of the agency's operational work.

IOM's expanding humanitarian engagement: background

After its establishment in 1951, PICMME transformed in 1952 into the Intergovernmental Committee for European Migration (ICEM), rebranded in 1980 as the Intergovernmental Committee for Migration (ICM), and finally emerged in 1989 as the International Organization for Migration. IOM and its precursors were tasked with facilitating orderly migration flows generally, including the "migration of refugees" (ICEM Constitution, Article 1.3). IOM has never had an explicit legal mandate to protect the rights of migrants. That is, it does not have a formally assigned, specific responsibility to defend migrants' rights, and is not tasked with overseeing international laws on migrants' rights – indeed, there is no comprehensive international convention on migrants' rights (the International Convention on the Protection of the Rights of Migrant Workers and Members of their Families applies to only a relatively small subset of people on the move worldwide). Some of IOM's member states see this as a key strength of the organization; for its part, "IOM has come to see protection falling within its mandate, although others might contest the extent of the agency's commitment to protection principles."[28]

IOM's Constitution indicates that its member states must have a "demonstrated interest in the principle of free movement of persons."[29] While minimalistic, for decades this expression of normative commitment served the important political function of precluding the membership of Communist states that prevented citizens from leaving their territories. Like UNHCR, the organization's work was initially focused on Europe, but this restriction was eventually lifted in light of the need for coordinated responses to migration further afield. As Elie points out, both UNHCR and PICMME were "offsprings of the IRO [International Refugee Organization]," the body established in the aftermath of World War II to deal with the millions of refugees spread across Europe, "but neither were its true successor."[30] UNHCR was delegated to take on IRO's legal protection work, but the United States, which dominated negotiations over the establishment of both UNHCR and PICMME, opposed the creation of an operational UN agency with responsibility for (forced) migrants. Indeed, the US Congress decreed in 1951 that no American funding for responding to displacement and population challenges in Europe could be "allocated to any international organization which has in its membership any Communist-dominated or Communist-controlled country."[31] This initially precluded a strong operational role for UNHCR, and prompted the establishment of PICMME outside of the UN system, with no Communist member states. PICMME inherited the IRO's fleet of ships, and started using them to move migrants, including refugees, from Europe to the Americas, Australia, and New Zealand.

Although IOM (and its precursors) has long represented itself as a migration agency with a broad interest in the movement of people, in the contemporary context and throughout much of its history, the organization has worked predominantly with displaced persons, whether refugees or IDPs, and with migrants in precarious circumstances, such as migrant workers affected by the outbreak of war.[32] For instance, by 1974 some 90 percent of those supported by ICEM were refugees.[33] Despite the agency's long history of engagement with displaced populations, it has often "been dismissed by scholars as a significant international actor in its own right. Throughout its existence, in fact, it frequently has been derided as a 'travel agency,' booking passages for all kinds of migrants."[34] When the IOM Constitution was adopted in 1989, several of its objectives pertained directly to the organization's work with forced migrants, and in the humanitarian sector generally, providing a foundation for more recent expanded humanitarian engagement. According to Perruchoud, the objectives guiding the development

6 Introduction

of the IOM Constitution included fortifying the organization's "basic humanitarian character and orientation," and underscoring the importance of cooperation among states and international agencies on refugee issues, and on migration more broadly.[35]

IOM's sometimes contradictory and controversial activities reflect not only its lack of an explicit legal protection mandate, but also its governance structure, and its historical status as an inter-governmental organization outside – but closely linked to – the UN system. IOM has to a significant extent adopted human rights discourse; for instance, its most important institutional policies released over the last 15 years explicitly cite human rights standards and commitments, and the majority of speeches delivered by senior IOM officials in the 12-year period from 2006 to 2017 refer to migrants' rights and protection.[36] Yet views on IOM's roles and responsibilities vary significantly within the organization, particularly between its two main operational divisions, the Department of Migration Management and the larger Department of Operations and Emergencies. The former concentrates on "mainstream" migration – that is, movement outside of emergency situations – while the latter is responsible for IOM's humanitarian operations, although both departments affect forced migrants in a range of situations.[37] IOM's member states, which govern the organization through the IOM Council, have for much of the agency's history valued and capitalized on IOM's ability to work on the edges of the UN system, where it can execute programs that states wish to see implemented, unfettered by rigorous formal protection responsibilities. The agency is almost entirely dependent on project-based funding; while many IOs receive funding from states to implement programs encompassing a diverse range of activities, states pay IOM to provide particular services, packaged as discrete projects. More than 97 percent of contributions to IOM are earmarked to particular projects.[38] In the context of this funding structure, IOM has agreed to implement initiatives that arguably constrain rather than advance migrants' rights and well-being, fostering the perception that IOM is simply a servant of its state masters. At the same time, key member states and leaders within IOM itself have advocated more explicit protection commitments and a closer relationship with the UN, culminating in the 2016 Agreement between the United Nations and the International Organization for Migration, through which IOM became a related organization in the UN system, unanimously acknowledged by member states as an "essential contributor in the field of human mobility, [including] in the protection of migrants."[39]

Preceding these developments, in 2007 IOM member states adopted a new vision for the organization that identified twelve strategic priorities, many of which relate to an increased role for the agency vis-à-vis forced migration. These include enhancing "the humane and orderly management of migration and the effective respect for the human rights of migrants in accordance with international law"; increasing efforts to tackle human smuggling, trafficking, and other forms of "irregular migration"; participating in coordinated inter-agency humanitarian operations by providing migration services and other support in emergency and post-crisis contexts; and facilitating the voluntary return and reintegration of refugees, IDPs, and other migrants.[40] By 2011, projects undertaken in emergency and post-conflict contexts represented the majority of IOM's US$1.27 billion budget.[41] While it is difficult to determine the precise proportion of IOM funding that goes towards humanitarian aid and work with forced migrants, it is clear that this work now accounts for the majority of IOM's budget.[42] IOM participates actively in the Inter-Agency Standing Committee (IASC), the main mechanism for coordinating international agencies' humanitarian action; operates in the field as part of UN country teams; and contributes to UN humanitarian country team planning, as well as to longer-term developmental responses related to displacement, such as disaster risk reduction.[43] An influential 2008 evaluation of IOM's humanitarian assistance efforts conducted by the Swedish donor agency, Sida, catalyzed a series of internal policymaking efforts, including a detailed humanitarian policy development process that resulted in the 2015 release of a new policy entitled "IOM's Humanitarian Policy – Principles for Humanitarian Action," which is now being implemented, alongside a series of related policy-development processes.[44] These initiatives, among others, reflect IOM's efforts to systematize its engagement in responses to forced migration, and in the humanitarian system more generally.

Given these developments, existing explanations for why states turn to IOM increasingly appear underdeveloped. IOM's dramatically expanded involvement in forced migration crises has unfolded against the backdrop of the recent growth in humanitarian emergencies, particularly in the Middle East and sub-Saharan Africa, and the expanded scope and functioning of the forced migration regime, with the emergence of IDPs and migrants in crisis situations as key categories of concern alongside refugees.[45] However, these factors alone cannot explain IOM's expansion. This is evident, for example, in IOM's calculation that between 2011 and 2014, the number of individuals receiving assistance through the DOE nearly doubled from 10 million in 2011 to almost 20 million in 2014 – a rate of growth that far outpaces rising displacement levels globally.[46] Some scholars suggest that states call on IOM principally "because it is outside of the UN frameworks and therefore unencumbered by the human rights obligations and state scrutiny the UNHCR faces."[47] While these factors have certainly influenced state decision-making, such explanations sit in tension with how powerful member states such as the United States and European states supported IOM joining the UN system, and encouraged the agency to develop policies that more expressly tie it to core human rights and humanitarian principles. Further, such explanations overlook the significance of IOM's own concerted efforts to position itself to respond to emerging challenges (a strategy driven in part by IOM's constant drive to raise money through projects, given its lack of core funding). Such approaches also discount the significant interactions between UNHCR and IOM in the context of evolving international arrangements for responding to forced migration, in which member states have restricted UNHCR's engagement with "newer" forms of displacement such as forced migration linked to the effects of climate change, and have turned to IOM to help paper over persistent gaps.[48]

8 Introduction

IOM's growth is significantly attributable to its efforts to strategically position itself, leveraging its malleability and its reputation for logistical efficacy and efficiency to entrepreneurially expand into new areas of work. Like many international organizations, IOM has a long history of entrepreneurial behavior. For example, in the agency's early years it was focused on facilitating the movement of Europe's so-called "surplus population" – the thousands of would-be workers, including refugees, who were seen to exceed labor needs on the continent, but who could help meet the demand for migrants in Australia, New Zealand, and the Americas. As interest in this service declined, ICEM identified complementary and alternative activities it could undertake, such as pre-departure training and post-arrival integration support.[49] Today, IOM picks up the slack on a remarkably wide range of issues in emergency and post-crisis contexts (some only tangentially related to migration), filling gaps on issues including disarmament, demobilization, and reintegration of former combatants; disaster risk reduction and mitigation; the management of reparations and land claims programs; and even the response to the 2013–2016 Ebola outbreak in West Africa.

As an organizational entrepreneur in the humanitarian sector, IOM capitalizes on its reputation for being able to execute complex logistical projects in challenging circumstances, and more generally as an efficient, nimble body that can mobilize rapidly to respond to requests for assistance. In identifying new areas for expansion, IOM also leverages its ability to be flexible, given its very broad mandate and the fact that the IOM Constitution (unlike, for example, the UNHCR Statute) does not specifically define the populations that are to be the focus of the agency's work. The Constitution does call on IOM to "concern itself with the organized transfer of refugees, displaced persons and other individuals in need of international migration services," but the definitions of these groups are left open.[50] From the outset, the "mandate of ICEM was not limited to refugees in the strict sense, but extended to other persons in refugee-like situations."[51] Foreshadowing the increased role the agency would come to play in relation to IDPs, a document brought before the ICEM Council in 1979 noted that the "organization has also been called upon to assist a growing number of so called 'potential refugees,' i.e. persons who find themselves in the condition of refugees in their own country."[52]

While IOM has thrived as a jack-of-all-trades, a core element of its entrepreneurial strategy has also been to carve out distinctive niches that can be parlayed into more structural responsibility, influence, and growth. For example, IOM has assumed progressively greater levels of responsibility for emergency evacuations; collecting data on displaced populations; and assisting migrant workers displaced or trapped in emergency contexts, such as in Kuwait after the Iraqi invasion and Gulf War, and in Libya during and after the 2011 revolution. IOM has additionally become a major player in disaster-induced displacement. It has conducted extensive research and facilitated discussions on migration associated with the effects of climate change, and has taken on major operational roles in post-disaster displacement crises. By 2010, IOM had conducted over 500 projects in this field, spanning emergency response as well as recovery, mitigation work, and preparedness efforts.[53] Since 2010, IOM's involvement in this area has increased dramatically, with massive disaster response efforts in countries such as Pakistan, the Philippines, and Haiti. The IASC's cluster system identifies key issues requiring coordinated humanitarian response in conflict and disaster situations, and assigns responsibility for spearheading the response in each "cluster" to a particular agency. By assuming responsibility for post-disaster IDP camp coordination and management in the context of the cluster system, IOM solidified a major new role, which it has leveraged to further expand its institutional footprint.

From the margins to the center: rethinking IOM through its humanitarian engagements

IOM looks very different when its extensive work in conflict and disaster situations in the global South is moved from the margins to the center of the analytical frame – no less curious or concerning, but undeniably different, reflecting unresolved tensions between principles, practices, values, and interests. This book does not attempt to provide a comprehensive look at IOM's work in areas such as economic migration policy, migrant health, and convening international dialogues on migration. Rather, by focusing on IOM's underexamined but influential engagement in the humanitarian sphere, this volume aims to enable a more nuanced and complete understanding of IOM. As involvement in humanitarian emergencies and post-crisis response now comprises the majority of IOM's budget, staff, and field engagement, I contend that understanding this work is essential to understanding the organization itself. At the same time, understanding IOM's growing role in emergency, post-conflict, and post-disaster situations is increasingly critical to understanding global governance efforts, particularly as they pertain to forced migration and humanitarianism. Indeed, just as conceptions of IOM's organizational character and dynamics shift when its humanitarian activities are taken into account, the humanitarian system and the constellation of actors involved in responding to forced migration appears more complex and contested when IOM is brought into the picture as an ambitious and progressively more influential organization. IOM's influence has often been underestimated because states are generally reluctant to cede control over migration to external actors – meaning that IOM does not directly control or govern migration. Yet IOM shapes migration governance in subtler ways, particularly through its work in humanitarian contexts – but because IOM is often mistakenly assumed to be primarily focused on international, economic migration, its impact is sometimes missed. In the following chapters, I explore some of the diverse ways in which IOM's influence is manifested, from ratcheting up competition over funds and turf, to constituting new "populations of concern," collecting data to underpin major humanitarian initiatives, and papering over cracks in the international humanitarian architecture relating to groups such as IDPs.

IOM's humanitarian identity and engagements have evolved considerably over the course of the past 25 years. Despite lacking a formal protection mandate

10 Introduction

or responsibility for a particular population, I argue that IOM has prospered by acting as an entrepreneur, particularly in the humanitarian sphere, carving out distinctive roles for itself at the same time as key leaders within the organization have pushed for increased recognition and internalization of humanitarian and human rights principles. Some scholars charge that, "Unlike IOs with a normative mandate, IOM never criticizes its member-states and is unlikely to resist implementing projects that would be incompatible with its (non-existent) standards."[54] In contrast, I offer a more complex account, examining how norm advocates within IOM have pushed for the organization to "grow up" – and, in turn, lay the foundation for continued growth – by articulating commitments to the core principles and standards that legitimize organizations in the humanitarian sphere, including through a series of key internal policy development processes. In this connection, I suggest that understanding IOM's evolution in the humanitarian sphere requires attending to both external and internal dynamics and power struggles, considering how its structure, culture, and relations with other actors in the humanitarian system shape its behavior.

IOM's institutional development is not linear. Many member state representatives, UN officials, and even human rights advocates emphasize that IOM is not the organization it once was, and welcome its efforts to mature into a more reliable actor that more consistently raises and addresses protection concerns, and declines requests from member states that are incompatible with international human rights and humanitarian norms. Yet in many cases, IOM takes two steps forward and one step back. As the following chapters demonstrate, IOM's emergence as a serious humanitarian actor is compromised by the negative human rights and humanitarian implications of some of its "migration management" work, but also through its sometimes acutely competitive behavior, its pronounced deference to states, and a willingness to play fast and loose with protection terminology when it suits member states and its own institutional interests.[55] Notwithstanding the concerning ways in which IOM has at times failed to uphold its professed humanitarian and human rights principles, my goal is not to try to tally up IOM's successes and failures in the humanitarian sphere. Instead, my aim is to explore how involvement in this arena has propelled and shaped IOM's development and influence. This examination suggests that while some have called on IOM's new director general, António Vitorino, to shift the "narrative away from crisis, emergency or global tragedy," this is unlikely, as this is the narrative and field of work that has underpinned IOM's expansion, and that pays its bills.[56] Starkly put, as IOM has virtually no core budget, it relies on overhead from its humanitarian operations – usually financed more abundantly than other migration policy and management activities – to fund much of its work at its headquarters, and even to sustain some of the migration policy programs for which it is more well known.[57]

Focusing on IOM's engagements in the humanitarian sphere does not minimize the importance of other aspects of its work, or the ethical concerns raised by activities such as so-called "assisted voluntary returns." Examining IOM's humanitarian activities does, however, challenge the assumption that this side of the agency's work is simply benign, or a foil for efforts to control migrants. Rather, humanitarianism itself is a form of management and control. Humanitarianism is and has always been a morally vexed enterprise, in which the drive to save lives and alleviate suffering sits in tension with paternalistic impulses to manage and control.[58] IOM has often been depicted as an institutional outlier given its longstanding place on the margins of the UN system and its propensity – attributed to its lack of a clear protection mandate – to engage in normatively contentious work. While recognizing IOM's distinctive organizational attributes, and without excusing its shortcomings, this analysis suggests that in many ways IOM has more in common with other IOs and humanitarian actors than is sometimes assumed. Longstanding leaders in the agency's emergency operations suggest that IOM is often called upon to play a highly imperfect, inevitably compromised role of bringing victims "out of the fire, into the frying pan" – for example, by facilitating returns from abusive detention centers, or evacuating besieged populations who may never be able to go home.[59] In negotiating the moral dilemmas associated with such work, IOM is not so much an outlier as it is emblematic of humanitarianism as an enterprise that melds care and control, in which even the best-intentioned are often consigned to search for the least-worst options.

I develop these arguments through analysis of IOM's history, policies, and practices. The book is also informed by observation of the IOM Council, and themes drawn from a series of in-depth interviews conducted between 2015 and 2019 with 62 mid-level to senior IOM officials, IOM member state and donor representatives, human rights advocates, independent experts, and representatives of major humanitarian NGOs and UN agencies.[60]

Structure

IOM's institutional culture, internal politics, and member state dynamics remain largely unexplored.[61] In Chapter 1, I respond to this gap in the literature and lay the groundwork for my examination of IOM's evolving engagement in the humanitarian sphere by analyzing the organization's structure and governance. I introduce and analyze the IOM Constitution, highlighting how the organization's "permissive" founding document and the absence of a formal protection mandate have shaped its work. I then provide a brief overview of IOM member state politics, emphasizing the decisive influence of the United States, before explaining IOM's organizational structure and some of its defining institutional attributes, including its decentralized, project-based model, its deference to member states, the role of the director general, and the tensions between its two main operational divisions, the Department of Emergencies and Operations and the Department of Migration Management.

Statist examinations of international organizations typically consider them simply as servants of states, rather than as potentially autonomous and even powerful actors.[62] The assumption that international organizations merely execute the wishes of their principals has been amply refuted in the international relations

12 Introduction

literature, with scholars such as Loescher, Barnett, and Finnemore convincingly demonstrating how agencies such as UNHCR have autonomously shaped international responses to forced migration.[63] Yet the assumption of unmitigated state control remains particularly strong vis-à-vis IOM, given its reliance on project-based funding, its lack of a formal protection mandate, and its own oft-professed deference to its member states. Notwithstanding these constraints, in Chapter 2 I consider how IOM has strategically cultivated increased autonomy and influence in the humanitarian sector, in turn enabling its dramatic expansion. I examine IOM as a humanitarian entrepreneur, considering how its embrace of human rights rhetoric and its strategic expansion in areas such as data collection, support for migrant workers in crisis contexts, and work with IDPs in disaster settings have provided a foundation for its growth. Particularly since 2011, IOM has engaged in a series of strategic policy development processes, promoted by internal norm advocates with a view to improving responses to humanitarian crises and shoring up the organization's credibility, and in turn, its authority and prospects for continued growth by more explicitly tying IOM to the humanitarian principles and human rights standards that legitimize actors in the field. I analyze these processes as a window into the evolution of IOM's humanitarian identity.

In recent years, IOM has worked to build a reputation for itself as a responsible, dynamic humanitarian actor, yet the organization faces a number of challenges and controversies, often linked to tensions between its multiple mandates. Chapter 3 examines these issues through two cases: IOM's engagement in Haiti before and after the 2010 earthquake, and its involvement in Libya before, during, and after the fall of the Gaddafi regime. Chapter 4 explores the process and implications of IOM "joining the UN family" as a related organization, setting this development in the context of IOM–UN relations from the 1950s to the twenty-first century. The book concludes with reflections on the consequences of IOM's evolution, identifying areas for future research, and drawing out the implications of this study for policy and practice. In particular, I stress the importance of using the agency's recent policy development processes to insist on increased accountability and higher expectations for this increasingly influential actor.

Notes

1 IOM, *About IOM*, www.iom.int/about-iom; Jérôme Elie, "The Historical Roots of Cooperation between the UN High Commissioner for Refugees and the International Organization for Migration," *Global Governance* 16 (2010): 345–360; and Anne Koch, "The Politics and Discourse of Migrant Return: The Role of UNHCR and IOM in the Governance of Return," *Journal of Ethnic and Migration Studies* 40, no. 6 (2014): 905–923.
2 IOM, *IOM Becomes a Related Organization to the UN*, 2016, www.iom.int/news/iom-becomes-related-organization-un.
3 IOM, *About IOM*, 2018, www.iom.int/about-iom.
4 Ibid.
5 Ibid.; Martin Geiger and Antoine Pécoud, "The Politics of International Migration Management," in *The Politics of International Migration Management*, eds. Martin Geiger and Antoine Pécoud (Basingstoke: Palgrave Macmillan, 2010), 3.

Introduction **13**

6 Megan Bradley, "The International Organization for Migration (IOM): Gaining Power in the Forced Migration Regime," *Refuge* 33, no. 1 (2017): 97; Report of Director General, 109th Session of IOM Council, 27–30 November 2018.

7 Ibid.; IOM, *IOM Snapshot 2019* (Geneva: IOM), 1.

8 Antoine Pécoud, "What Do We Know About the International Organization for Migration?" *Journal of Ethnic and Migration Studies* 44, no. 10 (2018): 1621.

9 On IOM and the concept of migration management, see e.g. Martin Geiger and Antoine Pécoud, eds., *The Politics of International Migration Management* (Basingstoke: Palgrave Macmillan, 2010); Ishan Ashutosh and Allison Mountz, "Migration Management for the Benefit of Whom? Interrogating the Work of the International Organization for Migration," *Citizenship Studies* 15, no. 1 (2011): 21–38; Rutvica Andrijasevic and William Walters, "The International Organization for Migration and the International Government of Borders," *Environment and Planning D: Society and Space* 28, no. 6 (2010): 977–999; and Fabian Georgi, "For the Benefit of Some: The International Organization for Migration and its Global Migration Management," in *The Politics of International Migration Management*, eds. Martin Geiger and Antoine Pécoud (Basingstoke: Palgrave, 2010): 45–72. On IOM's involvement in returns, see e.g. Koch, "Migrant Return"; and Frances Webber, "How Voluntary Are Voluntary Returns?" *Race and Class* 52, no. 4 (2011): 98–107.

10 See e.g. Alexander Betts, "Institutional Proliferation and the Global Refugee Regime," *Perspectives on Politics* 7, no. 1 (2009): 54; Andrijasevic and Walters, "Government of Borders"; Georgi, "Benefit of Some"; and Ashutosh and Mountz, "Migration Management."

11 On the latter point, see e.g. Ashutosh and Mountz, "Migration Management"; Julien Brachet, "Policing the Desert: The IOM in Libya Beyond War and Peace," *Antipode* 48, no. 2 (2016): 272–292; and Asher Lazarus Hirsch and Cameron Doig, "Outsourcing Control: The International Organization for Migration in Indonesia," *International Journal of Human Rights* 22, no. 5 (2018): 681–708.

12 For discussion of IOM's predecessor organizations' involvement in humanitarian action, see Elie, "Historical Roots"; and Line Venturas, ed., *International "Migration Management" in the Early Cold War: The Intergovernmental Committee for European Migration* (Corinth: University of the Peloponnese, 2015).

13 Interviews, IOM officials 3, 4 and 5, November 2015; Interview, IOM official 14, December 2016.

14 Ashutosh and Mountz, "Migration Management," 24.

15 On the power of crisis-talk, see e.g. Janet Roitman, *Anti-Crisis* (Durham: Duke University Press, 2013).

16 Michael Barnett, *Empire of Humanity: A History of Humanitarianism* (Ithaca: Cornell University Press, 2011), 16. For more detailed discussions of humanitarianism, and the relationship between humanitarianism and human rights, see Barnett, *Empire of Humanity*; Michael Barnett, "Humanitarian Governance," *Annual Review of Political Science* 16 (2013): 379–398; Michael Barnett and Thomas Weiss, "Humanitarianism: A Brief History of the Present," in *Humanitarianism in Question: Politics, Power, Ethics*, eds. Michael Barnett and Thomas Weiss (Ithaca: Cornell University Press, 2008), 1–48. Portions of this introduction draw on Bradley, "Gaining Power."

17 See for example Michelle Ducasse-Rogier, *The International Organization for Migration: 1951–2001* (Geneva: IOM, 2001).

18 Amnesty International, Human Rights Watch, Refugees International and other influential advocacy NGOs regularly release reports that address UNHCR's activities, but rarely cover IOM. For exceptions, see e.g. Human Rights Watch, "The International Organization for Migration (IOM) and Human Rights Protection in the Field: Current Concerns," Submitted by HRW at the IOM Governing Council Meeting 86th Session, 18–21 November 2003, Geneva; and Human Rights Watch, *Rot Here or Die There: Bleak Choices for Iraqi Refugees in Lebanon* (New York: Human Rights Watch, 2007).

14 Introduction

For analysis of how human rights advocacy organizations have reported on IOM, see Megan Bradley and Merve Erdilmen, "Speaking of Rights: Rights Talk, Protection Commitments and the IOM," Paper presented at the International Studies Association Conference, Toronto, 27 March 2019.

19 Pécoud, "What Do We Know," 1621–1622.

20 Ibid.

21 Pécoud, "What Do We Know," 1623. On the history of IOM, see e.g. Venturas, *Migration Management in the Early Cold War*; Rieko Karatani, "How History Separated Refugee and Migrant Regimes: In Search of Their Institutional Origins," *International Journal of Refugee Law* 17, no. 3 (2005): 517–541; Richard Perruchoud, "From the Intergovernmental Committee for European Migration to the International Organization for Migration," *International Journal of Refugee Law* 1, no. 4 (1989): 501–517; and Elie, "Historical Roots." On the influence of the IOM director general, see Nina Hall and Ngaire Woods, "Theorizing the Role of Executive Heads in International Organizations," *European Journal of International Relations* 24, no. 4 (2017): 865–886, and Ngaire Woods, Nina Hall, et al., *Effective Leadership in International Organizations* (Geneva: World Economic Forum, 2014).

22 Stephen Castles, Hein de Haas and Mark Miller, *The Age of Migration: International Population Movements in the Modern World* (Basingstoke: Palgrave, 2014), 18; Susan Martin, *International Migration: Evolving Trends from the Early Twentieth Century to the Present* (Cambridge: Cambridge University Press, 2014), 124; and Pécoud, "What Do We Know," 14.

23 On IOM and borderwork, see e.g. Philippe Frowd, "Developmental Borderwork and the International Organization for Migration," *Journal of Ethnic and Migration Studies* 44, no. 10 (2018): 1656–1672; Philippe Frowd, *Security at the Border: Transnational Practices and Technologies in West Africa* (Cambridge: Cambridge University Press, 2018); Andrijasevic and Walters, "Government of Borders; and Shoshana Fine, "Liaisons, Labelling and Laws: International Organization for Migration Bordercratic Interventions in Turkey," *Journal of Ethnic and Migration Studies* 44, no. 10 (2018): 1743–1755. On IOM's role in the Global Compact on Migration process, see Elizabeth Ferris and Katharine Donato, *Refugees, Migration and Global Governance: Negotiating the Global Compacts* (London: Routledge, 2019).

24 IOM, *Who Is a Migrant?*, www.iom.int/who-is-a-migrant.

25 IOM, *IOM Key Statistics 2011–2014* (Berlin: IOM Global Migration Data Analysis Centre), 2. Some senior IOM officials discouraged the public release of these numbers, as they crystallize the discrepancy between the scale of IOM's engagement in "traditional" migration management work and its much more extensive involvement with IDPs in humanitarian, post-conflict and post-disaster operations. Interview, IOM official 10, November 2015.

26 IOM, *Key Statistics 2011–2014*, 2. IOM indicates that in 2014 it also completed 300,000 migrant health assessments.

27 See for example Daniel Wunderlich, "Europeanization Through the Grapevine: Communication Gaps and the Role of International Organizations in Implementation Networks of EU External Migration Policy," *Journal of European Integration* 34, no. 5 (2012): 485–503. Most research on IOM appears to have been conducted by researchers based in Europe.

28 Martin, *International Migration*, 124–125.

29 Constitution of the International Organization for Migration, Article 2(b).

30 Elie, "Historical Roots," 349.

31 Ibid., 350; Martin, *International Migration*, 125.

32 Throughout this text, I use "displaced persons" and "forced migrants" as synonyms to refer to those uprooted from their homes, whether inside their own countries or across borders. I use the term "refugee" to refer to those who have fled across an international border, and "IDP" to denote those uprooted within their own countries.

Introduction **15**

33 Elie, "Historical Roots," 351.
34 Miriam Feldblum, "Passage-Making and Service Creation in International Migration," Paper presented at the annual meeting of the International Studies Association, Washington, DC, 1999; Elie, "Historical Roots," 346.
35 Perruchoud, "Intergovernmental Committee"; see also Martin, *International Migration*, 132.
36 Bradley and Erdilmen, "Speaking of Rights."
37 *Migration Crisis Operational Framework*, IOM, 2012, MC/2355. See also IOM, *Department of Migration Management*, www.iom.int/migration-management.
38 Woods, Hall, et al., *Effective Leadership*, 13.
39 Agreement Concerning the Relationship Between the United Nations and the International Organization for Migration, Article 2(2). See also General Assembly resolution A/RES/70/296, 25 July 2016.
40 Martin, *International Migration*, 135–137.
41 Ibid., 143.
42 For instance, McGregor estimates that in the 2000–2016 period, almost 58 percent of earmarked contributions to IOM from the agency's top 10 donors were related to work in emergency situations, transportation and support for refugees (particularly resettlement), interventions with IDPs, natural disaster response, and "post-crisis" activities such as stabilization efforts and programs for ex-combatants. See Elaine McGregor, "Money Matters: The Role of Funding in Migration Governance," *International Migration Institute Network Working Papers* 149 (2019), 16.
43 Martin, *International Migration*, 149.
44 Anders Olin, Lars Florin and Björn Bengtsson, "Study of the International Organization for Migration and its Humanitarian Assistance," *Sida Evaluations* 40 (2008): 1–96; and IOM Humanitarian Policy: Principles for Humanitarian Action, IOM Council, October 2015, C/106/CRP/20.
45 On the emergence of IDPs as critical global governance challenges, see Thomas Weiss and David Korn, *Internal Displacement: Conceptualization and its Consequences* (London: Routledge, 2006). On migrants in crisis situations, see e.g. Migrants in Countries in Crisis (MICIC), *Guidelines to Protect Migrants in Countries Experiencing Conflict or Natural Disaster* (Geneva: MICIC, 2016) (an initiative supported by IOM itself); and Susan Martin, Sanjula Weerasinghe and Abbie Taylor, eds., *Humanitarian Crises and Migration: Causes, Consequences and Responses* (London: Routledge, 2014).
46 IOM, *Key Statistics 2011–2014*, 5.
47 Betts, "Institutional Proliferation," 54.
48 For a detailed discussion of this issue, see Nina Hall, *Displacement, Development, and Climate Change* (London: Routledge, 2016).
49 Feldblum, "Passage-Making and Service Creation"; and Elie "Historical Roots," 351.
50 IOM Constitution, Article 1.1(b).
51 Perruchoud, "Intergovernmental Committee," 505–506.
52 Ibid.
53 Martin, *International Migration*, 137, 147–148.
54 Pécoud, "What Do We Know," 9.
55 For instance, in its early engagement with Rohingya who fled Myanmar into Bangladesh, IOM referred to members of this population as "undocumented Myanmar nationals" rather than refugees, reflecting Bangladesh's initial refusal to recognize the Rohingya as refugees, and leaving their rights in question. As IOM assumed a progressively more central role in the emergency response to the Rohingya in 2017, it started to refer consistently to the population as refugees – raising questions as to why IOM was playing such a central role in an operation that would typically fall under UNHCR's mandate.
56 Marta Foresti, "Welcome, Director General. There's a Lot to Do," *IRIN*, 2 July 2018.

16 Introduction

57 Interviews, IOM officials 1 and 13, November 2015; Interview, human rights advocate 5, December 2015.
58 Barnett and Weiss, "Humanitarianism"; Jennifer Hyndman, *Managing Displacement* (Minneapolis: University of Minnesota Press, 2000); and Michael Barnett, ed., *Paternalism Beyond Borders* (Cambridge: Cambridge University Press, 2016).
59 Interview, IOM official 3.
60 To enable open discussion of sensitive institutional concerns, all interviews were anonymous. As a fellow with the Brookings Institution, an independent policy research organization in Washington, D.C., I was involved in two studies undertaken by Brookings in cooperation with IOM on the resolution of displacement following the Haiti earthquake and Typhoon Haiyan (Yolanda) in the Philippines. See Angela Sherwood, Megan Bradley, Lorenza Rossi, Rufa Guiam, and Bradley Mellicker, *Resolving Post-Disaster Displacement: Insights from the Philippines after Typhoon Haiyan (Yolanda)* (Washington, D.C.: Brookings Institution/IOM, 2015); and Angela Sherwood, Megan Bradley, Lorenza Rossi, Rosalia Gitau and Bradley Mellicker, *Supporting Durable Solutions to Urban, Post-Disaster Displacement: Challenges and Opportunities in Haiti* (Washington, D.C.: Brookings Institution/IOM, 2014). For reflections on these research projects, including the interpretation of research findings, see Megan Bradley, Angela Sherwood, Lorenza Rossi, Rufa Guiam, and Bradley Mellicker, "Researching the Resolution of Post-Disaster Displacement: Reflections from Haiti and the Philippines," *Journal of Refugee Studies* 30, no. 3 (2017): 363–386. This research was undertaken after these studies, but was motivated in part by the recognition that the existing scholarly literature on IOM provided little insight into the questions and challenges associated with the organization's roles in such contexts.
61 Pécoud, "What Do We Know," 1621–1622.
62 Michael Barnett and Martha Finnemore, "The Power of Liberal International Organizations," in *Power in Global Governance*, eds. Michael Barnett and Raymond Duvall (Cambridge: Cambridge University Press, 2005), 162.
63 Michael Barnett and Martha Finnemore, *Rules for the World: International Organizations in Global Politics* (Ithaca: Cornell University Press, 2004); and Gil Loescher, *UNHCR and World Politics: A Perilous Path* (Oxford: Oxford University Press, 2001).

1

A SERVANT OF STATE MASTERS? IOM'S MANDATE, STRUCTURE, AND CULTURE

- *IOM Constitution and mandate*
  - *What's in a mandate? Humanitarian action and the protection mandate issue*
- *IOM and its member states*
- *Organizational structure and culture*
  - *Institutional structure and intra-organizational competition*
  - *The role of the director general*
  - *Staffing and generational differences*
  - *Projectization and decentralization*
- *Conclusion: building institutional autonomy on unlikely foundations*

Can international organizations (IOs) act autonomously? A wide range of IR scholars have compellingly refuted the assumption that IOs are merely servants of their state masters. For example, studies have shown how, in spite of member states' misgivings, UNHCR dramatically expanded its formal mandate and its involvement in responding to forced migration worldwide. Albeit with varying degrees of success, UNHCR has challenged restrictive and abusive policies towards refugees, even when they are backed by powerful states, and has shaped the refugee regime in ways unanticipated by its creators in 1950.[1] In contrast, in the limited literature on IOM, the organization is still often assumed to be entirely in the pocket of its member states, diligently implementing the programs they desire, and keeping mum on violations of migrants' rights.[2] This assumption is in some ways understandable: all IOs pledge faithful service to their member states, but IOM is strikingly deferential to governments, and overtly characterizes itself as a "member state-led organization."[3] In some ways, compared to more robustly mandated organizations like UNHCR, IOM's Constitution, institutional structure, and organizational culture provide weak or even antithetical

18 IOM's mandate, structure, and culture

foundations for autonomous action. And yet, in other senses, IOM's institutional characteristics and culture have proven to be surprisingly fertile grounds for organizational development, with varying degrees of autonomy.

In this chapter I introduce and analyze IOM's Constitution and mandate, member state politics, organizational structure, and institutional culture, with a view to understanding the possibility of autonomous action on the part of IOM. I first explore how IOM's "permissive" Constitution has enabled its engagement in a remarkably wide range of activities in emergency and post-crisis contexts, and the implications of the organization's lack of a clear, legally entrenched protection mandate. Second, I provide an overview of IOM member state politics, stressing the clear imprint of the United States on the organization, and the rising influence of member states from the global South. Third, I reflect on the relationship between IOM's organizational structure and culture, examining the role of the director general; IOM's decentralization and project-based funding model; and some of the tensions that shape the agency, including those between IOM's humanitarian-oriented Department of Operations and Emergencies and its Department of Migration Management, and generational differences between "old guard," operationally focused staffers and younger cohorts. Setting the stage for my discussion in Chapter 2 of how IOM has strategically evolved and entrepreneurially expanded in the humanitarian sphere, I argue that despite IOM's rather unlikely institutional foundations for independently shaping migration governance and, more specifically, humanitarian responses to displacement, the agency has strategically cultivated its capacity for autonomous action, at the same time as it remains highly deferential to states.

IOM Constitution and mandate

Established in 1951 as the Provisional Intergovernmental Committee for the Movement of Migrants from Europe (PICMME), the organization commenced work in 1952 as the Intergovernmental Committee for European Migration (ICEM). Its Constitution was only adopted in 1953, and entered into force on November 30, 1954. The Constitution "provides a framework for the purposes, functions, legal status, finance, membership, and other issues necessary for the functioning of the Organization."[4] Surprisingly, the organization's transformation into a global actor was officially effected in 1980 without formal changes to the Constitution. In November 1980, the Council adopted a resolution that removed "European" from the organization's name, making it the Intergovernmental Committee for Migration (ICM). According to an IOM institutional history, the resolution was adopted by consensus as the "modification was perceived as the recognition of an established fact and was not considered to imply any major changes in the Committee's mandate or the Constitution."[5] Later constitutional amendments addressed this change.

The current IOM Constitution incorporates the ICEM Constitution of 1953, as well as amendments that were adopted in 1987 and entered into force in 1989, when the organization was renamed IOM and became a permanent institution.

The Constitution also reflects amendments that were agreed to in 1998 and entered into force in 2013, which streamlined IOM's governance structures. Under the Constitution, the IOM Council, comprised of its member states, is the organization's highest decision-making body. Each member state has one representative and one vote on the Council.

IOM often describes itself as an organization "dedicated to promoting humane and orderly migration for the benefit of all."[6] Its purposes and functions are more formally articulated in a single article (Article 1) of the IOM Constitution, which indicates that:

1   The purposes and functions of the Organization shall be:

   (a) to make arrangements for the organized transfer of migrants, for whom existing facilities are inadequate or who would not otherwise be able to move without special assistance, to countries offering opportunities for orderly migration;

   (b) to concern itself with the organized transfer of refugees, displaced persons and other individuals in need of international migration services for whom arrangements may be made between the Organization and the States concerned, including those States undertaking to receive them;

   (c) to provide, at the request of and in agreement with the States concerned, migration services such as recruitment, selection, processing, language training, orientation activities, medical examination, placement, activities facilitating reception and integration, advisory services on migration questions, and other assistance as is in accord with the aims of the Organization;

   (d) to provide similar services as requested by States, or in cooperation with other interested international organizations, for voluntary return migration, including voluntary repatriation;

   (e) to provide a forum to States as well as international and other organizations for the exchange of views and experiences, and the promotion of cooperation and coordination of efforts on international migration issues, including studies on such issues in order to develop practical solutions.

This article reflects the organization's strong early focus on logistical support for transporting migrants – initially with ships inherited from the IRO – a line of work that led to the idea that IOM is a "glorified travel agency."[7] This is certainly a misperception. However, the Constitution, while generally short on substantive details, does linger on the details of transportation logistics. For example, the preamble underscores that "the movement of migrants should, to the extent possible, be carried out with normal transport services but that, on occasion, there is a need for additional or other facilities."[8]

The IOM Constitution is a remarkably short document. Beyond the sole article set out earlier that makes up Chapter I of the Constitution on IOM's Purposes and

20 IOM's mandate, structure, and culture

Functions, the rest of the document is devoted to formalities including membership (Chapter II), organs (Chapter III), the IOM Council (Chapter IV), administration (Chapter V), headquarters (Chapter VI), finance (Chapter VII), legal status (Chapter VIII), and "miscellaneous provisions" (Chapter IX) on issues such as voting procedures, and the interpretation, amendment, and application of the Constitution. Although Perruchoud argues that the amendments to the IOM Constitution in the 1980s aimed to more securely underpin the agency's "basic humanitarian character and orientation," the Constitution makes no direct reference to human rights, protection, or humanitarian principles.[9] Instead it stresses that, "The Organization shall recognize the fact that control of standards of admission and the number of immigrants to be admitted are matters within the domestic jurisdiction of States, and, in carrying out its functions, shall conform to the laws, regulations and policies of the States concerned."[10] While otherwise thin on explicit normative commitments, the Constitution emphasizes the need for international cooperation to address migration flows, and indicates that IOM's member states have "a demonstrated interest in the principles of free movement of persons."[11] As noted in the Introduction, this provision served as grounds to exclude Communist countries that restricted citizens' right to leave, staunching flows of would-be refugees to the west. This exclusion was critical to American support for the agency, and explains its creation outside the UN system. In 1951, the US Congress refused to approve funds to address the post-war displacement crisis in Europe by any IO with Communist members, a stance that initially undercut UNHCR's ability to respond operationally to refugees.[12] Instead, American support for resolving displacement and perceived "over population" in post-war Europe was channeled through agencies such as PICMME (subsequently ICEM). Since the end of the Cold War, IOM's membership has come to include China and other states that impede the human right to leave one's country, suggesting that members' "demonstrated interest" in free movement can now be merely theoretical.

What's in a mandate? Humanitarian action and the protection mandate issue

IOM has worked in relative anonymity for much of its history. One of the few widely known facts about the organization is that it lacks a formal protection mandate. What does this mean? The Inter-Agency Standing Committee (IASC), the central humanitarian coordination platform bringing together UN agencies, other IOs, and NGOs, offers a broad, influential definition of protection as "all activities aimed at obtaining full respect for the rights of the individual in accordance with the letter and the spirit of the relevant bodies of law."[13] A wide range of organizations involved in humanitarian action, both IOs and NGOs, understand themselves to have a responsibility to promote the protection of human rights, and to ensure that their interventions are sensitive to protection concerns. However, only some of these organizations have legal protection mandates. In this narrower sense, a protection mandate entails a formal legal responsibility, typically conferred by states and articulated in the organization's founding document, to advance rights protection. Protection mandates often focus on particular groups, and entrust the organization to act as the guardian and promoter of particular pieces of international law. Thus UNHCR's protection mandate, articulated in the UNHCR Statute, formally requires it to promote the protection of refugees, and makes it the "custodian" of international refugee law.[14] The International Committee of the Red Cross (ICRC) has a mandate to advance the protection of civilians in conflict, and is the guardian of international humanitarian law.

When viewed in comparison to robustly mandated protection actors such as UNHCR, IOM seems peculiar as it is not formally responsible under its Constitution for a particular population or convention, or for rights protection or adherence to humanitarian principles. IOM does, however, claim a humanitarian mandate. According to IOM, this is rooted in paragraphs (a) and (b) of Article 1 of the IOM Constitution, and affirmed by IOM's member states in two important recent policies, IOM's 2012 Migration Crisis Operational Framework (MCOF), and its 2015 Migration Governance Framework (MiGOF).[15] Notwithstanding the references in paragraphs (a) and (b) to refugees and displaced persons, on a straightforward reading, Article 1 does not explicitly address rights protection, and bears little direct relation to the remarkably wide range of work IOM now undertakes in humanitarian contexts. Taken in combination, IOM's lack of a formally and clearly articulated protection mandate, its historic status outside the UN, its tendency to engage in a diverse swath of activities, and its project-based funding model, have led to considerable confusion about the nature of the organization. Some mistake it for an NGO.[16] Yet as Barnett and Finnemore point out, IO mandates "are often vague or broad, or contain conflicting directives."[17] Examined from the vantage point of the study of IOs more generally, rather than in direct comparison to UNHCR, IOM is not so much an outlier as it is reflective of how IO staff imbue weakly mandated organizations with their own agendas, interests, and values.

The Constitution is "permissive" – that is, while IOM doesn't have a mandate to protect a particular, formally defined group, Article 1 enables the organization to provide assistance, without limiting the categories of people with whom it can engage.[18] As I discuss in greater detail in Chapter 2, the "embedded flexibility" or "constructive ambiguity" in the IOM Constitution has allowed the organization to strategically position itself to fill key gaps in the international humanitarian system, for example in relation to those displaced in disasters.[19] Some humanitarians working with UN agencies and NGOs recognize that, "If you didn't have IOM, you would have big gaps."[20] The flexibility inherent in the Constitution has been an asset for IOM, enabling the organization to expand its footprint and influence. As one longtime humanitarian worker put it, "It's good for them, but it's not clear it's good for the rest of the world," as IOM often competes aggressively for "turf," takes on work that may serve states' interests to the detriment of migrants' well-being, and has not – by many IOM staffers' own admission – historically had a strong protection orientation.[21] According to some critics, "The lack of mandate means they're basically a contractor."[22]

Over the course of IOM's evolution, its member states have certainly valued and capitalized on the agency's ability to work on the edges of the UN system, unfettered by strict protection mandates. However, in more recent years, many member state officials and IOM staff have come to see the agency as having a clear obligation to protect and promote human rights, and have had this explicitly recognized in several core institutional policies and frameworks. For instance, the MCOF seeks to rationalize IOM's diverse activities in crisis situations by clarifying their relationship to human mobility, and states that

> IOM adheres to humanitarian principles and is a formal and full member of the United Nations response and coordination system for humanitarian crises. IOM is further *bound and committed* to the existing legal and institutional frameworks contributing to the effective delivery of assistance and protection and ultimately to the respect and promotion of human rights and humanitarian principles.[23]

Building on the MCOF, IOM's Humanitarian Policy, subtitled "Principles for Humanitarian Action," was warmly welcomed by member states when it was presented to the IOM Council in 2015. As discussed in Chapter 2, the policy aims "to ensure that when the Organization is engaged in humanitarian action, it acts on the basis of robust principles and as part of the humanitarian response system."[24] While the policy is replete with deferential references to states, it also affirms the core humanitarian principles of humanity, impartiality, neutrality, and independence, and clarifies the agency's commitments regarding them.[25] In the policy IOM squarely identifies itself as a protection actor, declaring "Protection is at the center of IOM's humanitarian action," and articulates its commitment to protection mainstreaming.[26]

The 2015 MiGOF and the 2016 Agreement Concerning the Relationship between the International Organization for Migration and the United Nations, which made IOM a related organization in the UN system, also address IOM's roles and obligations vis-à-vis rights standards and protection. The MiGOF provides a structure for cooperation between IOM and states to address migration by distilling the "essential elements for facilitating orderly, safe, regular and responsible migration."[27] The Framework stresses that this must include "adherence to international standards and fulfilment of migrants' rights," and "effectively address[ing] the mobility dimensions of crises."[28] In the 2016 Agreement, IOM

> undertakes to conduct its activities in accordance with the Purposes and Principles of the Charter of the United Nations and with due regard to the policies of the United Nations furthering those Purposes and Principles and to other relevant instruments in the international migration, refugee and human rights fields.[29]

In addition, in the Agreement the UN recognizes IOM "as an essential contributor in the field of human mobility, [including] in the protection of migrants."[30] These provisions are remarkable given that, as recently as 2004, IOM contended in some prominent forums that it was not bound by international human rights law.[31]

These provisions sit uneasily with the identification of IOM in the 2016 agreement as a "non-normative" organization.[32] Is this designation compatible with the preceding provisions suggesting that although IOM does not have a clear protection mandate under its Constitution, it nonetheless has explicit roles and responsibilities vis-à-vis protection? "Non-normative" carries no commonly understood definition under international law, and some have suggested that this designation may be used to justify IOM undertaking work that is incompatible with human rights and humanitarian values.[33] Among senior IOM officials and member state representatives involved in negotiating IOM's entry into the UN system, "non-normative" is understood to carry a specific, shared connotation: that IOM is not a venue for setting binding standards. As one senior IOM official expressed it, "Member states don't want IOM to do convention negotiations to protect migrants' rights, to set standards that governments *have* to abide to."[34] For member states concerned that IOM may become another "finger-wagging"[35] organization, "'Non-normative' becomes a phrase that's used to calm people down. It's kind of a diplomatic thing."[36] From this perspective, IOM's "non-normative" designation is compatible with its recently-articulated protection commitments and obligations, but these understandings could change in the future, as migration continues to be hotly debated.

To be sure, IOM does not always systematically uphold the commitments made in the policies, frameworks, and agreements I have discussed, and these recent articulations cannot fully compensate for the exclusion of explicit references to human rights and humanitarian principles from the IOM Constitution. However, IOM is certainly not the only IO in the humanitarian sector that was created without a formal protection mandate, and has had to maneuver to address this concern as a clear commitment to protection is now arguably essential to recognition as a legitimate humanitarian actor. The World Food Programme (WFP), for example, does not have a formal protection mandate, but initiated a multi-year process to develop an official institutional protection policy that articulates its interpretation of and commitment to protection as an integral aspect of its work.[37] The UN Relief and Works Agency for Palestine Refugees in the Near East (UNRWA) was originally mandated only to assist, and not officially to protect, the world's most longstanding refugee population. Decried by many of its purported beneficiaries and their supporters for offering only material aid instead of protecting refugees' rights, UNRWA's commissioners-general gradually began to assert a protection role for the agency. This role was eventually recognized by member states, and since 1982 has been progressively developed through a series of General Assembly resolutions.[38]

Many researchers attribute IOM's moral failings, and its being beholden to states, to its lack of a protection mandate.[39] In contrast, some NGO and state officials – including outspoken protection proponents – dismiss the debate on IOM's lack of a protection mandate as a red herring, pointing out that robustly mandated agencies like UNHCR have had their own protection failures and moral fiascos, and that, more generally, "You don't need a formal, UN General Assembly-blessed mandate to do protection."[40] As one influential civil society representative expressed it, the protection mandate critiques are "where things maybe get a bit silly. Does [my NGO] have a formal protection mandate? . . . Quite honestly, I think it's irrelevant. Let's not get hung up on who has a protection mandate and who doesn't," but work to "ensure their programs live up to standards."[41]

Some argue that IOM should be granted a clearer, formal protection mandate from its member states – integrated, perhaps, into the IOM Constitution – in order to enable stronger oversight and accountability, and a more rights-focused response to migrants. Others insist that this would be a riskier move than it might first appear. As a seasoned diplomat and donor official expressed it,

> The fact that they don't have a protection mandate is not necessarily their fault. They were set up as a travel agency, not a protection agency. . . . And that's not to say that they haven't done protection work. Would their effectiveness and utility in the international community be enhanced if they had a protection mandate? And that's a question you have to think about hard

before suggesting constitutional amendments.[42] Such changes could land IOM on the "hit list" of states who purposefully obstruct traditional protection agencies, and undermine its ability to deliver aid in areas where actors like UNHCR are restricted. Conferring a protection mandate on IOM would also be difficult given member state opposition, the massive diversity within the "migrant" category, and the lack of normative consensus internationally on migrants' rights. To raise such concerns is not to excuse failures to live up to the human rights and humanitarian principles to which IOM has now committed itself. Rather, it is to recognize that ensuring that IOM supports consistent and effective protection for migrants, particularly in humanitarian crisis situations, is not simply a matter of its legal mandate.

Whether or not one believes that IOM could and should seek out a formal protection mandate from its member states through the amendment of its Constitution, the developments outlined earlier demand an updating of scholarly critiques of IOM's relationship to protection, and international human rights and humanitarian standards. As recently as 2018, scholars have argued that "IOM is indeed not bound by the human rights frameworks that form the basis of the UN's work," suggesting that "the underlying issue" explaining IOM's involvement in troubling activities such as returns to unstable and abusive states, is that "IOM has no 'protection mandate.' Being situated outside the UN system, it is not committed to international human rights law."[43] In fact, IOM has tied itself in a range of ways to these standards, and its member states have recognized and approved these commitments – even if the organization is not yet reliably held accountable to them. In this sense IOM has followed the path of many other IOs negotiating mandates that are ill-defined or only tangentially related to the roles the organizations aspire to play. As one influential human rights advocated expressed it, IOM is "the International Organization for Migration, not the International Organization for *Migrants*"; the agency still "takes its marching orders from governments" and "has not always been as supportive of migrants' rights as it purports to be."[44] But increasingly, "managing the delicate balance" between serving its member states and working for *people* has emerged as a defining organizational challenge.[45] Understanding how IOM manages this balance, and when it fails to do so, requires understanding the evolving politics of IOM's member states.

IOM and its member states

IOM nurtures its reputation as a member state-led organization. That is, IOM's direction is formally set by states through the IOM Council, and the organization is highly responsive to its members' views and requests. As a member state-led organization, IOM's "first responsibility is to their members," rather than to particular populations of concern.[46] Yet the transformation in IOM's membership over the last 20 years has changed what it means in practice for the agency to be member state-led.

A creation of the United States and a clutch of other like-minded states concerned with displacement and "over-population" problems in Europe after World War II, the organization was for decades primarily made up of western states. However, several directors general, including James Carlin, Jim Purcell, and particularly Brunson McKinley and William (Bill) Lacy Swing, concertedly worked to expand the organization's membership base. By courting new members, IOM has cemented its transformation into a truly global institution; shored up its claim to be *the* leading IO concerned with migration; and expanded its political reach, particularly in the global South, where the majority of migration unfolds.

These efforts have paid off for IOM, as it now boasts almost as many member states as the UN itself (173 members in 2019, compared to the UN's 193), and is much more regionally balanced than it was previously. Russia has still not formally joined – perhaps unsurprisingly, as the organization was created outside the UN specifically to exclude its involvement – but is an observer. China entered IOM in 2016, a development that seemed impossible in the 1980s, when "IOM was seen as an organization of western countries."[47] In addition to IOM's full members, it has eight observer states. Besides Russia, these include Bahrain, Bhutan, Indonesia, Kuwait, Qatar, San Marino, and Saudi Arabia. The IOM's weakest region in terms of membership is the Middle East. States that send or receive large numbers of refugees or migrants but have not, to date, joined IOM as a member or observer include Iraq, Lebanon, Syria, and the United Arab Emirates. In southeast Asia, Malaysia and Singapore have also not yet joined IOM.

The changed composition of IOM's member states, particularly the entry of large numbers of Southern, migrant-sending states, has come with changes in what

26 IOM's mandate, structure, and culture

members expect of IOM and increased complexity in charting the organization's course, as there are now many more views and interests in play. For instance, notwithstanding IOM's non-normative designation, some Southern member states want IOM to play an active role in setting new standards on migrants' rights, an aspiration that has largely been thwarted by more powerful donor states.[48] The member state expansion has also heightened the complexity of IOM intervening in returns, as the organization's European and African members have markedly different positions on this issue. IOM is now much more active in providing migration policy advice in response to requests from Southern member states. Some Southern members utilize IOM as a kind of quasi-governmental organization, leaning on IOM to execute policy work, border management activities, IDP assistance, and even infrastructure projects largely unrelated to migration. Two Southern member states, Peru and Colombia, rank among IOM's top donors in the 2007–2016 period (see Table 1.1). Colombia has engaged IOM to implement large IDP support programs and related youth and education initiatives, whereas the connection between migration and IOM's involvement in Peru is much more tenuous. The government of Peru has, for example, paid IOM to renovate the Lima town hall (2010, US$245 million); construct and equip a convention center in Lima (2014–2015, US$185 million); and help build the new Peruvian Central Bank headquarters (2015, US$80 million).[49] These activities have little if any connection to migration, raising the question of whether it is appropriate for IOM to provide these services – even if it can do so efficiently.

States have varied reasons for joining and supporting IOM, but many are motivated by the sense that IOM offers valuable opportunities for "increased coordination and cooperation on tough issues" surrounding migration, one of the foremost governance challenges of the twenty-first century.[50] IOM's member states prize its convening power (that is, its skill in bringing together diverse actors to discuss shared concerns); its ability to draw on its extensive field presence to keep members abreast of important trends; and its reputation for working effectively and efficiently. As one senior IOM donor state official expressed it, "States feel like they're getting value for money, or value for someone else's money, with IOM."[51] Like IOM itself, many of the organization's member states are grappling with how humanitarian principles and human rights obligations butt up against the drive to "manage" migration flows, and the recognition that the tools used to achieve this can have negative repercussions for the rights, dignity, and well-being of (would-be) migrants.[52] For many member states, IOM is an appealing venue for conversations on such challenges, as they feel that they have more control over it than they do over some branches of the UN; IOM can therefore create platforms for discussion of sovereignty-sensitive questions.[53] IOM is systematizing its commitment to human rights and humanitarian standards, and is now more likely than it was in the past to raise concerns about the rights and well-being of migrants in particular member states. It does this most often through direct discussions with government officials, but also through the press and through joint statements and reports with UN partners. In such efforts, however, IOM walks a fine line, preserving its position of deference to its member states. As IOM's head

IOM's mandate, structure, and culture **27**

of communications put it, "We're not in the business of lecturing member states or trying to be unhelpful in order to make a point."[54]

Many IOM member states have internal coordination struggles relating to their involvement in IOM because the agency's main interlocutors within its member states often come from ministries of the interior or related departments with responsibility for migration, rather than ministries of foreign affairs, where officials have more experience working closely with IOs.[55] (The US relationship with IOM is, however, managed through the US State Department, as is its relationship with UNHCR and other major IOs.) The tendency of many member states to delegate primary responsibility for their relationship with IOM to ministries of the interior rather than foreign affairs has meant that IOM's member state interlocutors may be less informed and sympathetic than their foreign affairs counterparts regarding the roles, operations, and contributions of IOs, including those in the UN system. This had important early implications for debates on the IOM–UN relationship – many representatives were dubious about the value of IOM becoming a related organization, as they see the UN as costly and overly preoccupied with standard-setting, and "don't want [IOM] to be contaminated by the bureaucracy of the UN system."[56] Although the proponents of IOM's entry into the UN system won their case in 2016, attending to the concerns of this skeptical cohort of member state representatives remains an ongoing concern for IOM.

As in other IOs, IOM's member states sometimes make incongruous demands of the organization. Perhaps most obviously, as one senior donor government official put it, member states "expect and demand a lot of IOM," but "pony up very little," with assessed contributions covering a tiny fraction of the operating budget – an amount insufficient to cover even the costs of IOM's bare-bones headquarters.[57] The incongruity of member states' demands are also evident in the ways in which some of IOM's European members have pressed the organization to become more assertive on behalf of migrants' rights in emergencies, at the same time as they expect it to compliantly implement return programs that may actively place migrants in emergency situations. Some members encourage IOM to be more coherent in its programming and turn down projects only tangentially related to migration, at the same time as they want the agency to be available to them as a flexible jack-of-all-trades, and openly applaud IOM's ability to avoid being hamstrung by mandate questions.

In recent years, IOM has engaged in a wide range of internal policy development processes intended, in part, to help the organization navigate such competing demands, and to provide guidance on the difficult question of saying "no" to requests for assistance from governments. These policy processes include, for instance, the elaboration of the MCOF, MiGOF, and the IOM Humanitarian Policy, discussed earlier and in Chapter 2. Internal proponents of a more principled, protection-oriented approach have used the development of these policies as an opportunity to more clearly (albeit still loosely) tie IOM to human rights and humanitarian principles, in ways unanticipated by the agency's founders and by scholars who assume that IOM's prime comparative advantage is

28 IOM's mandate, structure, and culture

being untethered to international norms. In these efforts IOM usually tries not to get ahead of its member states, but to "bring governments along as they do this work," preserving the agency's image as deferential to its members, if not entirely led by them.[58]

Any account of IOM's evolving relationships with its member states must consider the decisive influence of the United States. From its founding, there has been a tradition of American leadership in the organization: all but two of IOM's ten directors general have been American, and the United States has been IOM's largest funder, consistently contributing more than a third of the annual budget (see Table 1.1). US financial support for IOM has typically increased every year, with 2000–2016 seeing a tenfold increase. In this period, one-third to one-half of US donations funded the resettlement of refugees to the United States; the remainder primarily went to emergency response activities, as well as post-conflict and post-disaster reconstruction efforts.[59] While there are a range of IOs involved in migration issues, the United States has long "considered IOM as *the* international migration organization," as "the one, go-to shopping kind of place" for migration – a turn of phrase that is, perhaps, reflective of the sometimes transactional dynamic in the US–IOM relationship.[60] Given the United States' weight in IOM, some observers have dubbed it the AOM, the "American Organization for Migration," although US officials insist that IOM answers not to the United States but to all its member states. The expansion of IOM's membership, the diversification of its donor base, and the agency's own gradual cultivation of organizational autonomy means that IOM is certainly no longer a "100 percent US-owned entity."[61] The United States' own pre-Trump policy of encouraging multilateralism also facilitated this shift. As IOM's largest funder, the US government retains tacit veto power over some aspects of IOM, but the United

TABLE 1.1 Top donors to IOM: voluntary contributions to operational programs (member states and European Commission), 2007–2016

	2007–2011	*2012–2016*	*2007–2016*
1.	United States	United States	United States
2.	Peru	Peru	Peru
3.	Colombia	European Union	European Commission
4.	European Commission	Colombia	Colombia
5.	Australia	Australia	Australia
6.	United Kingdom	United Kingdom	United Kingdom
7.	Japan	Canada	Japan
8.	Canada	Japan	Canada
9.	Argentina	Germany	Netherlands
10.	Netherlands	Netherlands	Sweden
11.	Sweden	Norway	Germany
12.	Italy	Sweden	Italy

Sources: IOM Financial Reports, 2007–2016

States also recognizes that it cannot achieve its objectives in relation to IOs on its own, and so actively encourages a sense of shared investment among the member states, and a (modest) degree of independence for the organization.[62] The United States has thus been supportive of IOM recruiting new member states, and has encouraged IOM's regional secretariat functions, which have entailed IOM working with US funds, but not necessarily under direct US control.[63]

These changing dynamics in the US–IOM relationship were apparent in the negotiations over IOM's relationship with the UN system. Debate on the IOM–UN relationship was for a time stuck in a "stalemate" as member states including the United States had questions for IOM on why the organization should enter the UN system, and the implications.[64] Other members looked to the United States to lead on this question, but senior US officials wanted input from IOM on the issue to solidify its position; IOM was not initially forthcoming, as it wanted direction to come from its member states. While Washington's historic position on the IOM–UN relationship was, in one official's terms, "Never, over our dead body, will IOM join the UN," this position was more habitual than strategic.[65] It shifted as Director General Swing stepped forward to offer arguments for change that Obama administration officials found clear and convincing. With US support confirmed, the other member states in both the UN and IOM approved IOM's entry into the UN system as a related organization.

All told, the IOM–US relationship has in recent years been characterized by both continuity and change. The United States has long been pivotal to IOM's governance and operation, but its influence has been moderated, in part by Washington's own design. The Trump administration's anti-migration stance has cooled the US–IOM relationship, with the United States pulling out of the Global Compact on Migration that IOM was tapped to jointly service, and IOM member states rejecting Ken Isaacs, the US nominee for director general. Isaacs's rejection was attributed in part to his anti-Muslim and climate change-denying comments on social media, but it was also seen as a refutation of the Trump administration's policies, particularly the separation of migrant children from their families after crossing the US–Mexico border.[66] However, the longer-term influence of the Trump presidency on the IOM–US relationship remains to be seen.

Overall, as IOM's membership has expanded and the organization has evolved, IOM has become more confident in asserting itself vis-à-vis its member states. At the same time as it continues to portray itself as a "member state-led" organization, IOM's conception of its constituents is shifting, with some now recognizing that this must also include other IOs and NGOs as well as migrants themselves.[67] This analysis points to a certain incongruity in critiques of IOM, in that they are typically directed towards the IOM bureaucracy rather than its member states, although one of the leading accusations leveled against IOM is that it is hidebound to acquiesce to its members. If true, this would suggest that there is little IOM bureaucrats could do in response to criticisms, rendering them moot. This discussion suggests that there are sound reasons to critique the IOM leadership and bureaucracy for programs and positions that impede migrants' rights and well-being, as it has developed a significant capacity to act autonomously

30 IOM's mandate, structure, and culture

despite its continued reliance on project-based funding and its deferential rhetoric towards its members. For those interested in seeing change in the organization, there is a clear need to more closely analyze the increasingly complex, evolving relationships between IOM and its member states (and among the member states themselves), and to understand the levers of power that may be applied for more consistent and coherent responses to the rights and needs of migrants.

Organizational structure and culture

In IOM Council resolution 1309 of 2015, IOM's member states authorized the director general to negotiate a new relationship between IOM and the UN system. In Article 2, the member states also identified several institutional attributes that they prize, and want preserved as the IOM–UN relationship evolves:

(a) IOM is the global lead agency on migration and is an intergovernmental, non-normative organization with its own constitution and governance system, featuring a predominantly projectized budgetary model and a decentralized organizational structure. The Organization must, in addition to these features, also retain the following attributes to which its Member States attach importance: responsiveness, efficiency, cost-effectiveness and independence;

(b) IOM is an essential contributor in the field of migration and human mobility, in the protection of migrants' rights, and in operational activities related to migrants, displaced people and migration-affected communities, including in the areas of resettlement and returns. It has, over time, accumulated a wide and unique range of real world experiences. IOM must be in a position to continue to play this essential and experience-based role.

In this section I examine several of these attributes, and the institutional structure and organizational culture that give rise to them. I first explain IOM's structure and intra-organizational competition, before addressing the influence of IOM's directors general, staff dynamics, and the decisive significance of IOM's projectized, decentralized model.

Institutional structure and intra-organizational competition

As discussed, IOM is formally governed by its member states through the IOM Council. Alongside the Council, the Standing Committee on Programmes and Finance, comprised of member states, works closely with the director general to oversee budgets, policies, and programs. Some 97 percent of IOM's budget comes from voluntary donor support for particular projects, and only 3 percent of IOM staff are based at headquarters; the remaining 97 percent work in field offices, implementing these projects (for information on the geographic distribution of IOM's offices, see Table 1.2).[68] (In contrast, 12 percent of UNHCR staff are headquarters-based.)[69] Consequently, the organization's Geneva headquarters is remarkably small and operates on a shoestring, sustained by member states' extremely modest assessed contributions, and overhead from IOM's projects. IOM also operates nine regional offices in Nairobi, Dakar, Pretoria, Cairo, San José, Buenos Aires, Bangkok, Brussels, and Vienna, and two special liaison offices. The first, in New York City, focuses on the United Nations, while the second, in Addis Ababa, concentrates on the African Union – a mark of the increasing importance for IOM of Southern member states and their regional organizations. Like some other IOs looking to limit the high cost of doing business in Geneva, IOM maintains administrative centers in less pricey locations (Panama City and Manila), which handle functions such as finance support, staff security, project monitoring, and information technology. In addition, IOM has a range of other specialized offices and centers, including its Berlin-based Global Migration Data Analysis Center, which opened in 2015 and reflects the central role that data collection, management, and analysis has played in IOM's expansion.

IOM's headquarters is comprised of four departments. One, the Department of Resources Management, is largely administrative, and focuses on the organization's human, financial, and technical resources. Another, the Department of International Cooperation and Partnerships, concentrates on IOM's relations with its member states and donors, as well as with other IOs, NGOs, and the media. IOM is extensively involved in convening global forums and facilitating consultations and negotiations, such as the International Dialogue on Migration and the process leading to the 2018 Global Compact on Migration. The Department of International Cooperation and Partnerships spearheads these efforts, and is also tasked with promoting "awareness and understanding of international migration law."[70] The remaining two departments are operational, and map onto IOM's engagement in "the field." The mandates and concerns of the Department of Migration Management (DMM) and the Department of Operations and Emergencies (DOE) are intertwined, and relations between them have shifted over the years, at times acquiring a competitive edge as IOM's humanitarian engagement has grown, placing DMM in an arguably subordinate position.[71]

TABLE 1.2 Geographic distribution of IOM offices, 2019

Region	Number of offices
Africa	121 (30.8%)
Americas and the Caribbean	58 (14.8%)
Middle East	24 (6.1%)
Asia and Oceania	123 (31.3%)
Europe and Central Asia	67 (17.0%)
Total	393

Note: IOM operates smaller field locations in addition to the offices listed here. The number of offices in a region is not necessarily related to the size of these offices; e.g., IOM maintains several large offices in the Middle East.

Source: IOM Snapshot 2019.

32 IOM's mandate, structure, and culture

Perhaps the most opaque of IOM's departments, the DMM is "responsible for the development of policy guidance for the field; the formulation of global strategies; standard-setting and quality control; and knowledge management relating to 'mainstream' migration sectors."[72] (What makes some movements "mainstream" is unclear.) More concretely, DMM works on issues including labor migration, migration and development, migrant health, counter-trafficking, assisting vulnerable migrants, and the relationship between migration, environment, and climate change. The department runs the IOM Development Fund, through which IOM responds to requests for assistance from Southern member states, often for policy development assistance, for which it cannot secure donor support. DMM also spearheads some of IOM's most contentious work, on so-called "assisted voluntary returns" (AVR), and border management, sometimes critiqued as border control.[73] In contrast to DOE, which works extensively with IDPs, DMM focuses predominantly on cross-border migration. Although the literature on IOM rarely examines the organization's internal structure, it is striking that the majority of studies on IOM address activities that fall under DMM's remit.

In a statement reflective of its breadth of work and ambition, DOE indicates that it

> directs, oversees and coordinates IOM's resettlement work and transport programmes and is responsible for overseeing IOM's activities related to movement, logistics, preparedness and response in migration crises and humanitarian emergencies and to recovery and transitional settings. The Department coordinates IOM's participation in humanitarian responses and provides migration services in emergencies or post-crisis situations to address the needs of individuals and uprooted communities, thereby contributing to their protection. It provides technical support to efforts in the field, particularly in responding to forced migration and massive population movements, including protracted internal and cross-border displacement and refugee situations.[74]

Like DMM, DOE also claims a role in crafting policy and guidance for field operations. DOE is comprised of four divisions dedicated to preparedness and response; transition and recovery; resettlement and movement management; and land, property, and reparations. It also has a unit devoted to statistics and knowledge management, reflecting the centrality of data collection and management to IOM's expansion in the humanitarian sector.[75]

Much recent scholarship on IOs emphasizes their capacity for autonomous action, but in assessing their attempts to navigate their mandates and shape questions of global governance, IOs are often treated as monoliths.[76] IOM exemplifies the need to understand internal competition and fragmentation in order to understand IOs as dynamic agents. As IOM's humanitarian engagement has expanded, competition has emerged between DOE and DMM. This plays out most evidently at headquarters level, but also shapes internal politics in regional offices and, to a lesser extent, in field offices where all funded projects are assigned a code that defines the work as DMM or DOE turf.[77] While IOM has been involved in humanitarian responses to forced migration since its establishment, in the 1990s and early years of the 20th century, areas of work now associated with DMM, such as AVR, were particularly predominant. As DOE has grown, DMM's relative internal power has diminished. This is evident not only in differences between the departments' budgets, but also in everyday aspects of bureaucracy. A few decades ago, for instance, many staffers concentrating on humanitarian work were housed in an annex at IOM's headquarters, while those focused on migration management "used to have more visibility, they were seen to be the de facto lead department in those days."[78] Now, DOE occupies more prime real estate at headquarters, and is seen as the institutional "Cinderella," the "good guys" who often speak first at management meetings in virtue of their institutional power and esteem.[79]

Tensions between the departments have grown as some argue that IOM's role is increasingly and perhaps unduly weighted towards humanitarian activities. Some suggest that DOE is an internal "empire," and underscore the weakness of intra-organizational mechanisms to ensure that the department is held to account for high-quality interventions that adhere to its professed values and strategies.[80] Leaders within DOE concede that the department is "too much of an organization within the organization," which "can play against DOE, but people realize where the money comes from."[81] That is, much of IOM's headquarters and important initiatives, such as the IOM Development Fund, rely on overhead from humanitarian work.[82] Some distinguish between the "business mentality" primarily driving DMM and the "NGO mentality" that is more prominent in DOE (in the sense of being part of work with an overarching element of shared humanity, compassion or solidarity), recognizing the irony that despite its business mentality, DMM has in recent years had to fight for money to survive while DOE has an easier time securing funds, such that it can "afford" to talk about principles.[83] (The possibility that some within IOM consider human rights and humanitarian principles a luxury to be afforded, rather than an integral aspect of institutional identity and operations, distinguishes IOM from more traditional humanitarian actors where these principles are arguably baked into organizational mandates and characters.)

Tensions have further escalated with the perception that these principles may constrain the work DMM can take on. Some DOE leaders have pushed for the organization to adhere more clearly and systematically to human rights standards and humanitarian principles, framing this as part of IOM's maturation as an institution. Such maturation serves DOE interests by strengthening IOM's credibility as a humanitarian actor, but may limit other lines of work, such as AVR. Ultimately, the perception among many inside and outside the agency is that IOM – particularly at headquarters – is "like two organizations stitched together," and that one of its foremost challenges is "reconciling different sides of the house."[84] The development and uptake of the MCOF, which attempts to distill the relevance of IOM's different activities for migrants in crisis contexts, broke down some internal barriers by underscoring shared stakes in responses to humanitarian emergencies. Equally, DMM's development of the concept of "humanitarian border management" and engagement on counter-trafficking work in crisis situations, have fostered a sense of shared investment across the organization in emergency response – although some in DOE have interpreted such efforts as a DMM power grab.[85] Reflecting on the challenge of attempting to harmonize IOM's humanitarian work and other migration management activities, senior IOM officials point out that many multi-mandated organizations face comparable challenges as each "hat" the organization wears brings different expectations, incentives, and responsibilities. "Learning how to play those hats" is a matter of the "political maturity of an organization. We are growing up but we are not there yet."[86]

The role of the director general

Over the years, IOM's directors general have not only steered the institutional ship, but have rebuilt the ship as it sailed. Scholars of international relations are increasingly interested in the roles and imprints of the heads of major IOs, but in this emerging literature the characters, strategies, and contributions of IOM's directors general have not yet been extensively analyzed.[87] (See Table 1.3 for a list of the organization's directors general from 1951 to 2019.) Even IOM itself has not highlighted the history of this office. Exploring the approaches and influence of those who have occupied the organization's top post would undoubtedly deepen understanding of the institution's evolution and expansion, including in the humanitarian sphere. I cannot aspire to fill this gap here, but briefly introduce the office and its responsibilities, before discussing the distinctive contributions of Director General Swing to IOM's expanded engagement in the humanitarian sphere.

Since its establishment in 1951, the organization has had ten directors general, all men and all but two American. The director general and deputy director

TABLE 1.3 IOM directors general, 1951–2019

Director general	Nationality	Years of service
Hugh Gibson	American	1952–1954
Harold H. Tittman	American	1955–1958
Marcus Daly	American	1958–1961
Bastiaan Wouter Haveman	Dutch	1962–1969
John F. Thomas	American	1969–1979
James A. Carlin	American	1979–1988
James. N. Purcell Jr.	American	1988–1998
Brunson McKinley	American	1998–2008
William Lacy Swing	American	2008–2018
António Vitorino	Portuguese	2018–present

general are elected by the member states by a two-thirds majority vote, and may serve two five-year terms.[88] Under the IOM Constitution, the director general's mandate is expressed in brief but broad terms:

> The Director General shall be responsible to the Council. The Director General shall discharge the administrative and executive functions of the Organization in accordance with this Constitution and the policies and decisions of the Council and the rules and regulations established by it. The Director General shall formulate proposals for appropriate action by the Council.[89]

Several occupants of the office have used the latitude inherent in their mandate to effect major changes. During the latter years of the Cold War, various directors general were primarily preoccupied with keeping the organization afloat financially, as its original lines of work, supporting migration from Europe, dried up. Arguably, it is the two most recent directors general, McKinley and Swing, who most decisively transformed the organization from a shoestring operation into a multipronged, global enterprise. During his tenure as director general, Purcell developed a vision of IOM as a global organization, and encouraged the institution's work in a widening range of spheres. It was, however, McKinley who overhauled the agency and is "credited with – or blamed for – the franchise model of the field offices" that provide myriad services to IOM's member states through the projectization system.[90] Although McKinley came to IOM after a long career in the US diplomatic service, observers suggest that he revamped IOM "with a sledge hammer rather than any kind of finesse," and in the process "antagonized the whole UN system."[91] He also antagonized some of IOM's own donors, who "balked" at his "incursions" into the policy sphere.[92] Known as a strong-willed and ambitious leader, McKinley simply persevered in the face of such resistance, convinced that the project-based, service-oriented model could ensure IOM's survival and prosperity.[93] Under his tenure, IOM's operational budget more than quadrupled.[94] While the model fueled IOM's growth, it also propelled it further onto morally thin ice, as this quadrupling came in part through IOM's increased engagement in humanitarian operations, but also in contentious activities such as AVR.

Swing took over as director general in 2008. Like McKinley, Swing built his career in the US diplomatic service; both served as US ambassadors to Haiti. Swing was also US ambassador to South Africa, Nigeria, Liberia, the Democratic Republic of Congo (DRC), and Congo Brazzaville, providing him with in-depth experience in countries of the global South where, as IOM director general, he continued to expand the institution's footprint. Before coming to IOM, Swing spent five years as special representative of the UN secretary-general for the DRC. In this role, Swing oversaw the largest UN peacekeeping mission on record, and deepened his engagement in complex humanitarian operations, experiences that informed his approach as IOM director general. In this role, Swing sustained the operational models and growth patterns

36 IOM's mandate, structure, and culture

McKinley initiated, but also accomplished three key, interrelated developments. First, he shored up IOM's position as a serious player in the humanitarian sphere, including through the more systematic integration of rights and protection into the organization's rhetoric and policy frameworks. Second, in conjunction with other senior IOM officials, he strengthened the organization's diplomatic chops. Third, he improved IOM's relations with other organizations, particularly UN agencies, eventually enabling IOM's entry into the UN system in September 2016.

Moreso than his predecessor, in pursuing these goals Swing retained a highly deferential position vis-à-vis IOM's members, consistently presenting IOM as a member state-led organization. Drawing on his well-regarded diplomatic skills and his experience with humanitarian emergencies, he established a pattern of advocating for migrants' rights while reassuring wary governments that he "won't shut the door in front of the member states."[95] The relationship between Swing's interest in protection and the organization's ambitions for growth was epitomized in the quote emblazoned across the top of his bio page on the IOM website while he was director general: "One billion people are migrants. No longer can we merely count them; we must protect their rights."[96] Such rhetoric nods to IOM's growing role in data collection and research on migration, while positioning IOM as a protection-conscious IO that can be trusted to play a leading role in addressing the massive challenges – and reaping the institutional opportunities – that migration presents.

Increasingly, the director general publicly raises advocacy concerns through joint statements with the heads of other international organizations involved in humanitarian affairs, such as UNHCR and UNICEF. Between 2010 and 2018, for instance, Swing released at least 58 joint statements, usually on critical advocacy issues, with the heads of other IOs, especially UNHCR and UNICEF.[97] While underscoring the continued need for a more cohesive, systematic commitment to protection from IOM, many human rights advocates and humanitarian workers who have long been wary of IOM's ambiguous role recognize the achievements made in this respect under Swing's stewardship. As one bluntly expressed it, Swing was pivotal in making IOM a "more honest, less ridiculous player," particularly on the humanitarian front.[98]

The IASC was a particularly important venue for Swing to strengthen IOM's place in the humanitarian system and improve its diplomatic relations, particularly in relation to UN actors. IOM joined the IASC as a standing invitee upon its founding in 1992, and over time the IASC became a key platform for IOM to build up its credibility in the humanitarian sector, with IOM signing on to key IASC statements on protection and humanitarian values. The IASC provided a forum for Swing to improve IOM's relations with other humanitarian agencies, conveying the message that "We are going to play well with others, we're not going to be the cowboy people think we are."[99] Beyond working to improve IOM's reputation, emphasizing its desire to be a reliable partner and not just a competitor, Swing drew on his experiences in the DRC to become the "undisputed leader within the IASC on protection from sexual exploitation and abuse,"[100] and integrated challenges facing migrants in crisis situations into IASC discussions.

In terms of organizational developments, one of Swing's most significant accomplishments was to negotiate a small increase in the overhead IOM charges on its projects, bringing the overhead rate to 7 percent.[101] While this may seem like a trivial bureaucratic matter, it is in fact a major development, as it dramatically expands the amount of untied money flowing into IOM's coffers – mostly from big-budget DOE projects. These additional funds help IOM strengthen its presence in Geneva, undertake initiatives such as the IOM Development Fund, and lay the foundations for further strategic expansion. Member states' approval of this increase reflected their respect for Swing, particularly as the increase was negotiated at a time when many governments were focused on fiscal austerity, and at first blush the increase runs counter to IOM's reputation for cost effectiveness. In response to such concerns, Swing was able to convince skeptics that the increase was essential to IOM's ability to sustainably serve its member states.

Given the tradition of American leadership of IOM and the arrival of President Donald Trump in the White House, IOM faced "an obvious succession problem" at the conclusion of Swing's mandate as director general in 2018.[102] While it is too early to analyze Vitorino's influence as director general, early indications suggest that he is working in the broad spirit of Swing's approach.

Staffing and generational differences

Beyond the director general and the deputy director general selected by the IOM Council, the organization now employs more than 12,600 people, the vast majority in field operations in the global South.[103] Interlocutors stress that IOM "is not a monolithic organization; a lot depends on who's sitting at what desk or out in the field."[104] IOM's staffing practices and institutional culture are distinctively shaped by how it has responded to pressure from member states to operate as a lean, cost-effective alternative to UN agencies seen as bloated and inefficient. All IOM employees, from junior hires to the director general, travel economy class – a pointed signal of the organization's dedication to providing "value for money." (Interestingly, IOM management also framed this policy as a matter of solidarity with the migrants IOM transports, with Swing suggesting that, "If migrants fly economy, so do we.")[105] But the pursuit of cost-effectiveness also has more substantive effects on the organization's composition and operation. Given its reliance on project-based funding, IOM has a thinly staffed headquarters and a relatively low proportion of permanent staff. As IOM has expanded, it has become increasingly untenable for the organization to operate with such a small core staff team. Over the five-year period from 2013 to 2018, IOM aimed to increase the number of core staff by 61 percent, from 450 in 2013 to 723 in 2018.[106] Even with these increases, the institutional culture is strongly influenced by the lack of stability facing its employees, as staff move from contract to contract. This model affords perceived benefits and costs: IOM can in theory more easily shed poorly performing staff than other organizations, but the agency has also

38 IOM's mandate, structure, and culture

lost talented staff to employers offering greater stability. The constant turnover in IOM staff also creates problems in terms of ensuring thorough staff training, including in protection principles. This turnover is further exacerbated by the organization's rotation policy, which requires that its few permanent employees rotate positions on a regular basis. While this prevents disconnection between the field and headquarters, the policy privileges the cultivation of generalists rather than experts. As IOM moves further into highly specialized areas such as policy development and work on housing, land, and property issues, rotation, and the focus on generalization may come at the expense of sustained, credible expertise.[107]

In order to ensure its competitiveness as an employer – while also emphasizing that it "belongs" in the UN family – IOM has a longstanding policy of paying its staff on the UN's standardized salary scales. IOM staff also participate in the UN pension fund, and IOM labels its positions using the UN's professional categorizations. In contrast to other major IOs, however, it has a flatter organizational structure and hires relatively few senior managers, instead transferring major responsibilities to staff working at lower pay grades. For instance, in 2017 IOM had approximately 10,000 staff members and UNHCR had almost 11,000; only 49 IOM staff members held D-level positions (the most senior job category, with the exception of the executive-level positions occupied by the director general and deputy director general), while UNHCR had 163 staff members at D-level.[108] Longstanding observers note that IOM lacks "bench strength" at the top levels, risking burnout and creating major gaps when senior officials retire or move on, and reducing the organization's ability to strategically manage its own relentless expansion.[109] IOM has also struggled to promote and retain women at senior levels, and some staff members critique the organizational culture as hostile or unsupportive of women, particularly in leadership positions. While 46 percent of IOM staff are female, only 24 percent of D1 grade staff are women.[110]

Unlike major humanitarian IOs such as UNHCR, IOM does not generally use implementing partners, but rolls out its projects directly. In order to do so, IOM relies on extensive contingents of national staff members, who also work on temporary contracts, but at much lower rates than international staff. Many national staff members work with IOM for years, and senior officials recognize IOM's national staff as one of the organization's greatest assets. Tasks that UN agencies typically assign to senior international staff, IOM often undertakes with highly skilled local staff. Working extensively with national staff can also expand humanitarian access and open up important – if risky – possibilities for crisis response. For example, by working with national staff, IOM and the NGO Mercy Corps were among the very few agencies able to deliver aid in Raqaa, Syria when it was under ISIS control.[111] Some strong national staff do move up to work for IOM at the international level. Yet opportunities for international mobility for national staff remain limited, and ensuring consistent, in-depth training for national staff is a pressing challenge, particularly as national staff serve as IOM's frontline in emergency and post-crisis operations, where protection concerns are prominent.

Many within IOM stress the divisions and tensions between long-serving staffers and members of the younger generation, particularly in relation to protection and inter-organizational collaboration. The "old guard" are widely perceived to favor "gung ho," independent action focused on logistical efficiency, and relatively unrestrained by what they see as overly academic analyses of protection standards and principles. In contrast, among younger staff members and those who more recently assumed senior leadership positions, there are thought to be more "protection allies," support for IOM trying to be a "principled organization," and interest in cooperating with other inter-governmental agencies and NGOs.[112] As one advocate with a major human rights NGO expressed it, "The dinosaurs are on the top, and the new generation is much more switched on, but they have to pay deference."[113] While there is of course diversity within these groups, such tensions have made the transformation of IOM's ethos a much more gradual process than some would like. Whether the "new generation" will really be any better at addressing these challenges remains an open question. As IOM has become a bigger player in the humanitarian sector, its leaders are well aware that there is now an onus on the agency to coordinate with others, and better integrate understanding of and commitment to rights protection and humanitarian principles throughout the organization. However, they are equally aware that changing organizational culture and external perceptions is a long-term undertaking, especially as debates persist on exactly what humanitarian principles and protection standards entail vis-à-vis more controversial activities, such as returns and involvement in migrant detention centers.

Projectization and decentralization

The "projectized," decentralized model that McKinley promoted enabled IOM's rapid expansion and definitively shaped the organization – and, by extension, the humanitarian sector – in ways that continue to reverberate. IOM is in some modest ways stretching the strictures of this model, for instance through the IOM Emergency Fund, which it uses to start crisis response efforts before donor support is secured. However, the projectization model was entrenched in the agreement that brought IOM into the UN system in 2016, and there is every indication that it will remain IOM's definitive *modus operandi* in years to come. In this section, I briefly analyze some of the perceived benefits and costs of this approach.

The projectization model creates a "pay for play" system in which IOM functions as a service provider or "contractor" for its member states.[114] Through the projectization model IOM has become, in the words of one government official, the "consulting firm of the international community."[115] Whereas funding for most humanitarian IOs is heavily earmarked, this is rarely at the level of specific projects, but rather in relation to particular programs or national responses. The projectization model entails much higher levels of donor oversight – in other words, control – over how funds are used, which is appealing for many donors. IOM heads of mission shape the process by building relationships with funders and drumming up interest in proposed projects. The constant need to

40 IOM's mandate, structure, and culture

pitch projects to prospective donors creates an incentive for IOM staff to package and brand certain types of interventions, such as the displacement tracking matrix (DTM) discussed in Chapter 2, and to establish niches that it can use as a foundation for different operations. This is particularly important as IOM lacks mandated responsibility for a particular, defined population, meaning that it has to compete to establish itself as a relevant player meriting donor support. Coupled with organizational decentralization under which regional directors and heads of mission have considerable autonomy, the projectization model has made IOM very "responsive" to its donors, as representatives must "get projects or perish."[116] This reality stands in contrast to much of the academic literature, which acknowledges IOM's projectized system but also often reflects the assumption that IOM makes largely unfettered choices about where and how it allocates resources, rather than working where it can get projects funded, and stretching overhead from these projects to sustain a handful of other priority activities.

Proponents of IOM's decentralized, projectized model suggest that it keeps the organization focused, nimble, cost-effective, and results-oriented, encouraging innovation and ensuring that it can scale up quickly to respond to needs and fill important gaps. Senior IOM staff admit that while they don't particularly like working under this model, "we would all acknowledge that projectization has kept us sharp and forced us to deliver."[117] Some donors welcome how, in their view, projectization has kept IOM "hungry," and able to "hire, fire and deploy a hell of a lot faster than UNHCR."[118]

At the same time, IOM staff, donors, advocates, and humanitarians working with other agencies express many misgivings about projectization. Under this system, heads of mission have strong professional incentives to bring in lucrative projects, and relatively little oversight to ensure that these projects comply with rigorously interpreted protection standards, or a coherent vision of IOM's role. This has fostered a reputation for IOM in some circles as a competitive, scattergun, unreliable "cowboy." Critics charge that the model encourages a jack-of-all-trades approach that borders on dilettantism, and that it undercuts IOM's ability or willingness to speak up about protection concerns out of fear of jeopardizing their always-uncertain funding streams. It also creates problems with predicable and sustainable responses, as IOM works where it can get projects funded, and may disengage suddenly if funds dry up sooner than expected. The focus on selling services leads, some suggest, to a tendency to "over commit and under deliver," resulting in jadedness and inter-organizational tensions.[119] Activities such as in-depth staff training and policy development processes are difficult to adequately fund under this model, as is the maintenance of a robust headquarters, leading to staff burnout. At the same time, because IOM's senior level promotion systems put significant emphasis on fundraising, declining contentious but lucrative work is effectively disincentivized, particularly as there is little formal reward for scrupulously advocating and upholding protection standards.

Decentralization, similarly, has its proponents and detractors. A reform process initiated after McKinley's departure rebalanced the institution's approach to decentralization, putting more power in the hands of the regional offices, and somewhat less at the country level. Decentralization encourages responsiveness to member state concerns and keeps staff attuned to field-level concerns. Yet it can also generate unpredictability and credibility challenges as principles, policies, and commitments may be interpreted inconsistently, and partners cannot simply call headquarters for definitive answers. As one frustrated IO partner expressed it, "There's no recourse" if national and particularly regional offices fail to address important concerns, or espouse troubling interpretations of protection standards; "If you don't get it from the IOM regional director, you're not going to get it."[120] This amplifies the power and influence of heads of mission and, especially, regional directors, in shaping the quality and orientation of IOM's engagements.

Reflecting on decentralization and projectization, many IOM officials openly recognize that although the model has been an effective vehicle for expansion, it also creates certain problems for the organization. Many of these problems, such as hesitancy to critique governments that control humanitarian access and funding streams, are not unique to IOM, although they are heightened by this institutional approach. The model has generated particular vulnerabilities on questions of principle, fostering the perception in some quarters that IOM would take money for anything. One influential IOM official suggested that while the organization is now trying to mature, it is in some senses still like a "teenager": it wants everything now, it wants to do whatever it chooses, and yet also wants to be taken seriously as an "adult" organization, even though this means not always being able to do everything or have everything it might want.[121] Moving forward, this tension and the broader range of challenges associated with projectization and decentralization will continue to shape both IOM's internal culture and its position in the collection of actors involved in responding to migration and humanitarian crises.

Conclusion: building institutional autonomy on unlikely foundations

On several counts, IOM has inhospitable or even overtly hostile foundations for exercising institutional autonomy and influencing the governance of migration, particularly in hotly contested displacement situations. Marooned outside the UN system, for decades IOM toiled in relative obscurity in the UN's institutional shadow. The agency lacks a clearly framed mandate. Under its Constitution it has no formally articulated protection obligations or defined populations to represent. Even more so than other major IOs, IOM is highly deferential to its member states and dependent on their voluntary financial support under a decentralized, projectized institutional model that compels IOM officials to constantly package and sell the organization's services and tacitly discourages critique of the states on whose largesse the agency depends.

And yet IOM is not merely a servant of its state masters. Since its inception in 1951, and especially over the last 30 years, IOM has gradually cultivated its ability to autonomously shape responses to a wide range of migration-related

42 IOM's mandate, structure, and culture

issues, and its own place in the international system. This is manifested most obviously in IOM's dramatic expansion, including in terms of budget, areas of work, field presence, and membership. It is somewhat paradoxical that accruing more member states would help IOM achieve greater autonomy from the dictates of these very states – but the increase in the membership ranks has solidified IOM's transformation into a truly global agency, tempered (but not eliminated) its dependence on a small clutch of governments, and is changing what it means for IOM to be a "member state-led" outfit. IOM's expansion has been achieved despite the aforementioned constraints, but also in some senses *because* of them. That is, characteristics that appear at first blush to be constraints have proven to be key assets for IOM in its drive to grow as an institution and in terms of its influence. It has, for example, parlayed its imprecise, rather obscure mandate and its near-complete reliance on project-based donations into influential interventions in an ever-expanding range of activities – especially, as I discuss in the following chapter, in the humanitarian sphere. In leveraging its particular institutional characteristics to secure its own survival and in turn prosper, IOM is following a path well worn by other IOs. Although IOM is sometimes seen and portrayed as an outlier in the constellation of actors involved in responding to forced migration, in trying to understand IOM's evolution and dynamics it is thus also important to be attuned to the ways in which the agency is emblematic of broader trends and strategies shaping the politics of international organizations.

Notes

1 See for example Michael Barnett and Martha Finnemore, *Rules for the World: International Organizations in Global Politics* (Ithaca: Cornell University Press, 2004); Joel Oestreich, ed., *International Organizations as Self-Directed Actors: A Framework for Analysis* (London: Routledge, 2012); Gil Loescher, *UNHCR and World Politics: A Perilous Path* (Oxford: Oxford University Press, 2001); and Alexander Betts, Gil Loescher and James Milner, *UNHCR: The Politics and Practice of Refugee Protection*, 2nd Edition (London: Routledge, 2012).
2 See for example Antoine Pécoud, "What Do We Know About the International Organization for Migration?" *Journal of Ethnic and Migration Studies* 44, no. 10 (2018): 1621–1638; Ishan Ashutosh and Allison Mountz, "Migration Management for the Benefit of Whom? Interrogating the Work of the International Organization for Migration," *Citizenship Studies* 15, no. 1 (2011): 21–38; Rutvica Andrijasevic and William Walters, "The International Organization for Migration and the International Government of Borders," *Environment and Planning D: Society and Space* 28, no. 6 (2010): 977–999; and Fabian Georgi, "For the Benefit of Some: The International Organization for Migration and its Global Migration Management," in *The Politics of International Migration Management*, eds. Martin Geiger and Antoine Pécoud (Basingstoke: Palgrave, 2010): 45–72; Asher Lazarus Hirsch and Cameron Doig, "Outsourcing Control: The International Organization for Migration in Indonesia," *International Journal of Human Rights* 22, no. 5 (2018): 681–708.
3 Barnett and Finnemore, *Rules for the World*.
4 IOM, *Constitution and Basic Texts*, 2nd Edition, http://publications.iom.int/books/constitution-and-basic-texts-2nd-edition.
5 Michelle Ducasse-Rogier, *The International Organization for Migration: 1951–2001* (Geneva: IOM, 2001), 69.

IOM's mandate, structure, and culture **43**

6 IOM, *About IOM*, www.iom.int/about-iom.
7 Interview, IOM official 1, November 2015.
8 IOM Constitution, Preamble.
9 Richard Perruchoud, "From the Intergovernmental Committee for European Migration to the International Organization for Migration," *International Journal of Refugee Law* 1, no. 4 (1989): 501–517; and Susan Martin, *International Migration: Evolving Trends from the Early Twentieth Century to the Present* (Cambridge: Cambridge University Press, 2014), 132.
10 IOM Constitution, Article 1.3.
11 IOM Constitution, Article 2.b.
12 Jerome Elie, "The Historical Roots of Cooperation between the UN High Commissioner for Refugees and the International Organization for Migration," *Global Governance* 16 (2010): 345–360.
13 IASC IDP Protection Policy (1999). The relevant bodies of law include human rights law, international humanitarian law, and refugee law.
14 UNHCR also has a mandate to protect stateless persons.
15 See IOM Humanitarian Policy: Principles for Humanitarian Action, IOM Council, October 2015, C/106/CRP/20; IOM, Migration Crisis Operational Framework, 2012, MC/2355; IOM Council Resolution 1243, 101st session, 27 November 2012; IOM, Migration Governance Framework, 2015; IOM Council Resolution 1310, 106th session, 4 December 2015, C/106/RES/1310.
16 This will presumably become less common with IOM's enthusiastic rebranding as the "UN Migration Agency."
17 Michael Barnett and Martha Finnemore, "The Power of Liberal International Organizations," in *Power in Global Governance*, eds. Michael Barnett and Raymond Duvall (Cambridge: Cambridge University Press, 2005), 171.
18 Interview, IOM official 1.
19 Interview, IOM official 14; Interview, humanitarian actor 1 (UN), November 2015.
20 Interview, humanitarian actor 3 (NGO), November 2015.
21 Interview, humanitarian actor 5 (NGO), November 2015.
22 Interview, humanitarian actor 7 (UN), December 2015.
23 IOM, *Migration Crisis Operational Framework*, para 11, italics added.
24 IOM, *Humanitarian Policy*, para II.4.
25 IOM, *Humanitarian Policy*, para III.1a-d.
26 IOM, *Humanitarian Policy*, para IV.1, IV.5.
27 IOM, *Migration Governance Framework*, 1; see also IOM, *Emergency Manual: Migration Governance Framework Overview*, https://emergencymanual.iom.int/entry/26102/migration-governance-framework-migof.
28 IOM, *Migration Governance Framework*, 1.
29 Agreement Concerning the Relationship Between the United Nations and the International Organization for Migration, Article 2(5).
30 Agreement Concerning the Relationship Between the United Nations and the International Organization for Migration, Article 2(2). For a legal analysis of this agreement, focusing on its implications for rights protection, see Elspeth Guild, Stefanie Grant and Kees Groenendijk, "IOM and the UN: Unfinished Business," *Queen Mary University of London School of Law Legal Studies Research Papers*, no. 255 (2017): 1–24.
31 For instance, the IOM head of mission made this argument before the UK House of Lords EU Committee, in a session on the management of EU asylum claims. The Committee's view was that if IOM facilitated voluntary returns on behalf of the British government, then it should formally recognize itself as subject to international human rights law. See House of Lords European Union Committee, 11th Report of Session 2003–04, "Handling EU Asylum Claims: New Approaches Examined," HL Paper 74, 30 April 2004, paras. 121–124, discussed in Guy Goodwin-Gill, *A Brief and Somewhat*

44 IOM's mandate, structure, and culture

Sceptical Perspective on the International Organization for Migration, www.kaldor
centre.unsw.edu.au/publication/brief-and-somewhat-sceptical-perspective-interna
tional-organization-migration, 7 April 2019.

32 Agreement Concerning the Relationship Between the United Nations and the International Organization for Migration, Article 2(3).

33 Guild, Grant and Groenendijk, "IOM and the UN."

34 Interview, IOM official 9, November 2015.

35 Interview, IOM official 10, November 2015.

36 Interview, IOM official 9.

37 WFP, *WFP Humanitarian Protection Policy* (Rome: WFP, 2012).

38 Lance Bartholomeusz, "The Mandate of UNRWA at Sixty," *Refugee Survey Quar-
terly* 28, no. 2–3 (2010): 456; and Scott Custer, "UNRWA: Protection and Assistance
to Palestinian Refugees," in *International Law and the Israeli-Palestinian Conflict*, eds. Susan Akram, Michael Dumper, Michael Link and Iain Scobbie (London:
Routledge, 2011). UNRWA's claimed protection mandate remains disputed. See for
example Susan Akram, "Myths and Realities of the Palestinian Refugee Problem," in
International Law and the Israeli-Palestinian Conflict, eds. Susan Akram, Michael
Dumper, Michael Link and Iain Scobbie (London: Routledge, 2011).

39 Pécoud, "What Do We Know"; Hirsch and Doig, "Outsourcing Control."

40 Interview, member state official 2, December 2016. On UNHCR's failures to uphold
its own professed moral values, see Barnett and Finnemore, *Rules for the World*.

41 Interview, humanitarian actor 8 (NGO), December 2016.

42 Interview, member state official 11, July 2017.

43 Pécoud, "What Do We Know," 5, 12.

44 Interview, human rights advocate 10, December 2016.

45 Interview, humanitarian actor 5 (NGO).

46 Interview, independent expert 4, July 2017.

47 Interview, IOM official 14.

48 Interviews, IOM officials 2 and 9, November 2015; Interview, member state official
1, November 2015; Interview, member state official 4, December 2016.

49 Elaine McGregor, "Money Matters: The Role of Funding in Migration Governance,"
International Migration Institute Network Working Papers 149 (2019), 15, 21.

50 Interview, member state official 4; Interview, IOM official 2.

51 Interview, member state official 4.

52 Interview, IOM official 9.

53 Interview, member state official 4.

54 Kristy Siegfried, "How Will Joining the UN Change IOM?" *IRIN*, 12 August 2016.

55 Interview, IOM official 2; Interview, member state official 1; Interview, member state
official 12, July 2017.

56 Interview, IOM official 2.

57 Interview, member state official 4.

58 Interview, independent expert 3, December 2016.

59 McGregor, "Money Matters," 16–17.

60 Interview, member state official 7.

61 Interview, independent expert 3; Interviews, member state officials 1, 4 and 7.

62 For a discussion of this dynamic in relation to US involvement with UNHCR and
the refugee regime, see Susan Martin and Elizabeth Ferris, "US Leadership and the
International Refugee Regime," *Refuge* 33, no. 1 (2017): 18–28.

63 Interview, independent expert 3.

64 Interview, member state officials 5 and 7, December 2016.

65 Interview, member state official 5.

66 Marta Foresti, "Welcome, Director General. There's a Lot to Do," *IRIN*, 2 July 2018.

67 See e.g. António Vitorino, Message to IOM Staff, Geneva, 1 October 2018.

IOM's mandate, structure, and culture **45**

68 IOM, *Organizational Structure*, www.iom.int/organizational-structure; IOM, *IOM Snapshot 2019* (Geneva: IOM), 1.
69 Executive Committee of the High Commissioner's Programme, *Human Resources, Including Staff Welfare*, Standing Committee, 73rd meeting, 5 September 2018, EC/69/SC/CRP.14, 3.
70 IOM, *International Cooperation and Partnerships*, www.iom.int/international-cooperation-partnerships.
71 The names of these departments have changed over the years, but for simplicity I use DMM and DOE throughout this discussion.
72 IOM, *Migration Management*, www.iom.int/migration-management.
73 IOM defines AVR as "administrative, logistical, financial and reintegration support to rejected asylum seekers, victims of trafficking in human beings, stranded migrants, qualified nationals and other migrants unable or unwilling to remain in the host country who volunteer to return to their countries of origin." See IOM, *Key Migration Terms*, www.iom.int/key-migration-terms.
74 IOM, *Operations and Emergencies*, www.iom.int/operations-and-emergencies.
75 Ibid.
76 Erin Graham, "International Organizations as Collective Agents: Fragmentation and the Limits of Principal Control at the World Health Organization," *European Journal of International Relations* 20, no. 2 (2014): 366–390.
77 Interviews, IOM officials 6 and 9, November 2015.
78 Interview, IOM official 10.
79 Ibid.
80 Interview, human rights advocate 5, November 2015.
81 Interview, IOM official 13, November 2015.
82 Interview, IOM official 1. On the IOM Development Fund, and the ways in which IOM's migration management work benefit from the growth of its humanitarian engagement, see also Martin, *International Migration*.
83 Interview, IOM official 13.
84 Interview, humanitarian actor 5 (NGO); Interviews, IOM official 9, 10.
85 Interview, IOM official 9. On humanitarian border management, see Philippe Frowd, "Developmental Borderwork and the International Organization for Migration," *Journal of Ethnic and Migration Studies* 44, no. 10 (2018): 1656–1672.
86 Interview, IOM official 2.
87 See for example Kent Kille and Bob Reinalda, "The Evolvement of International Secretariats, Executive Heads and Leadership in Inter-Organizational Relations," in *Palgrave Handbook on Inter-Organizational Relations*, eds. Rafael Biermann and Joachim A. Koops (London: Palgrave Macmillan, 2017), 217–242; and Kent Kille, "Secretaries-General of International Organizations: Leadership Capacity and Qualities," in *Routledge Handbook of International Organization*, ed. Bob Reinalda (London: Routledge, 2013), 218–230.
88 IOM Constitution, Chapter V, Article 13(1).
89 IOM Constitution, Chapter V, Article 13(2).
90 Interview, independent expert 4.
91 Interview, independent expert 3.
92 Interview, independent expert 4.
93 Ibid.; Interview, member state official 11.
94 IOM, *Brunson McKinley, IOM Director General*, www.iom.int/jahia/webdav/shared/shared/mainsite/microsites/IDM/workshops/global_labour_mobility_0809102007/bios/bio_mckinley.htm.
95 Interview, IOM official 12, November 2015; Interview, humanitarian actor 5 (NGO); Interviews, humanitarian actors 8 (NGO) and 9 (UN), December 2016.
96 IOM, *Biography of William Lacy Swing, IOM Director General*, www.iom.int/director-general (Visited 22 August 2017).

46 IOM's mandate, structure, and culture

97 Megan Bradley and Merve Erdilmen, "Speaking of Rights: Rights Talk, Protection Commitments and the IOM," Paper presented at the International Studies Association Conference, Toronto, 27 March 2019.
98 Interview, humanitarian actor 5 (NGO).
99 Ibid.
100 Interview, humanitarian actor 8 (NGO).
101 IOM labels this is the "lowest rate of administrative support" charged by inter-governmental organizations. See IOM, *Organizational Structure*, www.iom.int/organizational-structure.
102 Interview, humanitarian actor 8 (NGO).
103 IOM, *Snapshot 2019*, 1.
104 Interview, human rights advocate 10.
105 Personal communication, July 2019.
106 IOM Council, *Programme and Budget for 2018*, 9 October 2017, 48.
107 Interviews, IOM officials 6 and 9; Interview, humanitarian actor 4 (NGO), November 2015.
108 UN Chief Executives Board for Coordination, *Human Resources by Grade*, www.unsystem.org/content/hr-grade; Executive Committee of the High Commissioner's Programme, *Human Resources, Including Staff Welfare*, Standing Committee, 70th meeting, 31 August 2017, EC/68/SC/CRP.26, 3. UNHCR also had some 4000 "affili-ates," such as interns, UN volunteers and consultants.
109 Interview, independent expert 4; Interview, IOM official 9.
110 IOM, *Gender Equity Policy 2015–2019*, 106th Session, IOM Council, 19 November 2015, C/106/INF/8/Rev.1, para 55.
111 Interview, human rights advocate 9, December 2016.
112 Interviews, IOM officials 1, 2, 9, 10, 11, 12, November 2015. On IOM staff members' ethos, see also Frowd, "Developmental Borderwork."
113 Interview, human rights advocate 5.
114 Interview, humanitarian actor 9 (UN); Interview, member state official 5.
115 Interview, member state official 3, December 2016.
116 Interview, member state official 1.
117 Interview, IOM official 4, November 2015.
118 Interview, member state official 11.
119 Interview, humanitarian actor 7 (UN). IOM has taken some steps to address this con-cern by mapping out in advance its anticipated funding requirements for each year. For instance, IOM now publishes a "Humanitarian Compendium" in which it lays out the interventions it proposes to respond to key needs, and reports on the extent to which the interventions have been funded. The Compendium does not, however, seem to be fully updated. Annual anticipated funding requirements, including in relation to the "mobility dimensions of crises" are also laid out in IOM's yearly Migration Initia-tives report.
120 Interview, humanitarian actor 9 (UN).
121 Interview, IOM official 13.

2
AN EVOLVING HUMANITARIAN ENTREPRENEUR

- *IOM's humanitarian entrepreneurialism*
  - *"Jack-of-all-trades" humanitarianism*
  - *Creating humanitarian niches*
  - *Cultivating populations of concern*
- *Growing up and growing out: IOM's evolving humanitarian identity*
  - *Humanitarianism and protection: IOM's conceptions and commitments*
  - *Policy processes: shaping IOM's humanitarian engagement*
- *Conclusion: implications for the governance of forced migration and humanitarian emergencies*

In recent years, IOM has provided humanitarian aid to internally displaced people in conflicts and disasters; evacuated migrant workers trapped in civil wars; constructed shelters for thousands uprooted by typhoons, earthquakes, and floods; run disarmament, demobilization, and reintegration programs in post-conflict communities; implemented major property restitution and compensation programs; become a leading source of data on displacement and migrant deaths; and resettled thousands of refugees. And this is only a tiny fraction of the interventions that IOM undertakes each year in relation to forced migration and humanitarian emergencies. In 2019 alone, IOM was involved in major humanitarian operations in Nigeria, Yemen, Syria, Venezuela, Bangladesh, the Democratic Republic of Congo, Cameroon, Chad, Somalia, South Sudan, Mozambique, Malawi, Zimbabwe, Iraq, Ethiopia, and Afghanistan, in addition to smaller missions elsewhere.[1] How has IOM come to play such a dizzying array of roles in countries around the world? What effect has this had on IOM and on international responses to forced migration?[2]

This chapter explores how IOM has expanded in the humanitarian sphere, and the implications of this expansion. In particular, I examine how conceptions of IOM's humanitarian roles and commitments, and its place in the international system, have developed inside and outside the organization. While some humanitarian actors and human rights advocates continue to harbor serious reservations about IOM, many also recognize that it is not the organization it once was. In contrast to its earlier reputation as a "cowboy" too quick to compromise individuals' rights to serve states' interests, IOM is, according to some observers, maturing into a more reliable, rights-respecting, collaborative member of the humanitarian system – if more slowly than some would prefer. IOM's evolution is hardly serendipitous. Rather, it is the product of strategic decisions made over the past 25 years, and gradual shifts in institutional stances and culture.

I present IOM's development in this field as the result of a two-pronged process. First, IOM has capitalized on many of the institutional characteristics discussed in Chapter 1, including its "permissive" Constitution, and its reputation for flexibility, efficiency, and logistical proficiency, to entrepreneurially expand the range of work that it undertakes in humanitarian emergencies and "post-crisis" situations. It has prospered as a jack-of-all-trades, but has avoided being a master of none by simultaneously developing distinctive niches which have provided footholds for further growth. IOM has, for instance, become a recognized leader in collecting data on displaced populations, and managing camps for IDPs in disaster situations. Through such efforts, IOM has positioned itself as an expert authority in a crowded field, lending legitimacy to its continued expansion.

Second, recognizing that (at least professed) fidelity to humanitarian principles and human rights norms is, increasingly, a *sin qua non* for acceptance as a legitimate actor in the field, IOM has attempted to recast itself as an organization that is explicitly committed to these standards and acts in support of them, notwithstanding its lack of a formal protection mandate. To this end, it has articulated commitments to humanitarian principles and human rights norms in internal policies, and has sought member state approval of these stances. IOM has also integrated "rights-talk" into its institutional discourse, and started to more regularly advocate for particular groups such as "migrants in crisis," for whom IOM wants to position itself as the natural representative – just as UNHCR is for refugees, and UNICEF for children. In pursuing these strategies, IOM has obvious self-interests that may seem at odds with popular conceptions of humanitarianism as an altruistic endeavor: IOM is looking to secure its organizational acceptance and in turn its prosperity, and affirm the legitimacy of its membership in the UN family. Yet such self-interest is a longstanding characteristic of the humanitarian enterprise which, as Barnett argues, has always been "about meeting the needs of others and meeting our own needs."[3]

I begin by discussing the contours of IOM's humanitarian entrepreneurialism – mapping out IOM's gap-filling role, some of the areas in which it has developed niches, and the "populations of concern" it is cultivating. I then explore the evolution of IOM's humanitarian identity, examining conceptions of IOM's humanitarian and protection commitments inside and outside the organization, and internal policy processes that have sought to inform IOM's humanitarian engagements. In concluding, I reflect on the significance of these developments for IOM, and for the governance of forced migration and humanitarian emergencies.

In light of this analysis, predominant explanations of why states work with and through IOM appear starkly underdeveloped. The idea that states turn to IOM primarily because it is outside the UN and unfettered by normative commitments, is now simply out of step with the reality of IOM as a "related organization" in the UN system with a relatively detailed set of agreements, policies, and frameworks that commit the agency to respect and advance human rights and humanitarian principles. Even before IOM entered the UN system, this explanation could not effectively explain why member states accepted and funded IOM's dramatic expansion in the humanitarian field, such that work related to forced migration in emergencies and their aftermath now comprises the majority of the agency's budget, staff, and field presence. Exploring IOM's evolution and struggles for legitimacy and influence in the humanitarian sector is not to condone or minimize the concerns associated with its continued involvement in activities in tension with humanitarian and protection principles, such as interventions that discourage or effectively restrict access to asylum.[4] Indeed, in a sense IOM's continued involvement in such activities is all the more troubling because the organization now clearly identifies as a humanitarian actor with protection obligations – meaning that it should know better and do better by the populations it claims to serve. I discuss tensions between IOM's humanitarian engagements and other migration management activities in greater detail in Chapter 3.

IOM's humanitarian entrepreneurialism

In his first speech as IOM's new director general, delivered to IOM's staff on his first day in office, António Vitorino reflected on the nature of IOM. In this address, he effectively acknowledged the entrepreneurialism that is in many ways the lynchpin of IOM's institutional character, and the characteristics that have fostered it, particularly in the humanitarian sector. Vitorino asserted,

> the advantages of IOM, that you know so well, [are] its flexibility, its effectiveness, its decentralized nature and being a cost-effective organization. . . . Of course [we] will also need to be very clear on one point: we stick to our very nature. We are an organization very much close to migrants, especially those who are more vulnerable and those who are in need of humanitarian assistance. And, we will stick to our very nature, to our DNA, being flexible in providing tailor-made solutions and being effective in contributing to the management of migratory flows, linking together countries of origin, of transit and of destination.[5]

As Vitorino recognized, IOM, like many other IOs, has a long history of organizational entrepreneurialism.[6] As demand has shifted for different kinds of work, and competition has emerged for limited donor funds, IOM (and its predecessor agencies) has recast itself, moving into new regions and fields of

50 An evolving humanitarian entrepreneur

work. IOM adopted this strategy at an early stage, as the need for work with displaced and "surplus" populations in post–World War II Europe dwindled.[7] IOM has grown through a practical strategy of analyzing gaps in existing systems and moving to fill them, creating demand for its own services by raising awareness of underexamined issues and even helping to constitute target populations for IOM interventions, such as "migrants in crisis."

"Jack-of-all-trades" humanitarianism

Longstanding IOM officials argue that IOM is and has always been a humanitarian agency.[8] However, IOM's sustained, largescale involvement in emergency operations really took off in the 1990s. This was catalyzed by increasing recognition of the links between migration, peace, and security, and by IOM's successful involvement in influential missions, such as the emergency evacuation of hundreds of thousands of migrant workers caught up in the Gulf War. In 1991, IOM's role in emergency response was recognized through a standing invitation to the IASC.[9] Yet many of IOM's member states were initially skeptical of the organization's ambitions in emergency response and humanitarian operations. For instance, an important strategic plan presented to IOM member states in 1995 included the objective that IOM would "provide migration assistance to persons affected by emergencies."[10] While the drafters of the strategic plan indicated that IOM did "not view itself primarily as an emergency response organization," this did not assuage the concerns of member states who worried that if IOM were to expand in this area, it would encroach on the work of other international organizations – a concern that resurfaced later in the 1990s, when IOM proposed taking on a more active role vis-à-vis IDPs in conflicts. Despite these concerns, IOM broke with its typical deference towards its member states, moving forward with its plans to expand in this area. In 1992, Director General Purcell established an Emergency Response Unit (ERU) at IOM's Geneva headquarters to strengthen the agency's ability to respond to emergency situations, building on experiences in the Gulf War operation. Between 1992 and 1998, the ERU shored up IOM's rapid deployment capabilities, but was disbanded in 1998 in the context of the organization's decentralization efforts, which saw responsibility for emergency preparedness and response efforts delegated to regional offices. This arrangement proved short lived. By 2000, with IOM extensively involved in crisis responses in East Timor and Kosovo, the unit was resurrected as the Emergency and Post-Conflict Division. As defined by McKinley in his statement to the November 1999 meeting of the IOM Council, the purpose of the division – a precursor of the current Department of Emergencies and Operations – was "to allow IOM to react more promptly and in a more systematic way to crises."[11]

While the humanitarian field has been a fruitful site for IOM's entrepreneurial ambitions, the organization's broad entrepreneurial ethos has often come into tension with humanitarian values and protection principles, bringing into question the legitimacy of IOM's claim to the humanitarian mantle. Indeed, officials who ardently defend IOM's humanitarian identity also acknowledge that the organization has sometimes undermined itself as such, particularly in the 1990s when, under McKinley's leadership, IOM pursued an agenda of almost unbridled expansion. IOM's entrepreneurial efforts in this period were facilitated by its decentralization and the implementation of the "projectization" model discussed in Chapter 1, whereby member states effectively contract IOM to carry out different activities. Heads of mission, operating with considerable independence and unrestrained by protection mandates and binding principles, had strong professional incentives to bring in lucrative projects. These dynamics, alongside increased transnational migration, saw IOM move far beyond its traditional logistics specialization, earning a reputation as a hungry, unscrupulous actor willing to undertake increasingly diverse activities, including morally troubling work such as involvement in offshore asylum claims processing. Especially in Europe, IOM became known as a returns organization, a reputation that overshadowed its innovative and less controversial humanitarian work. Although tempered in some ways, this tension continues to characterize IOM's role.

IOM's entrepreneurial efforts, including in the humanitarian sector, have been enabled by its "permissive" Constitution (as discussed in Chapter 1), which does not limit the organization to particular kinds of work, or to supporting a narrowly defined population. Complementing the flexibility allowed by its Constitution, IOM has strategically cultivated a reputation as a practical, "can-do" organization that is adept at executing logistically complex projects quickly and cost-effectively. IOM's member states and donors applaud the agency as an operationally focused, efficient, "lean," and "nimble" outfit that can rapidly scale up and down as needed. Initially, IOM prospered as a "jack-of-all-trades," ready and willing to take up a diverse range of work, even in areas where it did not have deep expertise and where the connection to migration was tangential at best. Consequently, IOM has at times been derided as the "poubelle" of the international system, the organization that accepts the work that doesn't fit under the more precise mandates of other agencies. Although some donors and other actors have chided IOM for accepting tasks that go beyond its expertise and have little, if any, connection to migration, others applaud the agency's "responsive" approach, and its refusal to be overly precious about mandate issues.[12] For instance, in a high-level panel on IOM's humanitarian activities at the 2015 IOM Council session, the head of the Office of US Foreign Disaster Assistance warmly saluted IOM for playing a key role in the response to Ebola in West Africa. The connection between migration and Ebola was limited, but rather than seeing this as a concern, US donors expressed appreciation for IOM's readiness to step into an extremely difficult situation, working in ways that gave donors clear oversight on the implementation of high-profile, high-risk interventions.[13]

IOM has responded to critiques of its work as scattergun in part through the development of tools such as the 2012 Migration Crisis Operational Framework, discussed in the following section, which maps out the connections between human mobility and IOM's wide range of work in crisis situations. Further, IOM staff insist that increasingly the agency does decline requests for assistance from its member states, whether on legal grounds, on the basis of moral or reputational concerns, or as a result of an insufficiently clear connection to migration.[14] IOM staff also point out that work on issues such as disarmament, demobilization, and reintegration (DRR) of ex-combatants, which has been criticized as overly removed from the agency's migration mandate, has proven to be integral to effective responses to forced migration, such as when the return of refugees and IDPs is hindered by the presence of disenfranchised former fighters. The UN's Emergency Relief Coordinator has sought out IOM's expertise on the relationship between DRR and displacement in cases such as the conflict in the Central African Republic – a vindication for IOM staff who have defended the appropriateness of the agency's engagement in this area.[15]

While IOM's jack-of-all-trades entrepreneurialism has sparked critiques of the agency as an insufficiency-discerning "yes man," by picking up the slack in the international humanitarian system, IOM has served important functions. By papering over gaps, IOM has helped respond to overlooked populations, and has enabled other agencies such as UNHCR to maintain more tightly focused mandates. The creation of the IOM Emergency Response Fund, which enables IOM to respond to crisis situations before donor commitments are confirmed, has enabled IOM to be a more reliable and rapid gap-filler. Rather than simply papering over gaps, it would (from a protection perspective at least) presumably be more desirable to actually *fill* them by attributing responsibility to particular organizations. To some extent, this has taken place through humanitarian reform processes, with IOM taking on formal responsibilities towards certain populations such as IDPs in disaster situations. However, as new fissures continue to emerge, IOM's gap-filling role remains salient, both for IOM itself as a growth opportunity, and for the humanitarian system more broadly.

Creating humanitarian niches

Not content to simply serve as a jack-of-all-trades in the humanitarian system, IOM has simultaneously cultivated niche areas of work that it can use as a springboard to bigger roles and more systematic influence. The following subsections sketch out some of the niches IOM has developed that have been particularly influential in underpinning its expansion and evolution.

Humanitarian people-movers: resettlement, evacuations . . . and returns?

Resettlement is the historic backbone of IOM's humanitarian work. If there is an iconic image of IOM's work, it is of refugees carrying blue plastic bags emblazoned with the IOM logo and filled with paperwork, as they make their way through international airports to resettlement countries. IOM has supported resettlement since its establishment in 1951; its contemporary resettlement services are a direct extension of its early efforts to help move displaced populations and other migrants in post–World War II Europe to new communities. While IOM now interprets Article 1 of its Constitution broadly, to underpin a wide range of work, much of Article 1 is clearly focused on supporting resettlement. Most explicitly, the Constitution calls on IOM to "concern itself with the organized transfer of refugees, displaced persons and other individuals in need of international migration services."[16] Over the last decade, IOM has facilitated the resettlement of more than 1.19 million refugees and other "vulnerable persons of concern" from some 165 locations worldwide.[17] In 2017, IOM assisted 42 states with the resettlement, relocation (within the European Union), and humanitarian admission of almost 138,000 forced migrants, including through major operations in Afghanistan, Jordan, Lebanon, Iraq, Turkey, Ethiopia, Uganda, Tanzania, Rwanda, Kenya, Nepal, and Greece.[18] This is bureaucratically intensive work that hews to IOM's traditional strengths in logistics and transportation. IOM cooperates closely on resettlement with UNHCR, which nominates refugees for resettlement, and with the member states who receive resettled refugees. IOM's four core resettlement services for member states are case management; health assessments and related assistance; movement management and operations (including the transportation of refugees to the resettlement country); and addressing integration through pre-departure activities such as cultural orientation and post-arrival support.[19]

According to IOM, the two overarching principles of its resettlement assistance are refugee-centered programming, and linking pre-departure and post-arrival support, where possible, to facilitate integration.[20] IOM identifies itself as an advocate for refugees in the resettlement process, but given its migration management approach, frames this as a matter of using "multi-level quality assurance controls" to prevent fraud and other challenges to the integrity of the process.[21] The agency underscores that

> Being vigilant about the quality of our work is the best way to advocate for refugees. Putting in place assurance controls at various stages in the process and by multiple actors helps us to minimize errors and enhance our value of service.[22]

This approach underscores that while resettlement is portrayed as a humanitarian undertaking, it also has important migration management functions. As Hyndman and Giles stress, through resettlement states can select the refugees they desire, legitimize refugees' containment in the global South, and enable the vilification of those with the temerity to actively seek out asylum in wealthy countries rather than patiently waiting for resettlement opportunities that, for the vast majority, will never come.[23] Indeed, IOM's resettlement assistance work serves as a reminder of the impossibility of separating out migration management and humanitarian action with displaced persons, in that care and control have always been the two sides of the humanitarian coin.[24]

Alongside its resettlement activities, IOM has become one of the leading actors worldwide in the complex work of emergency evacuations. As with IOM's resettlement efforts, emergency evacuations rely on the organization's expertise in logistics and transportation, and play to its reputation for efficient crisis operations. IOM has undertaken emergency evacuations involving a wide range of

54 An evolving humanitarian entrepreneur

groups, including IDPs and migrant workers who become displaced, trapped or stranded when conflicts break out. Because they are not fleeing their own states of origin, most migrant workers in conflict situations do not qualify as refugees and therefore do not fall under UNHCR's mandate – positioning IOM to step in to fill an important gap in humanitarian response. IOM's first major operation to assist migrants stranded or displaced in war started in the early 1990s in the context of Iraq's invasion of Kuwait and the subsequent Gulf War, when it evacuated some 250,000 migrants, particularly from South Asia, who were trapped in the region.[25] IOM's involvement in this area of work continued; for example, during the 2006 crisis in Lebanon sparked by clashes between Israel and Hezbollah, IOM evacuated some 13,000 third-country nationals from Lebanon, particularly people from developing countries without the means to facilitate their citizens' exit. As addressed in Chapter 3, IOM also played a prominent role in assisting and evacuating migrant workers caught in the violence accompanying the fall of the Gaddafi regime in Libya in 2011.[26] More recently, IOM has helped more than 4,000 migrant workers trapped inside Syria to escape the country's long-running civil war.[27] As discussed later, IOM's work in this area has helped the agency to constitute "migrants in crisis" as a vulnerable group that it now seeks to represent in humanitarian forums such as the IASC, and around which it has facilitated the clarification of norms and best practices.

In addition to evacuating migrant workers in emergencies, IOM has also been involved in supporting the relocation of IDPs in conflict and disaster situations. For example, alongside its efforts to evacuate migrant workers from the conflict in the Central African Republic (CAR), it was part of complex and sometimes controversial efforts to relocate displaced citizens of CAR who were at risk of violence.[28] IOM has helped to temporarily evacuate IDPs and other marginalized community members from high-risk areas in impending disasters such as incoming hurricanes, in order to reduce losses of life.

Beyond moving people in the relatively uncontroversial contexts of resettlement and emergency evacuations, IOM also applies its long experience in transportation, logistics, and (re)integration to the return of IDPs and the repatriation of refugees, rejected asylum seekers, and other migrants. IOM's involvement in repatriation movements began in earnest in the 1980s, when resettlement places began to decline in the twilight of the Cold War and states, UNHCR, and other actors began to reorient their attention to returns.[29] IOM and its member states have typically presented the facilitation of refugees' voluntary repatriation as a humanitarian undertaking. While UNHCR usually takes the lead in these processes, IOM has often played a supporting role, including through arranging transportation and offering reintegration activities. In contrast, IOM has generally not labeled its "assisted voluntary return" (AVR) programs as humanitarian, but rather as a separate element of migration management. Yet these programs have important humanitarian implications, as rejected asylum seekers and others who participate in them are often returning to instability. In some cases, however, IOM actively positions these efforts as explicitly humanitarian. For instance, as discussed in Chapter 3, IOM calls its involvement in the return of migrants,

An evolving humanitarian entrepreneur **55**

including would-be asylum seekers, from Libyan detention centers "voluntary humanitarian return," although some contend that these returns undermine or even represent the antithesis of humanitarian values.

Responding to internal displacement, particularly in disasters

Although it is rarely acknowledged, IOM's work with IDPs has fueled much of its growth, and its movement into the mainstream of the humanitarian system. In 2016, for instance, IOM assisted over 19 million IDPs – making IDPs IOM's biggest "beneficiary" population by far, and placing IOM among the most active intergovernmental organizations concerned with IDPs.[30] (In contrast, in 2016 UNHCR indicates that it assisted 13.9 million IDPs.)[31] As the IOM Constitution charges the agency to facilitate "the organized transfer of refugees, displaced persons and other individuals in need of migration services," IOM has strategically interpreted this as a mandate for a much broader range of work with IDPs.[32] In 2002, IOM released its first policy on IDPs, in which it opined that the "Constitution of IOM appears to be the only treaty providing a specific mandate for 'displaced persons' to an international governmental organization."[33] This document recognizes the 1998 Guiding Principles on Internal Displacement as a critical normative standard that "should be closely followed in all programmes benefitting IDPs, and in all attempts to address the issue of displacement."[34] In 2017, IOM released a new Framework for Addressing Internal Displacement, which explicitly integrates the Guiding Principles, and commits the organization to a rights-based approach, including "work[ing] towards effective respect for the human rights of migrants and uphold[ing] the human dignity and well-being of all mobile populations, which includes IDPs."[35]

While these strategic mandate interpretations and policy developments have helped IOM position itself to take on a larger role vis-à-vis IDPs, in practice its expanded engagement with IDPs was achieved through a combination of its jack-of-all-trades and niche cultivation approaches. This saw IOM become involved in activities ranging from providing shelter and aid packages to IDPs in crisis situations, to facilitating IDP return processes. At the same time, it became a major player in data collection on IDPs, as discussed in the following paragraphs. In particular, IOM invested heavily in work with IDPs in disaster situations, responding actively to disasters such as Hurricane Mitch, the 2001 Gujarat earthquake, and the 2003 earthquake in Bam, Iran. The 2004 Indian Ocean tsunami proved pivotal for IOM's involvement in disaster response; IOM was extensively involved in supporting IDPs in the emergency response and reconstruction period, setting the stage for more systematic involvement in subsequent disasters such as the 2010 Haiti earthquake, examined in Chapter 3. Since 2010, IOM has played a leading role in major disasters such as Typhoon Haiyan in the Philippines, massive floods in Pakistan, and a host of less well-known disasters. In addition to emergency relief and recovery work, IOM has supported disaster risk reduction and management initiatives intended to prevent large-scale and protracted displacement linked to natural hazards, and has conducted extensive research and convened policy discussions on displacement linked to the effects of climate change.[36]

Responding to IDPs in disasters has been a particularly fertile area for IOM's expansion because UNHCR is less actively involved in this space. In 2005, in the context of the humanitarian reform process that led to the creation of the "cluster system," IOM achieved a critical victory in its efforts to claim important roles in relation to IDPs. The cluster system was created in part to mitigate the problem of there being no international organization with clear responsibility for IDPs. The cluster system identified key areas of response in disaster and conflict settings, and allocated responsibility for leading the response in each of these "clusters." UNHCR and IOM were made co-leads of the camp coordination and camp management (CCCM) cluster, with UNHCR leading in conflicts and IOM in disasters. In taking on this role, IOM solidified an influential position in the humanitarian system, which it has leveraged to facilitate further growth and influence. As one senior humanitarian official observed, "They see it [CCCM] as their entry into humanitarian responsibility"; they were "strategically very wise to choose CCCM."[37] IOM staff concur. As one reflected, "embracing the cluster role was one of the most important [steps] from the humanitarian perspective," underpinning an expanding line of work and institutional influence, and consistently placing IOM among the largest humanitarian agencies in disaster settings.[38]

UNHCR and IOM's co-leadership of the CCCM cluster has been quite fractious, characterized by competition even though, in theory, it should be clear when each agency is to be in the driver's seat.[39] Although the division of labor is clear on paper, in the field there is more ambiguity, in part because UNHCR has not necessarily been consistent in advocating for activation of the cluster system. In such cases, IOM has sometimes stepped in and pressed for the system to be activated. At headquarters and in the field, IOM has positioned itself as "*the* CCCM agency who is ready, available and willing."[40] The tensions that have emerged in this arrangement reflect the outlook and character of each agency as they struggle for influence and power in humanitarian governance. Both compete and guard their turf, but UNHCR's characteristic approach is to defend its role by appealing to its formally mandated responsibilities. For IOM, in contrast, the best defense has been a good offense. Instead of adhering strictly to mandated roles, it has leveraged its CCCM role to take on greater responsibilities, even in conflicts where UNHCR is supposed to lead. UNHCR's position has been that if it is not delivering on its responsibilities, IOM should call it to account, rather than compete to take over the cluster in a conflict situation. IOM staff, in contrast, have asserted that although there is a clear distinction in CCCM responsibilities at the global level, at the field level the agency that is best positioned should take it up, saying, "There is nothing that should be given in this set up. We're talking about saving lives," not bureaucratic niceties.[41] As this suggests, for some within IOM, competitiveness is seen as more of a virtue than a vice. Perhaps reflecting its roots as a US-dominated agency, IOM arguably has greater institutional faith in the value of market-based competition as a driver of timely and efficient response.

Data and research

IOM has cultivated its influence – and a major revenue stream – in the humanitarian sector through research and data collection. This is part of IOM's broader effort to carve out a leadership role in migration data collection, dissemination, and analysis. This is unfolding against the backdrop of the rise in "data-driven" policymaking and practice, including in the development and humanitarian sectors, and the penchant for indicators and benchmarks, epitomized by the UN Millennium Development Goals and the subsequent UN Sustainable Development Goals.[42] The thirst for data to undergird migration governance is epitomized by the fact that the very first of 23 commonly agreed upon "Objectives for Safe, Orderly and Regular Migration" in the 2018 Global Compact for Migration is to "Collect and utilize accurate and disaggregated data as a basis for evidence-based policies."[43]

IOM's Constitution explicitly mandates the agency to promote "cooperation and coordination of efforts on international migration issues, including studies on such issues in order to develop practical solutions," positioning it to play a major role here. IOM has, by its own count, published some 1,250 reports on migration issues between 2001 and 2015, including the influential World Migration Report series.[44] These studies often feature data collected or crunched by IOM itself. In 2015, at Germany's invitation, IOM opened its Global Migration Data Analysis Centre (GMDAC) in Berlin, which aims to "contribute to IOM's overall effort to compile, analyze and share data on international migration."[45] The GMDAC operates the Migration Data Portal, which provides data from a wide range of agencies on migration-related issues including migration governance, migrant deaths, human trafficking, migration training, resettlement, IDPs, irregular migration, assisted voluntary returns, migration and the environment, and migrant health.[46] Perhaps the most distinctive element of IOM's entrepreneurial efforts in relation to data and statistics is that IOM both creates demand and sells the product – that is, it convinces states of the need for data in order to ensure the effective management of migration, and then secures contracts for a wide range of data collection projects and activities. This data entrepreneurialism reaps particular benefits for IOM. Through its data work it has positioned itself as a key node in the migration policy world; it can also showcase its value for governments and signal concern for migrants' rights and well-being, such as through its Missing Migrants work, while sidestepping sharp political and normative controversies in favor of what is perceived to be a technocratic approach.[47]

The centerpiece of IOM's data work in the humanitarian sector is the Displacement Tracking Matrix (DTM). IOM describes the DTM as

> a system to track and monitor displacement and population mobility. It is designed to regularly and systematically capture, process and disseminate information to provide a better understanding of the movements and evolving needs of displaced populations, whether on site or en route.[48]

The DTM was originally developed in Iraq in 2004, where it was used to inform needs assessments and monitoring activities relating to the massive IDP population created by the US invasion of Iraq and the country's subsequent descent into widespread conflict. The tool has since been refined and deployed in a wide range of circumstances, including in other conflicts, disasters, and in "complex emergencies."[49] Branded under the slogan "Understanding Displacement," the DTM has several components, which are deployed depending on donors' desire for data on different aspects of particular displacement situations. The components include "mobility tracking," which "aims to quantify the presence of population categories within defined locations."[50] Through ongoing rounds of "mobility tracking" assessments, IOM can provide macro-level or fine-grained information on the movements of particular displacement populations, and baseline assessments of the characteristics and needs of displaced populations in defined areas such as camps and return communities. Alongside other humanitarian actors, IOM uses information from the DTM to conceptualize and propose interventions to donors.[51] The DTM's registration and survey components can also be used to gather more detailed information on the needs, perspectives, and protection concerns of particular groups.

The DTM has been a remarkably powerful tool for IOM as it has sought to expand in the humanitarian sector. According to data specialists with other agencies, the DTM has "been the showcase, the Ferrari of IOM."[52] The tool brought the organization to a much higher level of influence in the humanitarian system, as many other agencies have come to depend on IOM for data to underpin their interventions. In this sense, in IOM's humanitarian expansion, "The DTM is the backbone. Everything else is the cherry on the cake," built on the data.[53] The difficulty is that the quality of the data gained through the DTM can vary dramatically, depending on factors including the nuance of the tools used, the skill of the staff, operational constraints, and the degree to which data is fully and openly shared.[54] And yet even when the data is of questionable quality, the DTM has significantly shored up IOM's influence and power in the aid world.[55] For instance, through the DTM, IOM identifies and counts people as members of particular groups, such as IDPs. This in turn can put IOM in a position to represent this group, and fundraise in their name. Effectively echoing Barnett's observation that "Knowledge is the trump card" in contemporary humanitarian governance, one former IOM staff member reflected, "Data gives you power. It's not just about moral authority anymore, data gives you the power."[56] In other words, as a human rights advocate expressed it, "Data is one of their chief commodities, it's more valuable to them than anything else they are doing."[57]

Just as IOM's "people-moving" efforts in humanitarian situations are shot through with tensions (some inherent to humanitarianism itself, some unique to IOM), so too is its data collection work. As in other fields, many in the humanitarian sector are committed to evidence-based responses, monitoring, and evaluation efforts, and are enthused about the prospects of applying new technological innovations in data collection to relief efforts. But data collection in humanitarian settings is not necessarily positive or even benign. While data collection can potentially helpfully inform humanitarian programming and be used to identify and constitute groups whose rights can theoretically then be more clearly and effectively represented, DTM data can be manipulated to surveil and control the displaced, who are often on the wrong side of state authorities. Although IOM has developed a Migration Data Governance Policy and Data Protection Principles, some critics charge that "IOM has done nothing to prevent them [data] from being used for policing purposes. IOM puts numbers out there and they create a reality," but without carefully considering the consequences as

> they are so focused on selling this as a big tool. .... You can't stop the conversation at, 'We collect data and that's automatically good.' You have to think about protection, and broader politics, and the implementation process.[58]

There is also insufficient attention to how the DTM "marginalizes the people who are being counted," given that in some cases, forced migrants may benefit more from being able to remain under the radar than from being identified and assisted by humanitarian authorities.

Despite these critiques, qualms raised about the DTM and IOM's broader data collection work rarely appear to translate into reduced influence or funding. The numbers and categorizations produced through the DTM are widely cited as authoritative, including by leading advocacy NGOs, and IOM steadily expands its work in this area, in cooperation with donors, member states, and other humanitarian actors. This suggests that despite ongoing moral concerns in some circles regarding the human rights implications of some of IOM's activities, its data work helps position the agency as an accepted, influential authority in the humanitarian system.

Other niches

The activities outlined earlier are not exhaustive of the niches IOM has developed in the humanitarian sector and post-crisis contexts. While the full range of IOM's interventions cannot be discussed in detail here, three additional areas deserve particular mention. First, building on its long record of work on anti-trafficking, IOM rolls out programs intended to identify, discourage, and clamp down on trafficking in many conflict and post-disaster environments. The logic here is that in emergencies, heightened socio-economic pressures and frayed community safety nets may increase vulnerability to trafficking. For example, in the Philippines in the early aftermath of Typhoon Haiyan, a category 5 superstorm that devastated some of the poorest areas of the country in 2013, IOM was actively involved in transporting families out of the affected areas until basic services could be restored. Specialized screening efforts were undertaken to help ensure that individuals moving outside the region were doing so voluntarily, and would not be coerced into undesired work upon arrival.[59]

Second, and again bridging to IOM's migration management work through the DMM, in recent years IOM has developed the concept of "humanitarian

60 An evolving humanitarian entrepreneur

border management." This refers to the creation and implementation – typically in cooperation with national customs and immigration services – of policies and practices to address the rapid arrival of large numbers of people seeking to cross national frontiers in emergency situations, as occurred on the borders of Egypt and Tunisia during the 2011 Libyan revolution.[60]

Third, IOM has become a major player in addressing displaced persons' housing, land, and property (HLP) concerns. IOM has been involved in administering several large property restitution and compensation programs that aim to remedy losses experienced by displaced persons, forced laborers, and other victims of major human rights violations from the post–World War II era through more recent conflicts in the Balkans, the Middle East, Colombia, and elsewhere.[61] This is a highly normative, legalized area of work with a strong focus on protection of HLP rights, and by extension other rights such as the right of return. Within the community of HLP specialists in Geneva, the clutch of key staff who led IOM's work in this area are recognized for their leadership in this field. They are respected for efficiently administering highly complex reparations programs, and for effectively applying protection principles and standards in ways that practically address thorny HLP disputes and avoid endless quarrels over competing claims.[62] And yet, as some critics have pointed out and as IOM's HLP experts are well aware, where property ownership patterns are deeply inequitable and even unjust, privileging the restoration of private property rights may not necessarily be conducive to protecting impoverished and landless displaced persons.

Cultivating populations of concern

Alongside its efforts to develop niche services, IOM has strived to establish itself as the representative of particular groups or concerns. This is both a way of carving out "turf" in a competitive sector, and a means of cultivating moral authority – that is, the ability to achieve deference from other actors on the basis of moral claims.[63] Moral authority is a critical resource for many IOs in the humanitarian sphere, and hinges on the perception of upholding shared values, typically with transcendent or universal dimensions. Moral authority is often particularly salient when an IO is seen to speak for groups who are assumed to be "weak and vulnerable," such as refugees or children.[64] Representational functions are built into the mandates of many IOs well known for morally-driven activities, such as UNHCR and UNICEF, but the IOM Constitution does not provide a clear basis for asserting moral authority through the representation of particular groups: it names refugees, displaced persons, and "other individuals in need of international migration services" as groups of concern for IOM, but does not define these groups or charge IOM with promoting their rights.[65]

Nonetheless, IOM has worked to position itself as a flagbearer for migrants, and for particular groups of people on the move such as trafficking victims and IDPs (particularly in disaster situations, leveraging its CCCM role). IOM has made interventions on migrants' rights and well-being in popular media and national and international forums, including in the context of the negotiation of the Sustainable Development Goals, the 2016 World Humanitarian Summit, and the 2018 Global Compact on Migration. Alongside its attempts to stake out broad territory as a representative for migrants writ large, IOM has drawn on expertise cultivated through its extensive involvement in field operations, research, and data collection activities to constitute new groups and issues it can then represent. For example, building on its experiences assisting migrant workers displaced in the Gulf War and during the Libyan revolution, IOM has helped establish "migrants in crisis" as a new category of concern, defined and addressed in detail through the state-led, IOM-convened Migrants in Countries in Crisis Initiative.[66]

IOM's attempts to position itself as a representative for migrants have sparked heated debates with UNHCR. With its legal mandate to protect refugees and its role as custodian of international refugee law, UNHCR objects to the conflation of the terms "refugee" and "migrant" as legally incorrect and practically dangerous, as it risks eroding refugees' sacrosanct status.[67] In contrast, IOM considers refugees a subset of migrants. In recent years IOM's media engagement on the "migration crisis" – rather than "refugee crisis" – in the Mediterranean has been a particular flashpoint, as has its high-profile "i am a migrant" campaign, which features the life stories of refugees and other migrants, without clearly distinguishing between the two.[68] Such definitional wrangling may seem petty, but is revealing of tensions in how IOM has sought to position itself in the humanitarian sphere, and its relationships with other key actors. For some within UNHCR, this conflict demonstrates IOM's continued lack of well-honed protection sensibilities. And yet given the complex motivations of people leaving their homes, the intermingling of different "categories" of people struggling to cross borders, and the impossibility of stretching narrow provisions of international refugee law to protect all those in need, UNHCR's steadfast adherence to legally mandated orthodoxies has been questioned by many influential actors in the system, while IOM's representational efforts have often been welcomed. As one government official expressed it, in such an environment, "IOM could really play that" – *not* having an explicit protection mandate for a particular population – "as a strength. I'm so fed up with all the damn mandates. There's no one institution that can do everything that every population needs."[69] Or, as a prominent human rights advocate vented, "Frankly, I'm tired of UNHCR trying to claim no one can ever, ever, ever, ever, ever encroach on their mandate," as a broader approach is required that recognizes the connections between groups and the limits of traditional categories.[70] These critiques suggest that IOM's efforts to cultivate populations of concern that it can represent in international forums, policy debates, and field missions may meet with success not so much despite, but because of, UNHCR's traditional dominance in this field.

Cultivating populations of concern and voicing concerns about the protection of their rights may also serve useful institutional functions for IOM. For example, these practices convey the message that IOM belongs among the clutch of influential international organizations that justify themselves in terms of their support for "vulnerable" populations, and perhaps tempers some of the reputational

62 *An evolving humanitarian entrepreneur*

problems created by migration management activities such as AVR. This further consolidates IOM's efforts to position itself as a humanitarian actor, and to access lucrative funding streams associated with emergency interventions.

Growing up and growing out: IOM's evolving humanitarian identity

IOM's concerted humanitarian entrepreneurialism has made the last 25 years a time of great change for the organization. As recently as 2002, IOM's head of mission in Jakarta, Indonesia, informed Human Rights Watch that IOM "is not, strictly speaking, a humanitarian organization."[71] Such an opinion would have been questioned within the organization even at the time, but would now be strenuously rebuffed by IOM leaders determined to preserve and strengthen the organization's place in the international humanitarian system in which IOM plays an increasingly influential role. IOM is still met with suspicion and pointed critique in much of the academic literature. However, among other humanitarian actors, human rights advocates, donors, member state officials, and other observers, there is broad – but by no means unanimous – recognition that IOM has grown considerably in recent years. The growth is in terms of IOM's size, but also in the quality and coherence of its contributions, and acknowledgement of fundamental normative standards. At the same time, the agency's maturation remains, inevitably, a work in progress. This section begins by considering IOM's conceptualization of its own identity as a humanitarian actor, and of the notion of protection. It then analyzes a series of policymaking processes that tie the organization more firmly – on paper, if not always in practice – to key human rights and humanitarian principles.

Humanitarianism and protection: IOM's conceptions and commitments

IOM's humanitarian identity and its conception of protection have been definitively shaped by the organization's pronounced operational focus. IOM's ethos, as expressed by one long-serving official, is that "We *do* things. . . . If you ask the older generation [of IOM staff], they'll say, 'There's a job to be done and we're going to go in and do it.'"[72] That is, IOM has concentrated primarily on providing concrete assistance, such as shelter, transportation, or health services. In contrast to this pragmatic "boots on the ground" approach, to many within IOM the idea of protection has seemed vague, intangible, academic, or legalistic.[73] While UNHCR's operational work stemmed from its protection role, IOM's institutional development has followed the reverse trajectory: its protection activities and sensibilities have emerged from its operational role.[74] Inside and outside the organization, IOM's operational engagements and protection responsibilities are increasingly seen as closely linked, and IOM is investing in protection mainstreaming, particularly in relation to its emergency and post-crisis work.[75] In many forums IOM has asserted its particular view that the provision of concrete assistance is a form of protection insofar as it helps ensure respect for rights such as shelter, food, and health.

Because IOM lacks a formal protection mandate and undertakes controversial migration management work, some have been incredulous of IOM's self-presentation as a humanitarian actor that takes protection obligations seriously, suggesting that while some of IOM's protection interest seems "authentic," it is also getting on the "protection bandwagon" to ingratiate itself with donors.[76] The "biggest problem," some suggest, is that much of IOM's protection work happens "below the surface, but it's not something they can always rely on, and others can't rely on."[77] That is, the extent to which IOM steps up on protection depends on the leadership of the head of mission, the skills and outlook of its staff, and on IOM's ability to raise funds for sustained engagement in protection activities.

IOM's deferential stance towards its member states has further prompted some to question the veracity of its claimed humanitarian identity and protection commitments. Senior IOM staff characterize the agency as a "discrete organization," and suggest that its role, particularly in crisis situations, is usually one of "quiet diplomacy" rather than naming and shaming.[78] While many humanitarian organizations are reticent in engaging national authorities, in IOM, "People are not shy of approaching governments."[79] Although working with national authorities, particularly those complicit in human rights violations, can raise complex moral questions, such engagements are a point of pride for some IOM staffers. As one declared, "I like the fact that we are humanitarians not afraid of national authorities."[80] As another expressed it, "That's our culture, to work with governments and solve problems."[81] In some operations, however, this approach has had troubling consequences. In some countries where the systematic abuse of migrants is a major concern, IOM has represented itself to government officials as available to undertake human rights monitoring, but without the more stringent reporting requirements and transparency standards associated with the practices of other international organizations such as the International Labour Organization (ILO).[82] This approach can also blur the boundaries between IOM and government interventions in ways that would be unacceptable for more traditional humanitarian actors. For example, IOM was one of the largest actors involved in responding to Typhoon Haiyan in the Philippines; IOM's fleet of vehicles that were used throughout the disaster zone were jointly branded with the logo of IOM and the Department of Social Welfare and Development, the branch of the Philippines government with primary responsibility for the disaster response and recovery process. This could create confusion about who was actually delivering particular interventions, and the basis for these interventions – a government acting on its responsibilities towards its citizens, or an international organization offering humanitarian response. Alongside quiet diplomacy and direct engagement with government officials in developing and delivering interventions, IOM has become somewhat more forthright in advocating for the protection of migrants' rights, such as through joint statements on protection issues with other IOs, and by partnering with human rights organizations to produce reports and recommendations

64 An evolving humanitarian entrepreneur

addressing protection concerns. IOM has also sought to incorporate protection standards into policy development efforts it undertakes in cooperation with national governments.[83]

Since the early 1990s, IOM's humanitarian identity has been shaped by its participation in a range of prominent "clubs" of other humanitarian actors, such as the IASC, the UN Humanitarian Country Teams, and the Global Protection Cluster. Being accepted into these groups has helped socialize IOM into the protection discourse and standards of the field, and legitimize IOM's claim to belong in the international humanitarian system.[84] IOM's involvement has also tempered its inclination for independent action that has stemmed from its focus on efficiency and "responsiveness." Although it has not always come naturally to IOM, the agency now works in a "shared environment" that demands cooperation and coordination with others. This requires that IOM rein in its drive to go it alone, and instead cultivate awareness of its rights and obligations in complex multi-agency operations, and train staff for work in which "partnership is higher in the modus operandi."[85]

At the same time as IOM has become a member of the international humanitarian system, has developed new policies and frameworks on its humanitarian and protection commitments, and is promoting protection mainstreaming, many within and outside the organization have pushed for IOM to retain its distinctive, pragmatic, and operationally focused approach. Whereas some human rights–focused actors promote comprehensive analyses of and responses to human rights challenges, IOM has often favored targeted interventions that don't purport to address all the concerns at hand, but make gradual progress towards the attainment of rights standards. Such interventions may be dissatisfying from the perspective of integrated human rights advocacy, but IOM staffers insist that, "If we lose this pragmatism, we lose the capacity to really help. . . . That level of flexibility is something really important, because at the end of the day, waving your documents just doesn't help."[86]

Reflecting on IOM's protection reputation, some staff recognize that the organization is "still perceived as the ones who don't get some of the critical protection concepts," and don't participate enough in collective actions to strengthen the protection of forced migrants.[87] Protection-focused staff admit that it is still a "struggle in-house to bring protection onto the agenda," and see a "long road" to clarifying and maximizing IOM's role and contributions to protection.[88] However, alongside internal divisions and resistance, there is a growing cohort of protection "allies" inside the agency. Serious protection proponents have had to contend with efforts, motivated in part by a desire to legitimize controversial migration management activities, to label everything IOM does as contributing to protection, however tangentially. Protection protagonists within IOM fear that this approach undermines the organization's credibility. In developing the policies and frameworks discussed next, internal norm entrepreneurs at IOM have taken a different approach, striving to articulate clearer commitments to core human rights and humanitarian principles, to underpin the evolution and expansion of the agency's humanitarian identity and protection work.[89]

Policy processes: shaping IOM's humanitarian engagement

Over the last fifteen years, IOM has engaged in a remarkable – but, in the academic literature, little remarked upon – series of internal policy development processes that have sought to clarify the organization's commitments, principles, and approaches.[90] Many of the resulting policies and frameworks pertain especially to IOM's work with forced migrants during and after emergencies. Several different kinds of policies and frameworks have been created. First, IOM has crafted overarching institutional frameworks that have been brought before the IOM Council for formal member state approval. For instance, the 2012 Migration Crisis Operational Framework (MCOF) aims to rationalize and explain the connections between IOM's wide range of interventions in emergency contexts by mapping out their links to human mobility. The 2015 Migration Government ment Framework (MiGOF) creates a structure for cooperation between IOM and national governments to address migration by identifying the key elements of efforts to facilitate "orderly, safe, regular and responsible migration."[91] Both frameworks articulate commitment to the relevant bodies of international law, and have become major touchstones for the organization, including as it negotiated its entry into the UN system as a related organization. The MCOF is particularly important to understanding IOM's evolution and self-positioning in the humanitarian sphere and the tensions associated with this, as the framework explicitly "combines IOM humanitarian activities and migration management services," asserting that "Migration management activities are not traditionally part of humanitarian responses, but can help tackle migration aspects of a crisis more effectively."[92] The framework identifies 15 sectors of assistance where IOM asserts that it has "a mandate to act and long years of experience."[93] These include camp management and displacement tracking; the provision of shelter and non-food items; transportation; humanitarian communications; health support; psychosocial support; (re)integration assistance; community stabilization and transition; disaster risk reduction and resilience building; land and property support; counter-trafficking and protection of vulnerable migrants; technical assistance for humanitarian border management; emergency consular assistance; diaspora and human resource mobilization; and migration policy and legislation support.[94] This array of activities reflects IOM's entrepreneurialism in the humanitarian sector, and its more recent, strategic step of attempting to bridge its humanitarian work and other migration management activities – perhaps lending an altruistic sheen to migration management initiatives that have been critiqued as forms of migration *control*, while inadvertently underlining the ways in which care and control are fused in the humanitarian enterprise.

Second, IOM has developed major institutional policies that address issues of broad concern for the organization, and have been formally brought before the IOM Council for member states' information, or for discussion but not necessarily formal approval. Examples include the 2009 document The Human Rights of Migrants: IOM Policy and Activities, the 2015 IOM Protection Policy, the Gender Equality Policy 2015–2019, and the 2015 Humanitarian Policy – Principles for Humanitarian Action, discussed in detail in the following section.[95] Third, IOM staff have developed more specific policies and frameworks that target particular populations, processes, or operational challenges. These include the 2016 Progressive Resolution of Displacement Situations Framework, the 2017 IOM Framework for Addressing Internal Displacement, the Key Principles for Internal Humanitarian Evacuations/Relocations of Civilian Populations in Armed Conflict, and the 2016 Guidance Note on the Inclusion of Protection Considerations when Planning and Implementing International Humanitarian Evacuations for Migrants Caught in Armed Conflict Settings. Most of these policies have not been formally brought forward to the member states, but some entail mandatory institutional compliance, and their implementation is supported by the development of a range of related field manuals and handbooks.

Why has IOM developed these policies and frameworks? Why have its member states formally approved or informally welcomed them? These standards deviate from IOM's reputation for reticence in discussing protection and the assumption that the agency has thrived precisely because it is unencumbered by normative commitments, and challenge the presumption that its members want it to stay that way. The answers to these questions lie largely in a combination of shifting opportunities for growth; recognition that acceptance and legitimacy, particularly in the humanitarian field (where IOM garners the majority of its budget), requires recognition of key norms; and the drive of internal norm entrepreneurs determined to see IOM "grow up" by taking a more consistent and principled approach. More specifically, it has gradually become clear that the humanitarian sector presents some of the most considerable opportunities for growth, but that gaining donors' confidence to undertake much larger projects, and working effectively in collaborative, inter-agency operations, required more thoroughly systemizing its commitment to humanitarian and human rights principles. According to their proponents, these policies rebuff the idea that IOM will "do anything for money," and help address some of the agency's reputational problems.[96] At the same time, some staff members were concerned on principled grounds to see IOM better serve its "beneficiaries" and mature as an organization by more clearly adopting and adhering to humanitarian and human rights principles.

This policymaking has also been a response to problems stemming from IOM's decentralization. While many senior IOM staff and member state representatives insist that IOM's decentralization is, overall, a strength, it has created problems in terms of consistency and reliability. One senior IOM leader expressed deep concern that influential donors have said, "I don't know which IOM I'm talking to when I go to the field," and so only fund heads of missions that they personally know and trust, rather than counting on the organization itself as a reliable partner. Reflecting on the obstacles to internalizing protection and humanitarian principles across a highly decentralized agency, the same official reflected, "Everybody has been talking about [how IOM could be made more like] a McDonald's franchise," where what's on offer is clear and consistent.[97] The new policies and frameworks have helped address this concern by providing a clearer direction from headquarters, although the McDonald's analogy betrays precisely the neo-liberal biases of concern for many IOM critics, suggesting that the drive to standardize, as it is with McDonald's, is ultimately a way of expanding – even with products of questionable quality.

Historically, IOM has engaged in internal policymaking processes to be able to navigate questions and concerns from its member states.[98] IOM's member states have gradually moved from some skepticism in the 1990s surrounding IOM's plan to expand its footprint in humanitarian operations, to acceptance and even active celebration of this role. These policies help secure and modestly advance these institutional gains. IOM's member states have generally been convinced by the case put forward by internal advocates of protection and humanitarian principles, but have also found that they can have their cake and eat it too. That is, while these policies have, to a certain extent, tied IOM to legitimizing normative standards, the binds remain sufficiently loose that it can still engage in contentious activities like AVR, and even normalize these interventions as broadly compliant with a rights-based approach.

IOM's humanitarian policy – principles for humanitarian action

IOM's Humanitarian Policy was presented to IOM's governing Council in 2015 and has been warmly welcomed by member states, donors, and other key players. While this policy is only one element in IOM's articulation of its institutional commitments, a closer analysis of it is instructive, as it illuminates many of the dynamics and tensions surrounding IOM's efforts to mature as a humanitarian actor. Like IOM's other recent policies and frameworks on issues such as gender, IDPs, and durable solutions, this is an internal policy. That is, it seeks to guide the agency's own operations and aspirations, but because it articulates IOM's interpretation of and relationship to humanitarian principles and standards, it may also be an important tool for external advocacy to ensure that IOM adheres to its own commitments. The development of IOM's Humanitarian Policy was triggered in part by an influential 2008 Sida review of its humanitarian assistance. This evaluation suggested that IOM was already well integrated in international humanitarian systems, and that in this context "IOM contributes to, endorses and follows the general accepted policy, principles and standards" of the field.[99] However, it recognized that IOM lacked clear policies binding it to humanitarian principles and standards, generating potential dissonance between its humanitarian actions and other work, particularly in countries grappling with instability, and urged the development of policies to address this challenge. Accordingly, IOM's Humanitarian Policy: Principles for Humanitarian Action was developed through a multi-year consultative process driven by well-regarded leaders within DOE and financed by the United States, Sweden, and Switzerland – countries that have, in other instances, relied on IOM to undertake projects that sit uncomfortably with humanitarian and human rights principles.

The policy aims "to ensure that when the Organization is engaged in humanitarian action, it acts on the basis of robust principles and as part of the humanitarian

68 An evolving humanitarian entrepreneur

response system."[100] The Humanitarian Policy clearly asserts a humanitarian mandate for the organization, grounded in an arguably creative reading of the IOM Constitution, and more obviously in the 2012 MCOF and the 2015 MiGOF. The use of "mandate" rhetoric in the Humanitarian Policy points to how policymaking processes may be marshalled to claim mandates, even in the absence of formal changes to an IO's constitution or statute. Additionally, the policy recognizes and unpacks IOM's interpretation of and commitment to the central humanitarian principles of humanity, impartiality, neutrality, and independence.[101] The policy expressly characterizes IOM as a protection actor, and lays out the organization's commitments in terms of protection mainstreaming.[102]

The policy reflects the complex work of interpreting humanitarian principles and the tensions they raise, particularly when trying to square them with states' expectations. IOM's member states have gradually come to support IOM's expanded humanitarian role, but they have consistently stressed that they expect the agency to remain available as a "one-stop shop" on migration-related issues, including returns.[103] In contrast to the policies and rhetoric of more robustly mandated humanitarian IOs like UNHCR, IOM's Humanitarian Policy has abundant deferential references to states, often the very actors responsible for causing humanitarian crises in the first place. As discussed, some IOM staff are proud of the organization's close work with governments, and applaud that "We don't get bolloxed up with theology."[104] However, such close relationships, coupled with the thirst to expand, can lead IOM to stifle criticism and shy away from commitments made in documents such as the Humanitarian Policy. As one former IOM staffer expressed it, "All UN agencies do it," that is, cozy up to governments,

> but IOM does it more. IOM is less confident to critique the government and that is probably due to its money-grubbing approach towards humanitarian affairs. . . . IOM is willing to embrace the language of rights, up to when it impacts their relationship with the state.[105]

That said, the same former staffer recognized that even before the conclusion of the Humanitarian Policy, moral and reputational arguments were increasingly employed by leaders within IOM to push back against involvement in contentious activities, such as facilitating Australia's containment of asylum seekers on Pacific islands.[106]

IOM is moving on to the even more challenging territory of implementing its Humanitarian Policy. This entails disseminating the policy, providing training, and ensuring accountability for abiding by it.[107] This stage may heighten conflict between the DOE and DMM as the policy may, at least theoretically, restrict certain work in the DMM's domain, while further strengthening DOE's hand. The policy does not explicitly address its relation to IOM's most criticized line of work, organizing purportedly voluntary returns to impoverished, unstable, and war-torn states. Some of the policy's architects suggest that it can and should be used to tackle the "hard question" of saying no to morally problematic projects, pointing out that the policy indicates that even when IOM is involved in non-humanitarian work in crisis-affected countries, the humanitarian principle of humanity must prevail, which requires IOM to protect life and human dignity, alleviate suffering, and ensure respect for rights.[108] "But," they acknowledge, "we were careful not to say this too loudly during the process of getting the policy approved."[109] In this way, the policy may serve as ammunition for internal critics hoping to steer the organization away from normatively vexed work on issues such as AVR, and towards a more consistent, rights-focused posture. Achieving this will, however, require systematic internalization of the policy and its values across the organization, which is particularly challenging in light of IOM's internal divisions and decentralized, project-driven nature.

Conclusion: implications for the governance of forced migration and humanitarian emergencies

IOM has evolved significantly as an organization, particularly over the last two decades. These changes have been significantly driven by IOM's humanitarian entrepreneurialism, combined with concerted recent policymaking efforts that help clarify the organization's normative commitments. What are the implications of these developments for IOM itself, and for the governance of forced migration and humanitarian situations?

By entrepreneurially "picking up the slack" on key issues from internal displacement in disasters to disarmament, demobilization, and reintegration, IOM has helped to paper over gaps in international humanitarian responses to forced migration. This has fueled IOM's own growth in significant but often underappreciated ways. As IOM has almost no core budget, the overhead charged on its projects is an essential source of funding for the organization's operations. IOM's humanitarian projects are among the organization's most lucrative, and a major area of growth. As director general, Swing successfully negotiated an increase in IOM's overhead rates with its member states, a major gain that further increases the institutional value of the agency's projects in the humanitarian sector. IOM has used revenue raised through operational work in the humanitarian sector to enable some of the migration management activities for which it is more well known, but sometimes struggles to fund. For example, through the IOM Development Fund, the agency responds to requests from Southern member states, often for assistance in the development of migration-related policies. The Development Fund is financed largely through overhead, the majority of which now comes from IOM's activities in emergency and post-crisis situations.[110]

Alongside these important internal implications, IOM's expansion in the humanitarian sector has enabled member states to ensure that other IOs such as UNHCR maintain more precisely forced mandates. In working to ensure a comprehensive response to the diverse and interconnected groups of people on the move in contemporary humanitarian emergencies, this cobbled-together system relies as much on inter-organizational competition and a thirst for ever-larger institutional budgets and influence as it does on precise legal mandates. What are the implications of this reality for forced migrants themselves, and for other

70 An evolving humanitarian entrepreneur

actors such as local NGOs? While these questions are outside the scope of the present discussion, this is a critical area for further research.

IOM's recent internal policymaking processes represent significant developments for an organization that has historically been hesitant to formally recognize and articulate its protection obligations. Coupled with IOM's more systematic integration into the international humanitarian system, these developments have prompted many observers to remark that IOM has matured significantly, progressively becoming a more reliable and accepted actor in the humanitarian system. For example, in his remarks to the 2015 IOM Council, John Ging, director of operations for the UN Office for the Coordination of Humanitarian Affairs (OCHA), applauded IOM as setting the "gold standard" for humanitarian responses to forced migrants.[111] Yet major challenges remain. Different ideas persist within IOM on what humanitarian principles and protection standards require, and what activities and values should be prioritized, with sometimes significant variations across different regions, missions, and departments. Despite IOM's adoption of human rights discourses and its formal acceptance of standards to which it may be held to account, these developments and policies are not yet well known outside the agency, beyond IOM's member states and donors. Prominent advocacy groups such as Amnesty International, Human Rights Watch, and Refugees International rarely analyze the protection implications of IOM's work, or hold the organization to account for its actions and positions.

This disconnect raises the possibility that IOM may be having its cake and eating it too. That is, IOM may be benefiting from the increased legitimacy – particularly in the eyes of its humanitarian donors – that comes from professed commitment to humanitarian and human rights principles, without being pressed for consistent and coherent adherence to these norms across all aspects of the organization's work. While this is certainly a concerning prospect, it must be recognized that many within IOM actively *want* their organization to live up to its professed standards. As director general, Swing reportedly invited the scrutiny of advocacy organizations, confident that IOM's programs could pass muster or be brought up to snuff.[112] Thus while IOM's adoption of human rights rhetoric and standards has sometimes been critiqued as mere "window dressing" or "blue-washing" intended to facilitate IOM's entry into the UN system, this is not all there is to the story.[113] Rather, these policy development processes, and IOM's broader evolution in the humanitarian sector, are better understood as an expression of tensions and competing interests – internal and external – in a complex institutional actor.

These developments require reappraisal of why states turn to IOM, and how the organization has grown. In contrast to explanations that focus on IOM's historic status outside the UN system, unencumbered by normative commitments, evidence from IOM's operations in the humanitarian sector suggests that states have engaged IOM because of its carefully honed reputation for efficient, timely, cost-effective, operationally focused, data-driven interventions. It has also cultivated and capitalized on its "responsive" posture, through which IOM presents itself as ready and willing to take on new challenges, from emergency evacuations to Ebola response, without being hide-bound by narrow debates on mandates. In addition, IOM has in recent years flourished precisely because it is now an established if not universally welcomed part of the international humanitarian community, with a new set of policies that help to explain, guide, and legitimize its engagement in the humanitarian sphere, and in the aftermath of emergency situations. Past efforts to grapple with why states engage IOM have often portrayed the agency as an outlier among IOs, given its status outside the UN, its lack of a formal protection mandate, and its projectized structure. This analysis suggests that while IOM remains in some ways singular, in its drive to grow – not only in its budget and field presence, but also in its influence and stature – it is following paths well worn by other organizations. In the following chapter, I explore these issues further through case studies of two of the largest operations in IOM's history, in Haiti and Libya.

Notes

1 *IOM Snapshot 2019* (Geneva: IOM), 5.
2 The implications of this expansion for forced migrants themselves is a critical question, but one I must largely leave to future investigations.
3 Michael Barnett, *Empire of Humanity: A History of Humanitarianism* (Ithaca: Cornell University Press, 2011).
4 See for example Asher Lazarus Hirsch and Cameron Doig, "Outsourcing Control: The International Organization for Migration in Indonesia," *International Journal of Human Rights* 22, no. 5 (2018): 681–708.
5 António Vitorino, "Message of Director General António Vitorino to IOM Staff," 1 October 2018, www.iom.int/speeches-and-talks/message-director-general-antonio-vitorino-iom-staff.
6 On IO entrepreneurialism, see e.g. Liliana Andonova, *Governance Entrepreneurs: International Organizations and the Rise of Global Public-Private Partnerships* (Cambridge: Cambridge University Press, 2017).
7 For an account of the agency's entrepreneurial efforts in the humanitarian sector from a former director general, see James Carlin, *The Refugee Connection: A Lifetime of Running a Lifeline* (London: Palgrave, 1989).
8 Interviews, IOM officials, 3, 4, 5, November 2015.
9 Michelle Ducasse-Rogier, *The International Organization for Migration: 1951–2001* (Geneva: IOM, 2001), 132–137.
10 Ducasse-Rogier, *International Organization for Migration*, 134; IOM, *IOM Strategic Planning: Towards the Twenty-First Century*, 9 May 1995, MC/1842, para 20.
11 Ducasse-Rogier, *International Organization for Migration*, 136.
12 Interviews, member state officials 2, 3, 4, 7, December 2016; Interview, member state official 11, July 2017.
13 Interviews, member state officials 8, 9, 10, December 2016.
14 Interviews, IOM officials 3, 4, 5, 13, November 2015.
15 Interview, IOM official 3.
16 IOM Constitution, Article 1(b).
17 IOM, *IOM Resettlement 2018* (Geneva: IOM, 2018), 10.
18 Ibid.
19 IOM, *Resettlement Assistance*, www.iom.int/resettlement-assistance.
20 IOM, *Resettlement 2018*, 36–37.
21 Ibid., 21.
22 Ibid.

72 An evolving humanitarian entrepreneur

23 Jennifer Hyndman and Wenona Giles, *Refugees in Extended Exile: Living on the Edge* (London: Routledge, 2016), 95–118; and Jennifer Hyndman and Wenona Giles, "Waiting for What? The Feminization of Asylum in Protracted Situations," *Gender, Place & Culture* 18, no. 3 (2011): 361–379.
24 See e.g. Michel Agier, *Managing the Undesirables: Refugee Camps and Humanitarian Government* (London: Polity, 2011); and Polly Pallister-Wilkins, "Hotspots and the Geographies of Humanitarianism," *Environment and Planning D: Society and Space* (2018).
25 Immigration and Refugee Board of Canada, *The Persian Gulf: The Situation of Foreign Workers*, 1 May 1991, www.refworld.org/docid/3ae6a8068.html; IOM, *IOM Allocates Emergency Funding to Begin Air Evacuation of Migrants Affected by Fighting in the Central African Republic*, 3 January 2014, https://reliefweb.int/report/central-african-republic/iom-allocates-emergency-funding-begin-air-evacuation-migrants; Ducasse-Rogier, *International Organization for Migration*, 137.
26 Khalid Koser, "Protecting Non-Citizens in Situations of Conflict, Violence and Disasters," in *Humanitarian Crises and Migration*, eds. Susan Forbes Martin, Sanjula Weerasinghe and Abbie Taylor (New York: Routledge, 2014), 267–286.
27 IOM, *IOM Allocates Emergency Funding to Begin Air Evacuation of Migrants Affected by Fighting in the Central African Republic*, 3 January 2014, https://reliefweb.int/report/central-african-republic/iom-allocates-emergency-funding-begin-air-evacuation-migrants.
28 On this process, see Josep Zapater, "Humanitarian Evacuations in the Central African Republic," *Humanitarian Exchange* 62 (2014), 12–14.
29 Ducasse-Rogier, *International Organization for Migration*, 86.
30 IOM, *IOM Framework for Addressing Internal Displacement* (2017), 5.
31 UNHCR, *Global Trends* (Geneva: UNHCR, 2016), 35.
32 IOM Constitution, Article 1.1(b).
33 IOM, *Internally Displaced Persons: IOM Policy and Activities* (2002), MC/INF/258, para. 6.
34 Ibid., para 13.
35 IOM, *IOM Framework for Addressing Internal Displacement* (2017), 8.
36 Nina Hall, *Displacement, Development, and Climate Change* (London: Routledge, 2016). Despite the synergies between the issues, IOM's work on migration and climate change appears to have developed in relative isolation from its operational engagement in disaster response.
37 Interview, humanitarian actor 2 (UN), November 2015.
38 Interview, IOM official 10, November 2015.
39 Interviews, IOM officials 11, 13, November 2015; Interviews, humanitarian actors 1 (UN), 2 (UN), 3 (NGO), November 2015; Interview, humanitarian actor 7 (UN), December 2015. See also Tim Foster, *CCCM Capacity Development Evaluation* (Geneva: CCCM, 2015).
40 Interview, humanitarian actor 2 (UN).
41 Interview, IOM official 13.
42 On this trend, see e.g. Sally Engle Merry, *The Seductions of Quantification: Measuring Human Rights, Gender Violence, and Sex Trafficking* (Chicago: University of Chicago Press, 2016); Sally Engle Merry, Kevin Davis and Benedict Kingsbury, eds., *The Quiet Power of Indicators: Measuring Governance, Corruption, and the Rule of Law* (Cambridge: Cambridge University Press, 2015); and Kevin Davis, Angelina Fisher, Benedict Kingsbury and Sally Engle Merry, eds., *Governance by Indicators: Global Power through Quantification and Rankings* (Oxford: Oxford University Press, 2012).
43 Global Compact for Migration, Objective 1. The centrality of data in the Global Compact is arguably reflective of IOM's influence in supporting the negotiations.
44 IOM, *IOM Key Statistics 2011–2014* (Berlin: IOM Global Migration Data Analysis Centre, 2015), 17.

45 IOM, *About GMDAC*, https://gmdac.iom.int/about-gmdac.
46 IOM, *IOM Data Overview*, https://migrationdataportal.org/themes/iom-data-overview.
47 Anne Koch, "IOM and Data," Presentation at "IOM: The 'UN Migration Agency'?" workshop, University of Oxford, Oxford, 2 February 2019; Stephan Scheel and Funda Ustek-Spilda, "The Politics of Expertise and Ignorance in the Field of Migration Management," *EPD: Society and Space* (2019): 1–19, First View. Creating statistics on migration may be perceived as technocratic, but is clearly political. For example, through analysis of IOM's Global Migration Flows Interactive App, Scheel and Ustek-Spilda examine how IOM creates the impression that expert knowledge (epitomized in the quantification of migration) can be applied to ensure the management of migration, despite the "widely acknowledged unreliability and noncoherence of migration statistics." See Scheel and Ustek, "Politics of Expertise," 1.
48 IOM, *Displacement Tracking Matrix*, www.globaldtm.info/global/.
49 Ibid.
50 IOM, *DTM Understanding Displacement*, https://displacement.iom.int/.
51 Ibid.
52 Interview, human rights advocate 2, November 2015.
53 Ibid.
54 Interviews, humanitarian actors 3 (NGO), 6 (NGO), November 2015.
55 On the "politics of ignorance" in migration data, see Scheel and Ustek-Spilda, "Politics of Expertise."
56 Interview, human rights advocate 5, December 2015.
57 Interview, human rights advocate 3, November 2015.
58 Interview, human rights advocate 5.
59 Angela Sherwood, Megan Bradley, Lorenza Rossi, Rufa Guiam and Bradley Mellicker, *Resolving Post-Disaster Displacement: Insights from the Philippines after Typhoon Haiyan (Yolanda)* (Washington, DC: Brookings Institution/IOM, 2015), 21, 38.
60 On IOM and humanitarian borderwork, see Philippe Frowd, "Developmental Borderwork and the International Organization for Migration," *Journal of Ethnic and Migration Studies* 44, no. 10 (2018): 1656–1672.
61 On IOM's involvement in restitution and compensation programs, see for example Heike Niebergall and Norbert Wühler, *Property Restitution and Compensation: Practices and Experiences of Claims Programs* (Geneva: IOM, 2008), and Peter Van der Auweraert, *Dealing with the 2006 Internal Displacement Crisis in Timor-Leste: Between Reparations and Humanitarian Policy-Making* (New York/Washington, DC: ICTJ/Brookings-LSE Project on Internal Displacement, 2012).
62 Interview, humanitarian actor 4 (NGO), November 2015; Interview, human rights advocate 4, November 2015.
63 Michael Barnett and Martha Finnemore, *Rules for the World: International Organizations in Global Politics* (Ithaca: Cornell University Press, 2004), 5.
64 Michael Barnett and Thomas Weiss, "Humanitarianism: A Brief History of the Present," in *Humanitarianism in Question: Politics, Power, Ethics*, eds. Michael Barnett and Thomas Weiss (Ithaca: Cornell University Press, 2008), 39.
65 IOM Constitution, Article 1(b).
66 See the Migrants in Countries in Crisis Initiative, https://micicinitiative.iom.int/. At the same time as IOM has been actively involved in constituting and positioning itself to represent particular groups of migrants, it retains a certain skepticism about categorization efforts. As one human rights advocate expressed it, "IOM is trying to become more nuanced in the way it applies aid in that it doesn't want to be *driven* by the categories." Interview, human rights advocate 5.
67 Interview, independent expert 2, December 2016.
68 See www.iamamigrant.org. See Sara De Jong and Petra Dannecker, "Managing Migration with Stories? The IOM 'i am a Migrant' Campaign," *Journal für Entwicklungspolitik* 33, no. 1 (2017): 75–101.

74 An evolving humanitarian entrepreneur

69 Interview, member state official 2.
70 Interview, human rights advocate 10, December 2016.
71 Human Rights Watch, *"By Invitation Only": Australian Asylum Policy* (New York: Human Rights Watch, 2002), 51.
72 Interview, IOM official 1, November 2015.
73 Ibid.
74 Interview, independent expert 3, December 2016.
75 Interviews, IOM officials 1, 5, 12, November 2015; Interview, independent expert 3. For IOM's presentation of its protection mainstreaming efforts, see www.iom.int/protection-mainstreaming-iom-crisis-response.
76 Interview, humanitarian actor 1 (UN).
77 Interview, independent expert 3.
78 Interviews, IOM officials 4, 5.
79 Interview, IOM official 11.
80 Ibid.
81 Interview, IOM official 4.
82 Personal communication, July 2019.
83 Interviews, IOM officials 1, 3.
84 For an analysis of IOM's institutional discourses as they relate to migration management more generally, see Antoine Pécoud, *Depoliticizing Migration: Global Governance and International Migration Narratives* (Basingstoke: Palgrave, 2015).
85 Interview, IOM official 14, December 2016.
86 Interview, IOM official 9, November 2015.
87 Interview, IOM official 12.
88 Ibid.
89 Interviews, IOM officials 9, 12; Interview, human rights advocate 5.
90 These policy processes complement IOM's practice of signing on to external policies, frameworks, and standards, such as the IASC Policy on Protection in Humanitarian Action, and the IASC Principals' Statement on the Centrality of Protection in Humanitarian Action.
91 IOM, *Migration Governance Framework*, 1. See also IOM, *Emergency Manual: Migration Governance Framework Overview*, https://emergencymanual.iom.int/entry/26102/migration-governance-framework-migof. The MCOF and MiGOF build on earlier overarching frameworks and strategies such as the 2007 IOM Strategy, which identified 12 key activities for IOM to focus on, including "enhance[ing] the humane and orderly management of migration and the effective respect for the human rights of migrants in accordance with international law" and "participat[ing] in coordinated humanitarian responses in the context of inter-agency arrangements in this field and to provide migration services in other emergency or postcrisis situations as appropriate and as relates to the needs of individuals, thereby contributing to their protection." See IOM Strategy, 9 November 2007, MC/INF/287, 3.
92 IOM, *MCOF Info Sheet*, www.iom.int/files/live/sites/iom/files/What-We-Do/docs/IOM-MCOF-Infosheet-10March2013-page2.pdf. See also IOM, *Migration Crisis Operational Framework*, 2012, MC/2355; IOM Council Resolution 1243, 101st session, 27 November 2012.
93 IOM, *MCOF Info Sheet*.
94 Ibid.
95 IOM, *The Human Rights of Migrants: IOM Policy and Activities*, 2009, MC/INF/298; IOM, *Gender Equality Policy 2015–2019*, C/106/INF/8/Rev.1; IOM, *Policy on Protection*, 2015, C/106/INF/9. I do not discuss all of these policies in detail owing to space limitations, and varying degrees of internal and external support.
96 Interview, member state official 4.
97 Interview, IOM official 3.
98 Interview, independent expert 3.

99 Anders Olin, Lars Florin and Björn Bengtsson, "Study of the International Organization for Migration and its Humanitarian Assistance," *Sida Evaluations* 40 (2008): 3.
100 IOM, *Humanitarian Policy*, II.4.
101 IOM, *Humanitarian Policy*, III.1a-d.
102 IOM, *Humanitarian Policy*, IV.1, IV.5.
103 Interview, member state official 7.
104 Interview, IOM official 1.
105 Interview, human rights advocate 5.
106 Ibid.
107 Interview, IOM official 3.
108 IOM, *Humanitarian Policy*, III.1.a, VI.13.
109 Interview, IOM official 13.
110 Susan Martin, *International Migration: Evolving Trends from the Early Twentieth Century to the Present* (Cambridge: Cambridge University Press, 2014), 139–145; Interview, IOM official 1.
111 John Ging, OCHA Director of Operations, Address to IOM Council, November 2015. Given pitched institutional battles between UNHCR and OCHA, this assessment was arguably intended as much as a disparagement of UNHCR as a celebration of IOM's accomplishments.
112 Interviews, human rights advocates 7 and 9, December 2016.
113 For such portrayals, see for example Ishan Ashutosh and Allison Mountz, "Migration Management for the Benefit of Whom? Interrogating the Work of the International Organization for Migration," *Citizenship Studies* 15, no. 1 (2011): 21–38; and Asher Lazarus Hirsch and Cameron Doig, "Outsourcing Control: The International Organization for Migration in Indonesia," *International Journal of Human Rights* 22, no. 5 (2018): 681–708.

3

IOM IN ACTION

Contributions and controversies in Haiti and Libya

- *IOM in Haiti*
  - *1994–2009: focus on community stabilization and migration regulation*
  - *2010–2019: earthquake response and aftermath*
- *IOM in Libya*
  - *1995–2010: before Gaddafi's fall*
  - *Responding to the 2011 revolution*
  - *Unending crisis? IOM in post-Gaddafi Libya*
- *Conclusion: implications for understanding IOM*

Against the contention that IOM is "hide-bound" by its history, I have argued that IOM's humanitarian identity and perspectives on protection have shifted over time, and continue to be shaped by external pressures and internal contestation and policymaking processes.[1] This chapter further considers IOM's identity and evolution through the lens of its work in Haiti and Libya. IOM defines itself as an operational agency. To understand the organization, it is essential to explore how it navigates not only in rarified meeting rooms in Geneva and New York, but especially in countries in the global South where the majority of IOM's staff are deployed.

IOM's operations in Haiti and Libya are of course not neatly representative cases, and must be considered in light of particular histories, socio-economic conditions and migration dynamics, structural constraints and incentives, and the influence of different personalities within and outside IOM. I have chosen to comparatively analyze IOM's activities in Haiti and Libya as these missions offer critical insights into the agency's development in the humanitarian sphere and more broadly. These operations are among the largest in IOM's history, and have shaped its involvement and approach in other countries. They bring into focus how IOM has positioned itself in different regions, and in different kinds of humanitarian crises, from earthquakes to civil war. To be sure, IOM's work in

Haiti and Libya has not been exclusively humanitarian. Rather, these cases bring into focus the tensions associated with IOM's position as a "multi-mandate" agency.[2] After examining IOM's operations in Haiti and Libya, I discuss their implications for understanding IOM.

IOM in Haiti

In the 1970s, ICEM transported small numbers of Haitian refugees, but the organization's in-depth involvement in Haiti began in 1994, and Haiti officially joined IOM in 1995.[3] Since then, IOM has implemented a panoply of activities in Haiti related in varying degrees to migration, from community stabilization and border management, to facilitating returns and responding to the 2010 earthquake. Much of this work was funded by the United States; notably, two IOM directors general, McKinley and Swing, served as US ambassadors to Haiti. This section first considers IOM's work in Haiti before the earthquake, and then analyzes its role in responding to the catastrophe.

1994–2009: focus on community stabilization and migration regulation

The September 1991 coup that ousted President Jean-Bertrand Aristide sparked mass displacement within Haiti and across its borders.[4] Thousands took to sea on rickety boats and rafts, hoping to secure shelter in the United States from violence, human rights abuses, and entrenched poverty. These movements led to

> some of the most bizarre experiments in US immigration history: over the course of a few years, US policy included interdictions and forcible returns, the search for other countries to be temporary safe havens, screening on Coast Guard ships and later processing at the US Naval Base at Guantanamo, in-country processing of Haitians fearing persecution, and special parole provisions.[5]

In this period, IOM worked "on behalf of the US government" by interviewing and collecting data on Haitian asylum seekers at Guantanamo Bay and on board the US Navy ship *Comfort*, transporting asylum seekers to countries offering temporary shelter, and moving the minority who were recognized as refugees on to the United States and other host states.[6] IOM was also involved in countertrafficking efforts, and in returning rejected Haitian asylum seekers and other migrants from the United States, Cuba, and elsewhere. The agency was particularly active in migration management efforts between Haiti and the Dominican Republic, including renovating border crossing facilities; encouraging coordination between border management agencies; strengthening the presence of the Haitian National Police in border areas; and offering reintegration programs for Haitian returnees.[7] While IOM ran modest programs promoting the rights of Haitian migrants in the Dominican Republic, its migration management projects

78 IOM in action

funded by donors such as Canada primarily tried to "keep Haitians in Haiti and out of the Dominican Republic."[8]

Alongside this explicitly migration-focused work, IOM was one of the lead implementing agencies for a major, US-funded Special Assistance Program for Haiti. In this context, from 1994–1996, IOM supported large-scale demobilization and reintegration efforts connected to Operation Uphold Democracy, the US-led multinational force that restored Aristide to power. IOM's role included providing technical and professional training to some 5,500 former soldiers, and rolling out 2,300 local development projects in an effort to address community concerns alongside the needs of individual returnees and demobilized soldiers.[9] The program was criticized as out of step with the scale of Haiti's problems, with IOM officials conceding that it was "too narrowly conceived to address any of the prevailing conditions affecting the lives of most of the Haitian beneficiaries," and suggesting that "what was needed at that time, rather than a militarily defined operation performed quickly, was a multi-year, multi-layered planning process for the country overall."[10] Haiti was only the second country in which IOM was involved in such large "post-conflict" community-based programs, and despite their stark shortcomings, the experience whetted IOM's appetite to work in this area.[11]

In 2004, following Aristide's second ouster and the establishment of the UN Stabilization Mission in Haiti (MINUSTAH), IOM revived its community stabilization efforts as a key actor in the multimillion dollar, US-funded Haiti Transition Initiative (HTI), later rebranded the Programme de Revitalisation et de Promotion de l'Entente et de la Paix (PREPEP). Running from 2004 to 2012, the program aimed to "enhance citizen confidence and participation in a peaceful transition; empower citizens and the Government of Haiti to address priority community needs; build cooperative frameworks between citizens and government entities; [and] promote peaceful interaction among conflicted populations."[12] While government ownership proved elusive, through this program IOM implemented scores of community projects, particularly infrastructure developments.[13] Alongside the American private security contractor DynCorp, IOM also became a primary implementing partner for the US-funded Haiti Stabilization Initiative (HSI), which sought to "bring security and economic improvements to some of the most difficult and dangerous neighborhoods in Port-au-Prince," particularly Cité Soleil.[14] IOM's role included running a small grant program intended to undercut gangs' control of volatile neighborhoods. HSI's coordinator explained that "we worked through IOM because there were no government ministries with either the personnel or will to take the risks entailed in working in the community."[15]

Beyond such community-based stabilization efforts, IOM also bolstered the Haitian security apparatus, receiving millions of dollars to train police; construct and refurbish prisons, jails, and police training facilities; and equip the Haitian National Police with "mobile offices" (containers) deployed in unstable neighborhoods and at the Malpasse border area.[16] The Haitian National Police were known for flagrant rights abuses, and while donors contend that these activities

IOM in action **79**

improved the police's human rights record, critics charge that because "policing reform, correction overhaul, and border security projects were not integrated, policing in the cities and on the borders intensified in advance of changes with prisons or courts, exacerbating human rights problems."[17]

As this overview suggests, much of IOM's work in this period was seemingly disconnected from migration, or only tangentially related to human mobility. Yet IOM's donors appeared largely unconcerned about potential mission creep, and were instead pleased to have an eager and able partner in a politically fraught and unstable operational context. The IOM administration did try to rhetorically link its stabilization and development work in Haiti to migration, albeit in ways that fed into its reputation for restricting rather than supporting mobility. For instance, Purcell's 1994 director general's report suggested that IOM's community stabilization projects "were likely to prevent future irregular migration."[18] In a similar spirit, IOM's retrospective on HTI/PREPEP indicates that "while not expressly designed to do so, the PREPEP contributed to reducing internal and cross-border migration by dramatically improving infrastructure and livelihoods."[19] Given the deep, structural roots of persistent poverty in Haiti, and Haitians' longstanding reliance on mobility as a coping strategy, these suggestions seem implausible if not far-fetched. Yet as IOM looked to expand its involvement in such activities beyond Haiti, this rhetoric provided a (tenuous) rationale for its participation.

2010–2019: earthquake response and aftermath

The 7.0 magnitude earthquake that hit Haiti on January 12, 2010, killed more than 100,000 people, destroyed some 300,000 homes, and uprooted over 1.5 million people who crowded into 1,500 camps across Port-au-Prince and the surrounding areas.[20] The camps ranged from massive sites at the airport and in public squares, to smaller clusters of tents clinging to hillsides and crammed alongside flattened buildings. Conditions were deplorable, with residents struggling to access adequate water, food, sanitation, shelter, and security. Already weak and more inclined to serve elite interests than the poor majority, the Haitian government was brought to its knees as more than a quarter of government officials in Port-au-Prince died in the disaster.[21] Humanitarian aid poured into Haiti, and billions of dollars were pledged in still unrealized promises to "build back better."[22]

IOM was at the heart of the international response to the earthquake, and the operation proved pivotal for IOM, shoring up its leading role in humanitarian responses to disaster-induced displacement. Building on its prior presence in Haiti, IOM mobilized and began deploying resources within 24 hours. At its peak, IOM had almost 100 international staff in Haiti and more than 600 Haitian employees, making it one of the largest teams in the earthquake zone.[23] IOM's crisis response efforts included distributing shelters and "non-food items," constructing emergency water and sanitation facilities, and responding to the autumn 2010 cholera outbreak. Three mainstays of IOM's role in post-earthquake Haiti,

80 IOM in action

discussed here, became camp coordination and camp management (CCCM), data collection and management, and facilitating camp closures.

In 2005 IOM took on responsibility for CCCM in disasters, in the context of the humanitarian cluster system. In Haiti, this meant that IOM deployed its own camp management teams, and spearheaded efforts to coordinate the hundreds of UN agencies and NGOs working in the camps.[24] This involved attempting to ensure the provision of basic services in the camps, and encouraging NGOs to step into the role of "camp management agency" (CMA). Ideally, each camp would have its own CMA responsible for coordinating services and addressing protection concerns, but given the scale of the disaster in Port-au-Prince, 80 percent of camps did not have a CMA, and IOM struggled to convince agencies to step into this demanding role.[25] IOM collected and circulated information on underserved and almost completely unserved camps, but faced the classic bind of humanitarian coordination efforts: it couldn't oblige other actors to coordinate or become CMAs. As Schuller laments, "no agency, be it the Haitian government, IOM or the UN was able to compel NGOs to work in underserved areas, since these institutions' accountability structures focus on foreign donors."[26] Many NGOs were particularly disinclined to work in areas such as Cité Soleil, despite extreme need, leaving IOM to attempt to fill the gaps as a provider of "last resort."[27] Faced with these limitations, IOM innovated by establishing roving management teams, each overseeing 50 to 100 sites. This stopgap measure was hardly ideal, and the CCCM cluster was pointedly criticized, especially in relation to protection concerns such as sexual violence in the camps, and eviction threats.[28] While the obstacles to effective protection were admittedly severe, IOM was criticized for deploying ill-equipped junior protection officers. Its model also positioned protection as simply "one of many services to be coordinated," rather than a concern that should inform all interventions in the disaster zone.[29]

IOM's CCCM work went hand in hand with its status as the central player in displacement data collection and management. In this role, IOM accrued significant influence and power as its numbers were cited as authoritative by almost all major actors, even when concerns arose about data quality. IOM's systematic data collection began in February 2010, with the goal of providing "baseline data in support of the planning and implementation of targeted and effective programs in camps, and timely and accurate statistical information to the CCCM and other clusters."[30] In cooperation with the Haitian Department of Civil Protection, IOM ran regular "rounds" of the Displacement Tracking Matrix (DTM), and released reports with detailed information on the camps and their residents. The DTM evolved considerably over the course of its use in Haiti, with the most recent assessment conducted in April 2018. Alongside the camp-focused DTM, IOM spearheaded parallel data collection efforts concentrated on earthquake-affected neighborhoods.

Through its data work, IOM wielded great definitional power. As IOM conducted the official counts of camp residents, it effectively defined the IDP population in Haiti. The UN Guiding Principles on Internal Displacement offer a broad conception of IDPs as those "who have been forced or obliged to flee or to leave their homes or places of habitual residence," including as a result of disasters.[31] Many displaced Haitians did not shelter in camps but pursued other options such as moving in with friends or family, and many of these people also needed assistance. However, international actors and the Haitian government were almost exclusively focused on the camps, and this is where most data collection happened, so being an IDP in Haiti was effectively conflated with living in a camp.[32] Whether a camp was counted as such in the DTM had significant repercussions for its residents, positive and negative. Concerned that residency numbers were inflated by people only claiming to live in the camps in order to access aid, draconian data collection tactics were sometimes employed, such as working with security services to "lock down" camps in the middle of the night before head counts, on the assumption that "legitimate" camp residents must be sleeping in their tents. Very small or far-flung camps could slip under the DTM radar, leaving their residents with little aid.[33] And yet being counted as IDPs, and using the DTM to characterize certain settlements as "camps," also came with risks, particularly in the context of efforts to shutter camps and resolve displacement.

As the emergency response wound down, much of IOM's work shifted to closing camps and supporting the "progressive resolution" of the IDP situation. The IASC Framework on Durable Solutions for IDPs identifies three avenues for resolving internal displacement – voluntary return, local integration, or relocation elsewhere in the country – and states that durable solutions have been achieved when former IDPs "no longer have specific assistance and protection needs that are linked to their displacement and such persons can enjoy their human rights without discrimination on account of their displacement."[34] The Framework identifies criteria that influence the attainment of durable solutions, indicating that IDPs who have accessed a durable solution will be able to equitably enjoy safety and security; adequate living standards (including water, food, housing, health care, and education); access to livelihoods; and mechanisms to restore lost homes and lands. To many aid workers with IOM and other agencies, these rights-based standards seemed almost impossibly ambitious in Haiti, where most citizens – displaced or not – did not enjoy these rights before or after the earthquake.[35] The notion of durable solutions seemed difficult to square with the reality that even before the earthquake, Port-au-Prince faced a massive housing shortage and chronic homelessness. Thus IOM's focus was not so much on durable solutions as ambitiously laid out in the IASC Framework, but on "progressive" steps towards resolving displacement – starting with closing camps.[36]

Camp closures were urgently pursued for various reasons: beyond concerns about their squalid conditions, some large camps occupied important public spaces which were needed for reconstruction to move forward. Others were located in unsafe, flood-prone areas or on private property that owners were determined to repossess – even by hiring gangs to torch the camps and drive everyone out.[37] At the same time, the Haitian government and some international actors often questioned the legitimacy of the IDPs' needs, painting them as opportunists out to game the aid system.[38] Against this backdrop, "IOM's

82 IOM in action

regularly conducted census," the DTM, "showing a gradual decline in the numbers of internally displaced [i.e. camp residents] became *the* barometer of the success of the international response."[39] IOM helped those IDPs who owned property but lost their homes to leave the camps primarily by erecting transitional shelters on their properties; it also provided more modest support for the reconstruction of permanent homes, and its legal team attempted to mediate land disputes and support the negotiation of land tenure agreements.[40] Yet these initiatives left behind the majority of IDPs without property on which to rebuild. For this group, camp closures were enabled primarily through the use of "rental subsidy cash grants," which IOM was pivotal in developing and implementing across Port-au-Prince. This initiative involved distributing US$500 minimum cash grants to IDPs in camps, to defray the cost of a first year of rental accommodation. The grants were ideally supplemented by training and skills development programs, and other forms of reintegration assistance.[41] Once all registered residents in a particular camp received the cash grant, the camp would be closed and cleared.

This approach helped some IDPs access decent rental accommodation, but for many, the intervention did not enable durable solutions or even sustainable progress towards them. Given the devastation of the city's housing stock, appropriate accommodation was often unavailable, and rents were unaffordable, prompting some to use the funds to move out to informal settlements springing up outside Port-au-Prince. The UN Special Rapporteurs on the right to housing and the human rights of IDPs expressed concern that this approach did not adequately promote IDPs' right to a durable solution, and risked facilitating evictions.[42] Despite such concerns, camp closures continued to be hailed as a sure sign of progress in an otherwise beleaguered international response, with IOM celebrating that over 90 percent had left the camps by 2014, a figure that rose to 97 percent by 2018.[43] This implies that leaving communities that were established as camps in 2010 was uniformly the best option for those displaced in the earthquake. However, some defied the pressure to leave, striving instead to transform former camps into permanent settlements where they may continue living and escape the relentless pressures of the rental market. These efforts are resisted by elites who claim private ownership of the land, and by their backers in the Haitian government. In the early years after the earthquake, IOM did in some instances promote "sites and services" models in attempts to "regularize" some former camps, and provide them with the infrastructure necessary to become permanent communities. More recently, however, IOM has effectively undercut some residents' efforts to remain living on disputed sites, by deploying the DTM – at the request of the government and donors – to count these sites as camps and their residents as IDPs, as a presumed prelude to using rental subsidy cash grants to displace them from places they have come to call home.

Almost ten years after the earthquake, the balance of IOM's work in Haiti has again shifted, with migration management activities between Haiti and the Dominican Republic taking a more prominent position, alongside continued involvement in a panoply of tasks from disaster risk reduction to electoral

IOM in action **83**

assistance. And yet the consequences of IOM's involvement in the earthquake response continue to reverberate, both within the organization and for those on the receiving end of its interventions.

IOM in Libya

As in Haiti, IOM's work in Libya reveals some of the limitations of humanitarian responses to forced migration, and tensions between its humanitarian identity and other aspects of its migration management mandate. In Libya, IOM "blurs the boundaries between protection and coercion, attention and persuasion, help and control, and thereby makes the different registers of intervention difficult to distinguish, and thus to evaluate critically."[44] While IOM represents its activities in Libya during and after Gaddafi's fall as largely humanitarian, Brachet argues that its "overall objectives" remain "the control of migrants and their systematic removal from Europe's southern borders."[45] IOM has certainly helped enable the European Union's restrictionist agenda, but a closer examination of IOM's work in Libya, including with IDPs, points to more diverse goals at play. For example, through its work in Libya, IOM has integrated itself more deeply into the UN system. IOM's engagements in Libya need to be understood in relation to the policies and practices of key actors including the European Union (EU) and the UN, particularly UNHCR, and in the regional context of North Africa and the Mediterranean.

1995–2010: before Gaddafi's fall

IOM appears to have first worked in Libya in 1995, when at UNHCR's request it repatriated 311 Eritrean and Ethiopian refugees from Libya.[46] In the 1990s, IOM began to analyze irregular migration and trafficking issues in North Africa, setting its sights on the region as an area for expansion.[47] This openness to engagement suited the Gaddafi regime, which used migration policy and governance as an avenue to help overcome its international isolation, cooperating with the EU and particularly Italy to control irregular migration, and encouraging migration from other African countries. Hundreds of thousands of workers moved to Libya, weathering discrimination, violence against black migrants, and periodic collective deportations.[48]

In 2002, Libya joined IOM as an observer, and IOM began working more actively with Libya. In October 2002, IOM played a major role in convening the first 5+5 Ministerial Conference on migration in Tunis with five North African states (Libya, Tunisia, Algeria, Mauritania, and Morocco) and five European states (France, Italy, Malta, Portugal, and Spain).[49] In 2004, Libya became a full member of IOM, and the Libyan General People's Committee for Public Security worked with IOM to convene a regional seminar on irregular migration, preceded by a training session for 100 Libyan officials and police officers that addressed border management and assisted voluntary returns.[50] The following year, IOM and Libya signed a cooperation agreement on irregular migration,

84 IOM in action

with little transparency about what this agreement entailed, or about IOM's role in subsequent work, such as facilitating returns from the Italian island of Lampedusa to Libya.[51] IOM also "initiated preparatory activities aimed at enhancing the Libyan Arab Jamahiriya's institutional capacity to tackle irregular transit migration," noting that such movement "poses serious challenges to the government," but saying little about the concerns associated with supporting a dictatorship that deftly used migration cooperation to strengthen its own hand, and vacillated between welcoming and viciously abusing migrants.[52]

IOM opened an office in Tripoli in 2006, focused primarily on irregular migration. Through projects on border management, returns, migration information campaigns, refurbishing temporary reception centers, and servicing migrant detention centers, Libya worked more closely with the EU and IOM on border control than any other North African state.[53] IOM bluntly justified these projects as necessary "to stop the growing trend in flows to Europe."[54] Some of these efforts eroded access to asylum in Europe, and heightened risk of refoulement – concerns that IOM acknowledged obliquely, if at all.[55]

Responding to the 2011 revolution

Before Gaddafi's fall in 2011, there were an estimated 1.5–2.5 million migrants in Libya, in addition to some 7 million Libyan citizens.[56] As violence erupted across the country, millions of Libyans and migrants headed for the borders. Most Libyans went to Tunisia, where they could enter without a visa, and relied on their own resources or help from UNHCR.[57] In contrast, many migrants in Libya were not legally entitled to enter and stay in neighboring states; many had to flee without their documents and other belongings, and could not afford to travel back to their countries of origin. As the displaced migrants were not legally refugees, they did not fall under UNHCR's mandate, and IOM stepped into a major role. Between February 2011 and January 2012, an estimated 790,000 migrant workers fled to neighboring countries, primarily Tunisia and Egypt but also Chad, Niger, and Algeria. IOM and UNHCR set up a Humanitarian Evacuation Cell to coordinate their efforts, and in cooperation with partners, IOM facilitated the evacuation of some 210,000 "vulnerable foreign workers," mainly from Chad, Bangladesh, Egypt, Nigeria, and Sudan.[58] Some six months after the revolution began, changes in the security situation enabled IOM to work more actively within Libya, where it evacuated 38,000 stranded migrants from Tripoli, Benghazi, Misrata, and other besieged communities, and provided emergency support for some 200,000 Libyan IDPs.[59] As in Haiti, in undertaking this work IOM emphasized its logistical efficacy and ability to execute projects in extremely difficult circumstances, as exemplified by press releases with titles such as, "Despite heavy shelling, IOM rescues several hundreds of migrants."[60]

This work has had important implications for IOM's institutional development. Hailed as a "compelling source of future best practice for addressing the humanitarian needs" of migrants in crisis situations, the mission led to emergency evacuations becoming a more prominent and regularized element of IOM's work.[61] IOM began speaking up more consistently in international forums on "vulnerable migrants" in crisis situations, cultivating this as a group the agency could represent.[62] (Speaking up about rights abuses may also have the institutionally useful effect of tempering some of the delicate or negative reputational concerns associated with work such as providing services in detention centers, or facilitating the return of failed asylum seekers to unstable countries.) The agency also established the Migration Emergency Funding Mechanism, to enable prompt responses to similar situations, even before securing donor support. Some of the major policies and frameworks discussed in Chapter 2, particularly the Migration Crisis Operational Framework and the 2015 Humanitarian Policy, were significantly influenced by experiences in Libya. The emergency response in Libya also provided IOM with critical opportunities to deepen its involvement with the UN system, particularly through "unprecedented cooperation" with UNHCR.[63] Inter-agency collaboration is still not always smooth or predictable, and behind the scenes of this unprecedented cooperation, inter-agency conflicts were reportedly intense.[64] Although UNHCR and IOM continue to scrap over terminology and turf, the mission demonstrated the potential complementarity between the agencies' mandates, and they have continued to work closely together in Libya, co-leading the Refugee and Migrant Platform, preparing a Joint Operational Framework for Humanitarian Response in Libya, and developing standard operating procedures that divide up responsibility for tasks such as assisting migrants and refugees upon disembarkation from intercepted vessels, in detention, and in the context of voluntary repatriation. The high commissioner for refugees and the IOM director general have delivered joint briefings on their agencies' work in Libya, with High Commissioner Grandi arguing at a 2017 joint briefing that "we have urgent work to do in Libya and can only do it together."[65]

Unending crisis? IOM in post-Gaddafi Libya

Since 2011, Libya has been "redefined as a geographic zone where crisis is permanent."[66] Gaddafi's ouster and NATO's botched intervention gave way to years of instability as militias battled for control, and the UN-recognized government has struggled to exert authority. With the fall of the Gaddafi regime, the policies and practices that staunched journeys to Europe from Libya's shores crumbled, and smugglers began moving thousands of refugees and other migrants over the desert, across the Mediterranean, and into Europe. Despite Libyan authorities' tenuous hold on power and their complicity in rampant human rights violations against migrants, the EU and particularly Italy have sought to re-engage Libya in defending "fortress Europe" – that is, in preventing irregular and unwanted migration into Europe. Under Libyan law, it is a crime to enter, stay in, or leave Libya without permission, upon penalty of indefinite detention pending deportation. Under this policy, tens of thousands of migrants and refugees are held in quasi-prisons, often controlled by Libyan militias and characterized by widespread ill treatment, torture, and rape.[67] Migrants in Libya have been traded as slaves, and killed in several attacks on detention centers. While Libya allows

UNHCR some latitude to work within its borders, it does not accept the Refugee Agency's mandate, has not ratified the 1951 Refugee Convention, and has no asylum system.[68] Nevertheless, Italy and other EU member states have equipped the Libyan Coast Guard to intercept migrant vessels and return them to Libya, and have cracked down on NGOs rescuing imperiled migrant vessels on the Mediterranean. This route has become the deadliest migrant passage in the world, with over 13,500 drownings between 2014 and 2016; 97 percent of these deaths befell migrants and refugees departing from Libya.[69] The violence and incompetence of the Libyan Coast Guard have only added to the risks migrants face on the Mediterranean: coast guard officials have beaten and abused migrants, and have caused migrant deaths by preventing NGO rescuers from saving drowning people, and by deploying sub-standard rescue techniques.[70]

IOM's role in this context is riddled with tensions: it portrays its activities in Libya and the surrounding region largely in humanitarian terms. Alongside UNHCR, it is active in responding to the rights and needs of more than 200,000 Libyan IDPs, including in highly complex cases such as the ethnic cleansing of the Tawergha.[71] IOM has become the main source of information on migrant deaths at sea through the Missing Migrants project, and has become progressively more vocal in speaking out against violations of migrants' rights.[72] For example, IOM helped to break news of slave markets operating in detention centers, and other egregious abuses of migrants in Libya, and has publicly taken positions at odds with donor states' perspectives, insisting for example that the Mare Nostrum rescue operation in the Mediterranean was not a "pull factor" enticing migrants to travel to Europe.[73] At the same time, IOM serves its European member states by helping to enable the restrictive policies that keep migrants locked in crisis conditions, including by providing capacity-building activities for Libyan authorities to "detect, prevent and manage irregular migration flows to or through the country."[74] While the UN high commissioner for human rights has argued that the EU's policy of "assisting the Libyan Coast Guard to intercept and return migrants in the Mediterranean [is] inhuman," IOM has provided training, equipment, and infrastructure for the Libyan Coast Guard.[75] This is an institution that, as the UN high commissioner for human rights decried, "has shot at NGO boats trying to rescue migrants at risk of drowning."[76] Do such interventions promote essential reforms in an institution that will operate one way or another? Or do they merely assuage European consciences and pave the way for more migrant apprehensions and detentions?

While the answers to these questions are a matter of debate, IOM's role in Libya has indisputably been shaped by its relationship with the EU as a major donor and member state bloc. Much of IOM's work in Libya unfolds under the auspices of the 2012 IOM–EU Strategic Cooperation Framework, and is linked to IOM's role as a key player in the implementation of migration governance-related agreements such as the 2015 Valletta Action Plan and the 2016 EU Migration Partnership Framework. That said, in contrast to its role in Libya a decade ago, when it offered almost unequivocal support for European efforts to curb unwanted migration, and was largely mum about related protection concerns,

IOM's approach has evolved in some significant ways. Reflecting its increased if not yet robust institutional autonomy, IOM has not mutely accepted the EU's frameworks, or acceded entirely to the roles that EU member states may want the agency to play in Libya. For example, the European Council's 2017 Malta Declaration expresses the Council's determination to "significantly reduce migratory flows along the Central Mediterranean route," and underscores the Council's wish to "ensure adequate reception capacities and conditions in Libya for migrants, together with the UNHCR and IOM."[77] In advance of the Declaration's conclusion, UNHCR and IOM issued a joint statement calling for the "creation of proper reception services" and "sustainable migration and asylum systems in Libya," but also insisting that "given the current contexts, it is not appropriate to consider Libya a safe third country nor to establish extraterritorial processing of asylum seekers in North Africa."[78] In this way, the agencies sought to fend off the possibility that they would be pushed into roles in Libya that are clearly legally inappropriate and at odds with the organizations' professed principles. By issuing their statement jointly, the agencies presented a united front, giving their position greater weight and (at least in this instance) breaking with past practices of states turning to IOM to implement policies opposed by other IOs with more robust protection mandates. In follow-up talks, the regional director for IOM's EU office appealed "to our Valletta partners to reinvigorate a rights-based approach to migrants, with more attention given to sustainable reintegration, protection and humanitarian assistance for all people of concern throughout their migratory process, regardless of their status, particularly the most vulnerable."[79] IOM also argued that "more opportunities for legal migration and mobility must become a greater part of a comprehensive approach to managing migration between Africa and Europe."[80]

IOM's contentious entanglement in restrictive European policies in post-Gaddafi Libya is exemplified by its work related to detention and returns.[81] IOM and UNHCR liaise with the Libyan Coast Guard and the Libyan Directorate for Combatting Illegal Migration (DCIM), which is in theory responsible for the detention centers, although several are outside DCIM control. IOM and UNHCR meet migrants when they disembark in Libya from intercepted vessels and, along with a handful of NGOs, they have limited access to the detention centers to provide basic humanitarian aid. IOM and UNHCR co-chair a Detention Task Force involving other IOs in Libya, and, in a twist on its usual data collection roles, IOM has started deploying the DTM to profile detention centers.[82] In very rare cases, IOM has been able to successfully lobby for highly vulnerable individuals to be released from detention, but more commonly, IOM facilitates migrants' ostensibly voluntary repatriation to their countries of origin.[83] With predominantly EU funding, IOM repatriated 2,775 migrants to their countries of origin in 2016, and 14,754 in 2017; over 80 percent returned from detention.[84] This uptick since 2017 followed a dramatic increase in the number of migrants in formal detention centers, from an estimated 5,000–6,000 detainees to more than 15,000 as many were transferred from unofficial detention sites.[85] Most returnees went back to sub-Saharan African countries, particularly Nigeria, Guinea, Gambia,

88 IOM in action

Mali, and Senegal. IOM's public presentation of relatively detailed data on these movements is an interesting contrast to the organization's past, less transparent practices in relation to returns, although there is still little analysis of conditions and experiences following returns. IOM's position now seems to be that whatever the controversies and complications attending these movements, they can and should be celebrated as humanitarian achievements.

In line with this view, IOM Libya has replaced the usual term assisted voluntary return (AVR) with voluntary humanitarian return (VHR). Funded primarily by European donors, IOM's VHR programs in Libya subvert the headquarters-level divide between the DMM, which is usually responsible for AVR, and DOE, which leads IOM's humanitarian activities, and epitomize the entanglement of migration management and humanitarian aid. Declaring the returns to be humanitarian – and thus, presumably, good – glosses over the difficult questions that plague repatriation efforts in such contexts. For example: Can returns be truly voluntary in the deeply coercive context of indefinite detention? Does IOM exacerbate risk of refoulement by returning migrants from detention centers in which they cannot reliably make asylum claims? Is this an acceptable risk in light of the alternative of prolonged suffering and possible death in indefinite detention? Is this really the only viable alternative? Amnesty International argues that while IOM's return program "certainly offers a lifeline to some," it cannot be and should not be promoted as the sole option for migrants stuck in Libya, as they include "tens of thousands of people in need of international protection for whom return is not an option."[86] According to Amnesty, the "extent to which these returns are genuinely voluntary remains questionable" given the excruciating conditions facing migrants in Libya, and the prospect of indefinite detention; without a functioning asylum system and full recognition of UNHCR's role, the risk of refoulement is pervasive.[87] Similar critiques have been expressed by Médecins Sans Frontières regarding "so-called voluntary returns."[88] The Office of the United Nations High Commissioner for Human Rights (OHCHR) and the UN Support Mission in Libya (UNSMIL) have further voiced concerns regarding detainee registration and IOM's role in this process, observing that

> IOM has introduced a registration system for migrants and refugees disembarked on Libyan shores following interception, which has been used by the [Libyan Coast Guard] since early 2018. Yet, it remains unlinked to any formal or informal registration undertaken by individual detention centers and is inaccessible to other United Nations entities or humanitarian actors, including UNSMIL. This registration system upon disembarkation does not include any measures for external oversight or data protection . . . there is a risk that international organizations working in DCIM centers are not able to provide adequate protection of the human rights of all detained migrants and refugees despite their efforts to identify vulnerability, conduct in-depth individual assessment and establish a referral system.[89]

Despite these concerns, UNHCR, OHCHR, and some major human rights advocacy organizations remain on balance supportive of IOM's efforts in detention and in relation to return, seemingly agreeing with Swing's view that "scaling up" IOM's "return programme may not serve to fully address the plight of migrants in Libya, but it is our duty to take migrants out of detention centers as a matter of absolute priority."[90] OHCHR, for example, has called for donors and destination countries to support "the activities of IOM aimed at ensuring voluntary, humanitarian and sustainable repatriation of migrants."[91] For its part, UNHCR recognizes that the "voluntary nature of . . . returns [from Libya] has been questioned given that the practice of detention often leaves no alternative. However," the agency insists, "the critical role of IOM's ability to support returns to their country of origin for stranded migrants is not in question."[92] Such public support for a delicate and still contentious intervention points to how engagements in Libya have more closely bound IOM and UNHCR together. These assessments also suggest that while returns have been a "thorn in the side" for IOM as it has struggled to cultivate its role in the international humanitarian system, in Libya the agency may have found a way to recast returns as humanitarian and thus more ethically palatable.[93] In so doing, experiences in Libya bring together the sometimes conflicted "humanitarian" and "migration management" sides of the IOM house.

The evolution of IOM's approach and the persistence of some of its older ways of working are crystallized in a 2019 statement that seeks to clarify IOM's position on returns to Libya, and the rationale for and limitations of its detention-related work, entitled Protecting Migrants in Libya Must Be Our Primary Focus. The statement reflects competing pressures to serve powerful states keen to engage IOM in executing restrictive migration policies, while also hewing to its asserted principles and identity as the newly-minted "UN Migration Agency." The statement seems intended to refute the suggestion that IOM's presence at disembarkation points signals support for the EU's interdiction policy, and opens by saying that, "With regard to its activities in Libya," IOM "would like to clarify that we follow the UN position indicating that Libya cannot yet be considered a safe port."[94] According to the statement, IOM meets intercepted vessels to "deliver primary assistance to migrants that have been rescued at sea," but that after disembarkation migrants are sent to DCIM-run detention centers over which IOM has no oversight or control.[95] IOM's failure to directly call out the EU for its policies and its euphemistic use of the term "rescue" reflects its traditional deference to states. While some migrants are pulled from the water by the Libyan Coast Guard before being shipped to Libyan detention centers, many are simply intercepted – not so much rescued as captured and condemned. However, the statement also breaks from IOM's reputation for deference and dissembling by clearly declaring that the "detention of men, women and children is arbitrary," and that conditions in detention are "unacceptable and inhumane."[96] IOM indicates that it "advocates for alternatives to detention," and that a "change of policy is needed urgently as migrants returned to Libya should not be facing detention."[97] This comparatively explicit, open critique is a notable shift from

90 IOM in action

IOM's longstanding practice of following states' leads, and urging changes in course only outside the public eye. It therefore challenges the view that IOM's structural dependence on states for project-based financing makes it incapable of mounting criticisms against them.[98]

Brachet suggests that post-Gaddafi Libya and IOM's efforts there reflect a "transformation" of the "nature of politics and humanitarian intervention at the international level."[99] However, in many ways the situation seems to be one of business as usual for the humanitarian system, insofar as humanitarian efforts in Libya are fraught with moral dilemmas, and humanitarianism is deployed – as it has been throughout its history – to maintain certain power imbalances, and to tamp down the costs of particular policy choices. The transformation is more evident in how IOM itself has navigated this case. Rather than unreservedly playing the part of docile servant, IOM has taken on a more ambitious but deeply fractured role. Attempting to play both sides of the system, IOM is embedded in restrictive EU and Libyan migration policies, at the same time as it has spoken up against these policies and their consequences in ways it hasn't done even in the recent past.

Conclusion: implications for understanding IOM

What are the implications of these cases for understanding the evolution and contemporary character of IOM? In Haiti and Libya, IOM made vital contributions to saving lives and relieving suffering. And yet some of its interventions – including some justified in humanitarian terms – endangered the populations IOM professed to serve. Notwithstanding the contested nature of interventions such as the rental subsidy cash grants in Haiti and "voluntary humanitarian repatriation" from Libyan detention centers, these operations were highly significant for IOM's evolution. Many international staff who now occupy influential positions within IOM worked on these missions and were shaped by them; experiences in Haiti and Libya have had clear imprints on subsequent operations as well as on internal policymaking efforts. In post-earthquake Haiti and post-revolution Libya, IOM cultivated major roles outside the purview of other IOs, including in data collection and management, CCCM, and work with "migrants in crisis," helping it to consolidate its international standing and influence.

IOM's work cannot be understood in isolation in either of these cases. IOM is part of the aid machine in Haiti and Libya. In some ways its activities and approach are distinctive, but in many others it has followed the familiar patterns and practices of established actors in the industry. While some stress how IOM gradually leads other actors to "share and adopt its own reasoning," in Haiti and Libya IOM shaped and was shaped by a broad constellation of actors, including other intergovernmental organizations.[100] IOM's integration into UN operations in these countries influenced its own discourses and willingness to question member states' policies, including through joint advocacy with UNHCR.

Experiences in Haiti and Libya raise questions about what it means to do "humanitarian" work in countries framed as places of perpetual crisis, where the line between emergencies and everyday life is razor thin. In both contexts, tensions arose as a result of IOM's role as a "multi-mandate" actor involved in humanitarian work alongside migration management efforts that are not necessarily intended to be humanitarian, and may be at odds with respect for humanitarian principles and human rights protection.[101] The concern here is that as a multi-mandate IO, IOM plays both sides of the system, enabling the restrictive and securitized policies that heighten migrants' precarity and set the stage for crises, and then stepping in as a central actor in alleviating the problems it helped to create.[102] On a certain level, this critique may overstate IOM's influence: states are remarkably resourceful in implementing restrictive agendas, and would presumably find alternatives if IOM refused involvement. IOM itself often suggests that the negative consequences for migrants of restrictive policies would be amplified without its engagement. For example, the Libyan Coast Guard would undoubtedly still operate without IOM's involvement, but perhaps with even less training and regard for migrants' rights and well-being. Yet this rationale creates a slippery slope that may justify institutional engagement in almost any circumstances. The question is whether involvement in contested activities is appropriate for an IO that asserts a humanitarian identity and is now part of the UN system. While I cannot offer a full analysis here, these tensions and challenges are built into IOM, and deserve close scrutiny moving forward. In order to avoid organizational complicity in harms against migrants, rigorous and transparent due diligence assessments, based on human rights standards, are required, in combination with concerted strategies to mitigate any risks or adverse impacts created by IOM's involvement.[103]

IOM's institutional character and structure – including its (in)famous flexibility, decentralization, and projectization – made it well suited to navigate some of the challenges it encountered in Haiti and Libya. IOM could respond quickly and sometimes innovatively to problems such as the need to close massive camps in public spaces in Port-au-Prince. The problem came when the rental subsidy cash grant mechanism devised to meet this need was used as a one-size-fits-all response. Although some IOM staff recognized the problems associated with this approach and tried at times to resist it, the organization had strong financial incentives to scale up the intervention, and to defer to the Haitian government by implementing it even in camps where residents did not want it, and where it risked legitimizing evictions and leaving people worse off.[104] This drive to scale up and "sell" interventions is common to many IOs and NGOs, but is perhaps particularly pronounced for IOM, and risks undermining its own contributions. IOM's thirst to secure funding and continually expand additionally meant that it took on incredibly diverse work largely unrelated to migration, such as constructing prisons in Haiti. Interestingly, IOM's donors do not generally seem to have critiqued the agency's broad array of activities in Haiti and Libya as mission creep, but rather took this as evidence of IOM pluckily rising to the occasion, overcoming operational obstacles that stymie other actors to get the job done, whatever it might be. The trouble lay, rather, in the potential negative implications of some of this work that IOM either overlooked or accepted as a reasonable trade-off.

92 IOM in action

The agency's service-oriented, entrepreneurial approach also led IOM to cultivate close relationships with repressive governments in Haiti and Libya, including the Gaddafi regime.[105] Working with governments is part of most IOs' job description, and IOM's close government connections sometimes helped it address protection concerns, such as when it could persuade Haitian officials to stave off arbitrary camp evictions. Behind the scenes, IOM may have weighed and tried to mitigate the ethical problems associated with strengthening the hand of authorities that at best ill-serve and at worst actively persecute their citizens and migrants under their control. In many instances, however, it appears that IOM's interest in bringing in projects overrode or minimized these concerns. All of this illustrates some of the benefits but also the risks associated with IOM's structure and entrepreneurial approach.

IOM is an evolving organization; experiences in Haiti and Libya both exemplify and have influenced important organizational developments, from the uses of the DTM to the creation of the policies and frameworks such as the Migration Crisis Operational Framework and the 2015 Humanitarian Policy. These polices and IOM's now more explicit commitment to humanitarian principles and human rights protection (discussed in Chapter 2) should inform its continued engagements in Haiti and Libya. However, the dynamic and demanding nature of these operational contexts, entrenched institutional cultures, continuous staff turnover, and lack of core budgets for across-the-board, protection-focused training, hinder the implementation and impact of these policies and commitments. These operations also advanced IOM's evolution by fostering its further integration into the international humanitarian system. Over the course of its engagements in Haiti, Libya, and worldwide, IOM has worked closely with other IOs, including some like UNHCR with explicit protection mandates. It has gradually become more transparent about activities such as returns, and more inclined to discuss human rights and protection issues, and to advocate more openly for the populations it claims to serve. Some dismiss these developments as mere talk, but these shifts represent an important step for an organization that has historically shied away from talking about rights.[106] As the next chapter discusses, IOM has now formally joined the UN system, a development that brings with it increased visibility and influence. It is therefore all the more important to ensure that as IOM carries on its work in Haiti, Libya, and elsewhere, it continues to raise these concerns, and to bring its operations more fully into line with its professed commitments.

Notes

1 Guy Goodwin-Gill, *A Brief and Somewhat Sceptical Perspective on the International Organization for Migration*, 7 April 2019, www.kaldorcentre.unsw.edu.au/publication/brief-and-somewhat-sceptical-perspective-international-organization-migration.

2 For a more general discussion of the role of multi-mandate organizations in humanitarian work, see Dorothea Hilhorst and Eline Pereboom, "Multi-Mandate Organizations in Humanitarian Aid," in *The New Humanitarians in International Practice: Emerging Actors and Contested Principles*, eds. Zeynep Sezgin and Dennis Dijkzeul (London: Routledge, 2017), 85–101.

IOM in action **93**

3 Michelle Ducasse-Rogier, *The International Organization for Migration: 1951–2001* (Geneva: IOM, 2001), 29.

4 For analyses of how colonialism, racism, and imperialism have translated into political instability, poverty, and displacement in Haiti, see for example Mark Schuller, *Killing with Kindness: Haiti, International Aid, and NGOs* (New Brunswick: Rutgers University Press, 2012), and Erica James, *Democratic Insecurities: Violence, Trauma, and Intervention in Haiti* (Berkeley: University of California Press, 2010).

5 Elizabeth Ferris, "Recurrent Acute Disasters, Crisis Migration: Haiti Has Had It All," in *Humanitarian Crises and Migration: Causes, Consequences and Responses*, eds. Susan F. Martin, Sanjula Weerasinghe, and Abbie Taylor (London: Routledge, 2014), 81.

6 Ducasse-Rogier, *International Organization for Migration*, 140.

7 On these activities, see e.g., Kevin Walby and Jeffrey Monaghan, "'Haitian Paradox' or Dark Side of the Security-Development Nexus? Canada's Role in the Securitization of Haiti, 2004–2009," *Alternatives* 36, no. 4 (2011): 273–287.

8 Walby and Monaghan, "Haitian Paradox," 276. On the rights protection initiative, see IOM, *IOM in the Caribbean*, 2002, http://publications.iom.int/system/files/pdf/caribbean_en.pdf.

9 Ducasse-Rogier, *International Organization for Migration*; Jonathan Dworken, Jonathan Moore and Adam Siegel, *Haiti Demobilization and Reintegration Program: An Evaluation Prepared for U.S. Agency for International Development* (Alexandria: Institute for Public Research CNA Corporation, 1997), 1–2.

10 Patricia Weiss Fagen, "The Long-Term Challenges of Reconstruction and Reintegration: Case Studies of Haiti and Bosnia-Herzegovina," in *Refugees and Forced Displacement: International Security, Human Vulnerability, and the State*, eds. Edward Newman and Joanne van Selm (New York: United Nations University Press, 2002), 226. See also Eirin Mobekk, "International Involvement in Restructuring and Creating Security Forces: The Case of Haiti," *Small Wars and Insurgencies* 12, no. 3 (2001): 100. For critical assessments of the program, see also Terry F. Buss and Adam Gardner, *Haiti in the Balance: Why Foreign Aid Has Failed and What We Can Do About It* (Washington, DC: Brookings Institution Press, 2009), 115.

11 Ducasse-Rogier, *International Organization for Migration*, 146, 150.

12 IOM, *HTI/PREPEP 2004–2012: The Journey to Stabilization* (Port-au-Prince: IOM, 2012).

13 Ibid. See also Buss and Gardner, *Haiti in the Balance*, 190.

14 David Becker, "Gangs, Netwar, and 'Community Counterinsurgency' in Haiti," *Prism* 2, no. 3 (2011): 138, 148. See also Robert Muggah, "The Effects of Stabilization on Humanitarian Action in Haiti," *Disasters* 34, no. 3 (2010): 451.

15 Becker, "Gangs," 145.

16 Walby and Monaghan, "Haitian Paradox," 278; Jeffrey Monaghan, *Security Aid: Canada and the Development Regime of Security* (Toronto: University of Toronto Press, 2017), 152. On IOM's involvement in police reform and training projects, see also the IOM, *2008 Report of the IOM Director General* (Geneva: IOM, 2009).

17 Walby and Monaghan, "Haitian Paradox," 283, and Monaghan, *Security Aid*, 152–156.

18 IOM, *Report of the Director General on the Work of the Organization for the Year 1994* (Geneva: IOM, 1995), para 104. See also Ducasse-Rogier, *International Organization for Migration*, 150.

19 IOM, *HTI/PREPEP*.

20 Angela Sherwood, Megan Bradley, Lorenza Rossi, Rosalia Gitau and Bradley Mellicker, *Supporting Durable Solutions to Urban, Post-Disaster Displacement: Challenges and Opportunities in Haiti* (Washington, DC: Brookings Institution/IOM, 2014), 6.

21 Ibid., 18.

22 For discussions of the earthquake response, see e.g., Mark Schuller, *Humanitarian Aftershocks in Haiti* (New Brunswick: Rutgers University Press, 2016); Mark Schuller and

94 IOM in action

Pablo Morales, eds., *Tectonic Shifts: Haiti since the Earthquake* (Sterling: Kumarian Press, 2012).

23 IOM, *IOM in Response to Haiti Earthquake: Update #8* (Port-au-Prince: IOM, 2010), and IOM, *Report on Human Resources Management* (Geneva: IOM, 2012). For an internally produced overview of IOM's activities in the first two years after the earthquake, see IOM, *Haiti: From Emergency to Sustainable Recovery, IOM Haiti Two-Year Report (2010–2011)* (Port-au-Prince: IOM, 2012).

24 IOM was also, at points, involved in leading shelter efforts. In September 2011, the Emergency Shelter and CCCM clusters were combined, with IOM continuing in a lead role. See IOM, *Sustainable Recovery*. For analyses of aid in the camps, see e.g., Mark Schuller, "Haiti's Disaster After the Disaster: The IDP Camps and Cholera," *Journal of Humanitarian Assistance* (2010); Elizabeth Ferris and Sara Ferro-Ribeiro, "Protecting People in Cities: The Disturbing Case of Haiti," *Disasters* 36, no. 1 (2012): 43–63; and Valerie Kaussen, "Do It Yourself: International Aid and the Neoliberal Ethos in the Tent Camps of Port-au-Prince," *NACLA Report on the Americas* 44, no. 6 (2011): 5–7. For discussion of IOM's psychosocial response work, as presented by former IOM staff members, see Guglielmo Schininà, Mazen Aboul Hosn, Amal Ataya, Kety Dieuveut and Marie-Adèle Salem, "Psychosocial Response to the Haiti Earthquake: The Experiences of the International Organization for Migration," *Interventions* 8, no. 2 (2010): 158–164.

25 Mark Schuller, "Kabrit ki gen twop mèt: Understanding Gaps in WASH Services in Haiti's IDP Camps," *Disasters* 38, no. 1 (2014): 1–24. See also Ferris and Ferro-Ribeiro, "Protecting People in Cities."

26 Schuller, "Understanding Gaps in WASH Services," 15.

27 Ibid., 16, 19; Schuller, "Haiti's Disaster After the Disaster."

28 Ferris and Ferro-Ribeiro, "Protecting People in Cities," 56; Shahla Ali, Governing Disasters: Engaging Local Populations in Humanitarian Relief (Cambridge: Cambridge University Press, 2016), 109; Refugees International, *Haiti: Still Trapped in the Emergency Phase* (Washington, DC: Refugees International, 2010).

29 Ferris and Ferro-Ribeiro, "Protecting People in Cities," 55; Refugees International, *Haiti: Still Trapped*.

30 IOM, *Sustainable Recovery*.

31 Guiding Principles on Internal Displacement, Introduction, para 2.

32 Sherwood, et al., *Supporting Durable Solutions*; Schuller, *Humanitarian Aftershocks*, 4–5.

33 Schuller, "Haiti's Disaster After the Disaster"; Schuller, "Understanding Gaps in WASH Services"; Schuller, *Killing with Kindness*, 172.

34 IASC Framework on Durable Solutions to Internal Displacement (2010). On the question of durable solutions to displacement in Haiti, see also Sherwood, et al., *Supporting Durable Solutions*; Megan Bradley and Angela Sherwood, "Addressing and Resolving Internal Displacement: Reflections on a Soft Law 'Success Story'," in *Tracing the Roles of Soft Law in Human Rights*, eds. Thomas Gammeltoft-Hansen, Stephanie Lagoutte and John Cerone (Oxford: Oxford University Press, 2016), 155–182; Angela Sherwood, "Grabbing Solutions: Internal Displacement and Post-Disaster Land Occupations in Haiti," in *Refugees' Roles in Resolving Displacement and Building Peace: Beyond Beneficiaries*, eds. Megan Bradley, James Milner and Blair Peruniak (Washington, DC: Georgetown University Press, 2019).

35 Sherwood, et al., *Supporting Durable Solutions*. Of course from a rights-based perspective, the presence of barriers to the enjoyment of human rights is no reason to lower the bar.

36 For IOM's compilation of its activities on this front, in Haiti and worldwide, see IOM, *IOM Contributions to Progressively Resolve Displacement Situations* (Geneva: IOM, 2016).

37 On evictions from camps, see Amnesty International, *Nowhere to Go: Forced Evictions in Haiti's Displacement Camps* (London: Amnesty, 2013).

IOM in action **95**

38 On expressions of this attitude among some CCCM participants and IOM staff, see e.g., Deepa Panchang, "'Waiting for Helicopters'? Perceptions, Misperceptions, and the Right to Water in Haiti," in *Tectonic Shifts: Haiti Since the Earthquake*, eds. Mark Schuller and Pablo Morales (Sterling: Kumarian Press, 2012), 185; Mark Snyder, "Vanishing Camps at Gunpoint," in *Tectonic Shifts: Haiti Since the Earthquake*, eds. Mark Schuller and Pablo Morales (Sterling: Kumarian Press, 2012).

39 Schuller, *Humanitarian Aftershocks*, 4–5.

40 See Boaz Desir and Alexandra Jackson, *Dealing with Land Barriers to Shelter Construction in Haiti: The Experience of the IOM Haiti Legal Team* (Port-au-Prince: IOM, 2012).

41 See e.g. Amy Rhoades and Leonard Doyle, "Rebuilding Lives and Livelihoods: Haiti's Long Road to Recovery through Skills Development and Training for Internally Displaced Persons," *Migration Policy Practice* 3, no. 1 (2013). As the training programs in vaunted initiatives such as the 16/6 Project were only 36 hours long, it is doubtful that they meaningfully equipped IDPs to successfully pursue new livelihoods upon leaving camps.

42 Bradley and Sherwood, "Resolving Internal Displacement"; Sherwood, "Grabbing Solutions."

43 IOM Haiti, *Shelter and NFI*, 2018, http://haiti.iom.int/shelter-nfi; IOM Haiti, *Camps and Returns*, 2018, http://haiti.iom.int/camps-returns.

44 Julien Brachet, "Policing the Desert: The IOM in Libya Beyond War and Peace," *Antipode* 48, no. 2 (2016): 286.

45 Brachet, "Policing the Desert," 274.

46 IOM, *Report of the Director General on the Work of the Organization for the Year 1995* (Geneva: IOM, 1996), 39.

47 Ducasse-Rogier, *International Organization for Migration*, 163–164.

48 Hein de Haas, "Trans-Saharan Migration to North Africa and the EU: Historical Roots and Current Trends," *Migration Information Source* (2006); Sara Hamood, "EU-Libya Cooperation on Migration: A Raw Deal for Refugees and Migrants?" *Journal of Refugee Studies* 21, no. 1 (2008): 19–42. Contrary to the assumption that most migrants in Libya are looking to move into Europe, most mobility in the Sahara occurs within and between countries in the region. See Brachet, "Policing the Desert," 275–276.

49 On the 5+5 conference and related regional processes, see Thomas Christiansen, Fabio Petito and Ben Tonra, "Fuzzy Politics Around Fuzzy Borders: The European Union's 'Near Abroad'," *Cooperation and Conflict* 35, no. 4 (2000): 404.

50 IOM, "Challenges and Responses to Irregular Migration in the Western Mediterranean," *Dialogue 5+5 Newsletter* 1 (2004): 4.

51 Rutvica Andrijasevic, "Deported: The Right to Asylum at EU's External Border of Italy and Libya," *International Migration* 48, no. 1 (2010): 150; Rutvica Andrijasevic, "Lampedusa in Focus: Migrants Caught Between the Libyan Desert and the Deep Sea," *Feminist Review* 82 (2006): 120–125.

52 IOM, *Programme and Budget for 2006* (Geneva: IOM, 2005).

53 de Haas, "Trans-Saharan Migration."

54 IOM, *Programme and Budget for 2007* (Geneva: IOM, 2006).

55 Andrijasevic, "The Right to Asylum at EU's External Border," 164.

56 IDMC, *Libya: Many IDPs Return but Concerns Persist for Certain Displaced Groups* (Geneva: Norwegian Refugee Council, 2011), 4–5. The lack of reliable data on the pre-2011 migrant population in Libya was an obstacle to assessing assistance needs after violence broke out in 2011. For an overview of the Libyan revolution, the NATO intervention and the international community's "light footprint" approach in post-Gaddafi, see Christopher S. Chivvis, *Toppling Qaddafi: Libya and the Limits of Liberal Intervention* (Cambridge: Cambridge University Press, 2013).

57 On protection concerns facing displaced Libyans that have generally gone under the radar of international organizations, see Megan Bradley, Ibrahim Fraihat and Houda

96 IOM in action

Mzioudet, *Libya's Displacement Crisis: Uprooted by Revolution and Civil War* (Washington, DC: Georgetown University Press, 2016).

58 IOM, *Migrants Caught in Crisis: The IOM Experience in Libya* (Geneva: IOM, 2012), 13.

59 IOM, *Policy in Brief: Returnees from Libya: The Bittersweet Experience of Coming Home* (Geneva: IOM, 2012), 2.

60 Brachet, "Policing the Desert," 273.

61 Alexander Betts, "The Global Governance of Crisis Migration," in *Humanitarian Crises and Migration: Causes, Consequences and Responses*, eds. Susan F. Martin, Sanjula Weerasinghe, and Abbie Taylor (London: Routledge, 2014), 354; IOM, *Annual Report 2015* (Geneva: IOM, 2016).

62 See for example IOM's work in support of the Migrants in Countries in Crisis Initiative.

63 Khalid Koser, "Protecting Non-Citizens in Situations of Conflict, Violence and Disaster," in *Humanitarian Crises and Migration: Causes, Consequences and Responses*, eds. Susan F. Martin, Sanjula Weerasinghe, and Abbie Taylor (London: Routledge, 2014), 279. For discussion of IOM-UNHCR collaboration in other contexts such as Turkey, see for example Shoshana Fine, *Borders and Mobility in Turkey: Governing Souls and States* (Basingstoke: Palgrave, 2019).

64 Interview, human rights advocate 5, December 2015.

65 UNHCR, *UNHCR, IOM Pledge Increased Support for Libya*, 2017, www.unhcr.org/news/press/2017/5/592d98ce4/unhcr-iom-pledge-increased-support-libya.html?query=IOM%20Libya.

66 Brachet, "Policing the Desert," 282.

67 OHCHR and UNSMIL, *"Detained and Dehumanized": Report on Human Rights Abuses Against Migrants in Libya* (Geneva: OHCHR, 2016); OHCHR and UNSMIL, *Desperate and Dangerous: Report on the Human Rights Situation of Migrants and Refugees in Libya* (Geneva: OHCHR, 2018).

68 OHCHR and UNSMIL, *Desperate and Dangerous*, 5.

69 IOM, *Fatal Journeys, Volume 3, Part 2: Improving Data on Missing Migrants* (Geneva: IOM, 2017), 7.

70 Charles Heller, Lorenzo Pezzani, Itamar Mann, Violeta Moreno-Lax and Eyal Weizman, "'It's an Act of Murder'": How Europe Outsources Suffering as Migrants Drown," *New York Times*, 26 December 2018.

71 As a predominantly black minority group in Libya, the Tawerghans have experienced generations of discrimination in Libya, but were generally seen as benefactors of the Gaddafi regime. After the revolution, they were collectively punished by Misratan militias through targeted violence and expulsion from their communities. On the IDP situation in Libya more generally, see Bradley, Fraihat and Mzioudet, *Libya's Displacement Crisis*; Human Rights Watch, *Libya: Ensure Safe Return of Displaced Tawerghans*, 2017, www.hrw.org/news/2017/06/20/libya-ensure-safe-return-displaced-tawerghans; Human Rights Watch, *Libya: Displaced Population Can't Go Home*, 2019, www.hrw.org/news/2017/06/20/libya-ensure-safe-return-displaced-tawerghans.

72 On the Missing Migrants Project, see https://missingmigrants.iom.int/. For information on the Mediterranean Missing project, a related collaboration between IOM and several academic institutions, see www.mediterraneanmissing.eu/. See also Simon Robins, "The Affective Border: Missing Migrants and the Governance of Migrant Bodies at the European Union's Southern Frontier," *Journal of Refugee Studies* (2019), First View.

73 Al Jazeera, "IOM: African Migrants Traded in Libya's 'Slave Markets'," *Al Jazeera*, 11 April 2017, www.aljazeera.com/news/2017/04/iom-african-migrants-traded-libya-slave-markets-170411141809641.html; IOM, *IOM Learns of 'Slave Market' Conditions Endangering Migrants in North Africa*, 11 April 2017, www.iom.int/news/

IOM in action **97**

iom-learns-slave-market-conditions-endangering-migrants-north-africa; IOM, *IOM Applauds Italy's Life-Saving Mare Nostrum Operation: 'Not a Pull Factor'*, 31 October 2014, www.iom.int/news/iom-applauds-italys-life-saving-mare-nostrum-operation-not-migrant-pull-factor.

74 IOM, *Programme and Budget for the Year 2014* (Geneva: IOM, 2013).

75 OHCHR, *UN Human Rights Chief: Suffering of Migrants in Libya Outrage to Conscience of Humanity*, 14 November 2017, www.ohchr.org/EN/NewsEvents/Pages/DisplayNews.aspx?NewsID=22393; IOM, *IOM Libya Brief* (2016), www.iom.int/countries/libya.

76 OHCHR, *Returned Migrants Are Being Robbed, Raped and Murdered in Libya*, 8 September 2017, www.ohchr.org/EN/NewsEvents/Pages/DisplayNews.aspx?NewsID=22039.

77 Malta Declaration by the members of the European Council on the external aspects of migration: addressing the Central Mediterranean route, para 6(d).

78 UNHCR and IOM, *Joint UNHCR and IOM Statement on Addressing Migration and Refugee Movements Along the Central Mediterranean Route*, 2 February 2017, www.unhcr.org/afr/news/press/2017/2/58931ffb4/joint-unhcr-iom-statement-addressing-migration-refugee-movements-along.html.

79 IOM, *Legal Migration, Rights, Protection for Vulnerable African Migrants Key to Implementation of 2015 Valletta Action Plan: IOM*, 7 February 2017, www.iom.int/news/legal-migration-rights-protection-vulnerable-african-migrants-key-implementation-2015-valletta.

80 Ibid.

81 For an overview of migrant and refugee detention in Libya, see www.globaldetention project.org/countries/africa/libya#_ftn65.

82 OHCHR and UNSMIL, *Detained and Dehumanized*, 13. On the DTM in Libya, including in relation to detention, see www.globaldtm.info/libya/.

83 OHCHR and UMSMIL, *Desperate and Dangerous*, 40.

84 IOM, *Voluntary Humanitarian Return (VHR) Assistance and Reintegration Support to Stranded Migrants in Libya*, 2017, https://twitter.com/IOM_Libya/status/938814598920228864.

85 IOM, *UN Migration Agency Moves to Relieve Plight of Migrants Trapped in Libya, Backing AU-EU Plan*, 1 December 2017, www.iom.int/news/un-migration-agency-moves-relieve-plight-migrants-trapped-libya-backing-au-eu-plan.

86 Amnesty International, *Libya's Dark Web of Collusion: Abuses Against Europe-bound Refugees and Migrants* (London: Amnesty International, 2017), 9, 52.

87 Ibid., 9.

88 MSF, *Stop Arbitrary Detention of Refugees and Migrants Disembarked in Libya*, 25 July 2018, www.msf.org/stop-arbitrary-detention-refugees-and-migrants-disembarked-libya. See also OHCHR, p. 40.

89 OHCHR and UNSMIL, *Desperate and Dangerous*, 41.

90 IOM, *UN Migration Agency Moves to Relieve Plight of Migrants Trapped in Libya, Backing AU-EU Plan*, 1 December 2017, www.iom.int/news/un-migration-agency-moves-relieve-plight-migrants-trapped-libya-backing-au-eu-plan.

91 OHCHR and UNSMIL, *Detained and Dehumanised*, 25.

92 UNHCR, UNHCR Position on Returns to Libya (Update II), para 23.

93 Interview, IOM official 3, November 2015.

94 IOM, *IOM Statement: Protecting Migrants in Libya Must Be Our Primary Focus*, 2 April 2019, www.iom.int/news/iom-statement-protecting-migrants-libya-must-be-our-primary-focus.

95 Ibid.

96 Ibid.

97 Ibid. Writing in 2017, the UK Independent Commission for Aid Impact suggests the search for alternatives is "at very early stages." See Independent Commission for Aid

98 IOM in action

Impact, *The UK's Aid Response to Irregular Migration in the Central Mediterranean* (London: ICAI, 2017).

98 On the view that IOM's structure precludes the agency serving as a "counterweight" to states by criticizing their policies, see Sandra Lavenex, "Multi-levelling EU External Governance: The Role of International Organizations in the Diffusion of EU Migration Policies," *Journal of Ethnic and Migration Studies* 42, no. 4 (2016): 554–570.

99 Brachet, "Policing the Desert," 274.

100 Ibid., 277; Fine, *Borders and Mobility in Turkey*.

101 Of course, as discussed, humanitarian responses to displacement have their own migration management functions.

102 For an examination of this dynamic in Indonesia, see Asher Lazarus Hirsch and Cameron Doig, "Outsourcing Control: The International Organization for Migration in Indonesia," *International Journal of Human Rights* 22, no. 5 (2018): 681–708. Relatedly, FitzGerald observes that IOM "cages" some would-be migrants, while facilitating the movement and reintegration of others. David Scott FitzGerald, *Refuge Beyond Reach: How Rich Democracies Repel Asylum Seekers* (Oxford: Oxford University Press, 2019), 145.

103 Personal communication, July 2019.

104 Sherwood, et al., *Supporting Durable Solutions*.

105 IOM typically frames its work, including in Haiti and Libya, in terms of supporting governments to execute their roles and obligations towards citizens and migrants. However government capacity was extremely limited in Haiti and post-Gaddafi Libya and IOM – like other aid agencies – sometimes simply substituted for the government, rather than strengthening it.

106 See Megan Bradley and Merve Erdilmen, "Speaking of Rights: Protection Norms, Rights-Talk and the International Organization for Migration," Paper presented at International Studies Association Conference, Toronto, March 2019.

4

THE UN MIGRATION AGENCY? IOM–UN RELATIONS

- *IOM–UN relations before 2016: ambiguity and rapprochement*
  - *IOM–UN connections in the twentieth century*
  - *Post-9/11: intensified tensions and debates*
  - *Renewed negotiations, new arrangements: 2014–2016*
- *Is IOM really in the UN system? The status of related organizations*
- *Joining the UN system: drivers, process, and misgivings*
- *What's new? Analysis of the agreement concerning the relationship between the United Nations and the International Organization for Migration*
  - *The "non-normative" designation*
- *Conclusion: uncertain implications*

At the Summit for Refugees and Migrants held at UN headquarters in New York on September 19, 2016, UN Secretary-General Ban Ki-moon and IOM Director General Bill Swing signed a new Agreement Concerning the Relationship between the United Nations and the International Organization for Migration. This agreement made IOM a "related organization" in the UN system. In his speech at the signing ceremony, Swing hailed the "historic agreement" for taking a "bold and visionary decision," through which the "United Nations now has a 'UN Migration Agency.'"[1]

Inside and outside IOM, many were surprised by the rapidity with which IOM's entry into the UN system was negotiated: less than a year earlier, there was "not even an emerging consensus" on whether IOM should join the UN system.[2] In his final report as UN special representative on international migration, Peter Sutherland reflected that IOM "has joined the United Nations system – a step that until quite recently was unthinkable, but is long overdue, and should strengthen both the IOM and the UN and benefit migrants."[3] While Sutherland's assessment is not unanimously shared, this development certainly challenges the received wisdom in the literature on IOM, which generally assumes that the agency has thrived precisely *because* it was outside the UN system, unfettered by principled commitments and obligations. If so, why would IOM undercut its own comparative advantage? This chapter explores the evolution of the IOM–UN relationship, the factors that prompted IOM's entry into the UN system, and the agreement through which this was achieved. Some have suggested that joining the UN was a longstanding, shared ambition of IOM staff, but question whether as a related organization, IOM is *really* part of the UN system.[4] In contrast, I recognize that IOM is indeed now part of the UN *system*, and bring into focus the diversity of shifting opinions on this issue among IOM officials and member states. The decision to join the UN system reflects a fluctuating set of cost–benefit calculations, with recent IOM leaders concerned about protecting their turf as "*the* global lead agency on migration" and convinced that IOM had become intertwined with and dependent on the UN, without reaping the benefits of membership in the UN system. Although the possibility of IOM formally entering the UN system seemed largely theoretical until 2015, when a confluence of factors dramatically accelerated the process, this development needs to be understood in the context of the long history of cooperation – and competition – between IOM and the UN, with close collaboration in the humanitarian sphere providing a foundation for recasting the IOM–UN relationship. Indeed, just as IOM's humanitarian engagements are critical to the organization's expansion and internal tensions, they are also central to apprehending this institutional realignment.

I begin by discussing the development of IOM–UN relations before 2016. Second, I examine whether IOM is actually in the UN system by exploring the status of related organizations. Third, I address the drivers that brought IOM into the UN system, and the process through which this was achieved, before analyzing the 2016 Agreement that effected this shift. In concluding, I consider some of the potential implications, risks, and benefits associated with this development.

IOM–UN relations before 2016: ambiguity and rapprochement

IOM's relationship with the UN has been a subject of periodic debate among member states and within IOM's ranks for decades. Over the years, the relationship between IOM and the UN – particularly key actors such as the UN Secretariat and UNHCR – has evolved considerably. These changes have been shaped by IOM's own development, and by the increasing engagement of a growing range of UN agencies in migration issues. UN agencies with significant roles in migration include the UN Development Programme (UNDP), the Department of Economic and Social Affairs (DESA), OHCHR, and UNICEF, among others. The Global Migration Group included some 22 UN and intergovernmental agencies; it was replaced in 2018 with the UN Network on Migration.[5] The IOM–UN relationship is thus multifaceted; IOM has developed relationships with individual agencies, at the same time as it has strived to carve out space for itself in the UN system writ large.

Overall, the story of IOM–UN relations leading up to 2016 is one of progressively closer rapprochement, alongside persistent tensions and "constructive

The UN migration agency? IOM–un relations **101**

ambiguity."[6] Different actors have benefited at different times and in different ways from this ambiguity, including IOM itself, but also states, UNHCR, and other UN agencies.[7] IOM has gained credibility, access to funds, and a place in important policymaking and planning processes through its association with the UN. At the same time, its independence has allowed it to undertake work unamenable to the mandates of existing UN bodies and, sometimes, to provide aid in communities inaccessible to UN agencies.[8] IOM's relationship with the UN, and specifically with UNHCR, is sometimes presented strictly in terms of competition, suspicion, and conflict. As discussed in previous chapters, both agencies deal with "refugee-like situations"; this has translated into competition for funding, visibility, and recognition in different humanitarian operations. However, they have also cooperated closely, particularly on contentious issues such as returns, where IOM's malleable mission and outsider status have enabled UN agencies to maintain more pristine, focused mandates.[9]

By the time IOM became a related organization in the UN system, its staff were already governed by the UN Staff Rules and Regulations, and were part of the UN's salary scales, security arrangements, and pension scheme. Over a period of decades, IOM negotiated memoranda of understanding and cooperation agreements with dozens of UN agencies. It became eligible to access funding through the Central Emergency Response Fund (CERF) as well as the UN Consolidated Appeals Process, and often operated as a de facto part of the UN Humanitarian Country Teams, building on its active involvement in the Inter-Agency Standing Committee (IASC). These developments bolstered the perception of IOM as "quasi-UN," an ambiguous status that brought advantages as well as deep frustrations both for IOM and its UN counterparts.[10]

IOM–UN connections in the twentieth century

Concerted efforts to remodel the IOM–UN relationship emerged in the 1990s. Yet the agency's imbrication with the UN system goes back to its founding, when a range of international organizations were involved in efforts to resolve displacement in Europe stemming from World War II. The UN Relief and Rehabilitation Agency tackled this challenge until 1947, when it was replaced by the International Refugee Organization (IRO), which in turn was dissolved in 1951. The IRO had no clear successor; rather, its responsibilities were meted out to several organizations. The International Committee of the Red Cross took up the IRO's family reunification efforts; the International Labour Organization (ILO) advised on connections between the resolution of the displacement situation in Europe and labor issues; UNHCR focused on the legal protection of refugees; and PICMME (later ICEM) focused on operational efforts to resolve displacement and Europe's perceived "surplus population" problem.[11] The determination of western states to exclude Communist countries that hindered free movement, particularly the flight of their citizens to western democracies, precluded the possibility of establishing PICMME within the UN system.[12]

102 The UN migration agency? IOM–un relations

Despite PICMME/ICEM's position outside the UN, one of its first major activities was the establishment in 1952 of a joint UNHCR/PICMME office in Hong Kong with responsibility for facilitating the resettlement of refugees of European descent. UNHCR and ICEM jointly ran this office until its closure in 1973.[13] Building on such early experiences, rapprochement between IOM and the UN often focused on work in the humanitarian sector, and gained pace beginning in the early 1990s. At this time, a combination of factors fueled IOM's expansion and increased involvement in humanitarian response, including the end of the Cold War, the emergence of new "complex emergencies," and the implementation of reforms led by Director General Purcell and continued under McKinley. At the 1991 IOM Council session, Purcell proposed that IOM should seek out observer status with the UN General Assembly on the grounds that "IOM collaborated increasingly with other organizations, particularly in the United Nations system" and "the international community encouraged and expected such inter-agency cooperation."[14] IOM's member states largely concurred, flagging "the need for an integrated approach and concerted and coordinated international action and solidarity to prevent, remedy or merely cope with the many and ubiquitous refugee and migration issues confronting the international community."[15] The 1992 resolution establishing IOM as an observer is perfunctory, and presents the desire for cooperation as, effectively, one-way, as it notes "the desire of the International Organization for Migration to intensify its cooperation with the United Nations."[16] This dynamic has threaded through the development of the IOM–UN relationship: as the outsider looking to safeguard its "territory" and prove itself as an accepted, legitimate peer agency, IOM has typically taken the lead in looking for opportunities to deepen and systematize connections between the institutions.[17]

1992 saw a second, key milestone in the development of IOM–UN relations: the establishment of the IASC, the main coordination platform for UN agencies, other inter-governmental organizations, and NGOs working on humanitarian issues. From the outset, IOM was a standing invitee to the IASC, which proved to be a key venue for developing, deepening, and mending relations with UN agencies. As director general, McKinley antagonized UN partners with IOM's unapologetically rapid expansion. In taking the organizational reins, Swing used the IASC as a forum to improve relationships, channeling the message that "We are going to play well with others, we're not going to be the cowboy people think we are."[18]

In 1993, IOM's integration into the UN-led humanitarian system took another step forward with the adoption of a UN General Assembly resolution that extended the scope of the CERF to include IOM. IOM celebrated this step, observing:

> This decision provides IOM with the possibility to draw on CERF to bridge the period between the beginning of an emergency operation and the receipt of contributions for the specific emergency. The decision also marks an important development, as IOM is the first and only non-UN

The UN migration agency? IOM–un relations **103**

organization authorized explicitly by the UN membership to make use of CERF. It confirms the level of integration IOM has achieved with the United Nations' coordinated approach to emergencies.[19]

By 2015, IOM had become the fifth-largest recipient of funding through CERF.[20]

A key 1995 policy document entitled *IOM Strategic Planning: Toward the Twenty-First Century* highlights the agency's increasingly close collaboration with the UN, especially in humanitarian response, and the increasing strains on this relationship. The plan asserts that

> IOM has participated in virtually every humanitarian emergency involving large-scale movement of people since it was founded. . . . Today, IOM operates as a member of the team of multilateral agencies which forms the global emergency response network under the leadership of the United Nations Department of Humanitarian Affairs (DHA). As part of that team, or as requested by Member Governments, IOM offers its services to vulnerable populations in need of evacuation, resettlement or return.[21]

And yet in this period, IOM increasingly sensed that its role and expertise were not fully recognized and respected by its UN counterparts. IOM's view that it was in some ways disadvantaged by its position outside the UN is evident in this assertion (however contestable) in the 1995 strategic plan:

> IOM respects and supports the roles and functions of each of [its] partner organizations, including areas in which they are assigned leadership responsibility in their functional specialities. In the same sense, IOM should receive reciprocal respect and support for its role and functions in the field of migration. Given current complexities and ambiguities in the migration field, this requires IOM Member States, which are also members of the United Nations organs and agencies, to establish and make clear such a policy decision. Only in that case would IOM's present institutional arrangement [in relation to the UN system] . . . provide a sufficient framework for accomplishing this strategic plan's objectives over the short to mid-term. Over the long term, the ongoing debate within the IOM membership on the formal ties that do or should bind IOM and the United Nations system would have to be pursued and brought to conclusion.[22]

This appears to be the first major policy document in which IOM leaders formally broach the question of recasting its increasingly fraught relationship with the UN.

Responding in part to these concerns, the following year Purcell and UN Secretary-General Boutros Boutros-Ghali signed the 1996 *Cooperation Agreement between the United Nations and the International Organization for Migration*.[23] The agreement declares that "The United Nations and the International Organization for Migration shall act in close collaboration and hold consultations regularly on all matters of common interest."[24] It encourages cooperation particularly in terms of attending meetings; sharing documentation, information, and legal and statistical analyses; administrative and technical arrangements; training; coordination between secretariats; and joint action on projects of shared interest. The rationale for the agreement centered on the organizations' history of cooperation, and the pressing need for coordination in response to forced migration and humanitarian emergencies. Purcell opined that the agreement "underscored the close ties between the two organizations and that its conclusion extended the promise of continued improvement in the international community's handling of issues of migration, refugees and displaced persons."[25] Boutros-Ghali similarly welcomed the agreement "as an important recognition of the need for close cooperation on global issues, especially those involving the movement of people affected by complex emergencies or natural disasters."[26]

In his 1996 address to the UN General Assembly, Purcell applauded the Cooperation Agreement and reinforced the message that the IOM–UN relationship had become progressively closer through the organizations' "recurring involvement in humanitarian emergencies, with consequent large movements of people."[27] In celebrating the agreement, Purcell demonstrated IOM's characteristic deference for states and its penchant for efficiency-focused management speak, reflecting that "Governments have the right to expect that international organizations will seek such collaboration, as well as rational divisions of labor."[28]

Post-9/11: intensified tensions and debates

Notwithstanding the organizations' pledge in the 1996 Cooperation Agreement to "strive for the maximum cooperation and coordination to ensure complementary action at headquarters and field levels," in the following years the IOM–UN relationship was marked by heightened competition alongside continued rapprochement.[29] In the early years of the twenty-first century, dissatisfaction within IOM's leadership regarding the IOM–UN relationship and discussions on the UN's engagement with migration in the post-9/11 context prompted a reinvigorated debate on IOM's place in the international system. IOM's anxieties were provoked in part by a September 2002 Report of the Secretary-General entitled *Strengthening the United Nations: An Agenda for Further Change*, which identified migration as one of a small number of major global governance challenges that deserved greater attention from the UN.[30] Building on this, Secretary-General Kofi Annan mandated his special advisor, Michael Doyle, to prepare an internal report assessing global migration challenges; areas where international organizations, particularly the UN, could advance cooperation; multilateral arrangements for addressing migration; and the adequacy of these arrangements. While the report did not recommend particular short-term reforms beyond improving consultation and coordination among the different IOs working on migration, it broached possibilities such as establishing a new, specialized agency within the UN focused on migration or converting IOM to this effect. While some senior IOM leaders broadly supported the idea of transforming IOM into a specialized

The UN migration agency? IOM–un relations **105**

agency, IOM officials appeared unnerved that the UN and its advisors, rather than the IOM itself, might drive this conversation.[31]

Accordingly, in December 2002, while IOM was under McKinley's leadership, the IOM Council established a Working Group on Institutional Arrangements, comprised of all interested member states, to "explore the place and role IOM could have in relation to the United Nations system."[32] In its communications to the Working Group, IOM endeavored to set the discussion in a broader frame than turf-wrangling with the UN, stressing that

> The Doyle report and discussions at the UN level are, however, only one part of the context in which this review is taking place. The reflection of being inside or outside the UN system is one which has been an issue for IOM since its creation. At that time, IOM was deliberately founded outside the system for Cold War, political reasons. Since the end of the Cold War, there has been some consideration within the Organization as to whether a change in IOM status should follow.[33]

In putting the IOM–UN relationship on the table and in its approach to advising the Working Group, including through the preparation of a detailed background study on the relative advantages of different options, the IOM administration strived to position itself as providing impartial information, and deferring to member states' discretion. For instance, in his 2002 address to the IOM Council, McKinley emphasized that:

> the IOM Administration is not campaigning either for or against a change. IOM has done well by our independence and can continue to prosper as we are. Alternatively, under the right arrangements – ones that preserve our Constitution, our individuality and our special characteristics – I believe we could also prosper as part of the United Nations system. It all comes down to weighing the advantages and disadvantages. Of course, this question is fundamentally one for the Council, not the Administration.[34]

In the study it prepared for the Working Group, the administration recognized the critical role that humanitarian work played in solidifying the relationship between the UN and IOM.[35] Cognizant of this reality, the administration fleshed out three main options for the Working Group to consider: (i) becoming a specialized agency; (ii) improving relations with the UN while remaining outside the system – the "improved status quo" option; and (iii) taking no action.[36] Alternate options such as merging IOM with an existing UN agency, such as UNHCR, were dismissed outright as unrealistic.[37] On member states' request, the study also briefly addressed the option of making IOM a related agency in the UN system. The report suggests that "for one reason or another" the related organizations "have not sought, or have not been accorded the status of 'specialized agency'" but are "still considered as part of the burgeoning 'UN Family.'"[38] The frame of this conversation implies that the natural and preferred option would be specialized agency status.

106 The UN migration agency? IOM–un relations

Indeed, despite its self-declared neutrality on the issue, and divided opinions within IOM's ranks on the wisdom of joining the UN system, on balance the administration's interventions underscored the limitations of its arrangements with the UN, and the potential benefits of becoming a specialized agency over other options. Specialized agencies are part of the UN system, but are independently governed and have separate legal status; examples include the Food and Agriculture Organization, the International Labour Organization, the United Nations Educational, Scientific and Cultural Organization (UNESCO), the World Health Organization, the World Bank, and the International Monetary Fund. For instance, the administration's report to the Working Group stresses that while integration of IOM into UN country teams in emergency and post-conflict situations is often "prompt and positive," the "initiative generally had to come from IOM and inclusion is never automatic nor as of right, and indeed is not always achievable even where it is highly justifiable."[39] While conceding that "the status quo is sustainable," McKinley argued that

> there are disadvantages to outsider status. IOM has to work harder to gain acceptance and recognition, to raise funds, to join inter-agency planning processes and assessment missions, and to acquire the international legal status that comes automatically to UN agencies. Decisions taken by the UN affect us heavily, but we have no voice in their formulation. Moreover, the international community has trouble understanding an international organization that is not part of the international system of governance.[40]

In analyzing the specialized agency option, the report optimistically concludes that

> [I]n general, none of the current relationship agreements [between the UN and its specialized agencies] have the effect of subjecting the agency to the 'control' of the UN or of placing them in a subordinate legal position. They are in the nature of agreements between equals, and the agencies retain to a large extent their independent character.[41]

Again, the administration tacitly suggests that this is the preferable option.

Nonetheless, in 2003 IOM's member states were unconvinced that it would be advantageous to bring IOM into the UN system. Although the Working Group did not issue a formal decision or recommendations on the issue, it was clear that member states preferred option two, "improving the status quo," which was seen as a route to tackle operational concerns without sacrificing IOM's flexibility and independence.[42] Member states stressed that IOM "should remain the central body providing policy advice and services to the international community on migration" – a win for the agency in its efforts to safeguard its position in an increasingly crowded governance arena.[43] The Chair of the IOM Council, Ambassador Amina Mohamed of Kenya, communicated this view in a May 2003 letter to UN Secretary-General Annan, essentially confirming that from the perspective of states who are members of both IOM and the UN, the gap in the UN's migration architecture identified in the secretary-general's *Strengthening the United Nations* report should remain, with IOM stepping into the void, however awkwardly.[44] While accepting its member states' decision, the administration sought to keep the door open to continued conversations on entering the UN system, concertedly pointing out the opinion of some of its members that

> IOM was now at a crossroads and its present status was no longer adequate to respond to needs, making an evolution necessary . . . it was [also] noted that IOM was still undergoing changes and had not completed its adaption, leaving a question mark as to the final form such an evolution should best take.[45]

In pursuit of an "improved status quo," technical and political discussions gained pace between IOM and the UN, at the same time as IOM's continued, dramatic expansion antagonized UN partners, many of whom perceived IOM as territorial, aggressive, and disrespectful of other agencies' mandates. The 2005 *Global Commission on International Migration Report*, and a report issued in May 2006 by the UN secretary-general in advance of the UN High-Level Dialogue on Migration and Development, contained recommendations for improving coordination, and field-level interactions between the organizations continued. However, the success of cooperation efforts were highly conditioned by the personalities and professional approaches of the individuals involved. IOM struggled to integrate itself into initiatives such as "One UN" – and rightfully so, some suggested, as IOM was not part of the UN itself, despite the ambiguity created by its entanglement with the UN system. IOM's interactions with humanitarian counterparts in the UN system were sometimes tense but comparatively smooth; more significant challenges were perceived in the development sector, where IOM was more often marginalized or shut out from UN-led planning processes and funding strategies. As IOM considers itself a multi-mandated agency, with legitimate roles in humanitarian response and longer-term development processes, this became a significant concern for the agency.[46]

In 2006, the IOM leadership resuscitated discussions on the IOM–UN relationship with the agency's member states. The 2007 document *Options for the IOM-UN Relationship: Additional Analysis of Costs and Benefits* offers a more expansive list of options to improve the IOM–UN relationship, including (i) full implementation of the existing cooperation agreement (essentially, continued pursuit of the "improved status quo"); (ii) becoming a related agency; (iii) transforming IOM into a UN program or fund (dismissed as radical and not viable); and (iv) specialized agency status.[47] Like IOM's analyses from 2002–2003, this assessment stresses that this decision is for member states to make, but in effect favors the specialized agency option. In 2007, IOM's administration was more forthright in setting out three explicit arguments for changing its relationship with the UN. Wary of undercutting its own success story, IOM walked a fine line in advancing these arguments, framing the debate in response to the question:

"If IOM is working well and growing at the same time, what is the argument in favor of changing its relationship to the UN?"[48] First, the administration argued, "IOM is at present at an unfair practical disadvantage vis-à-vis its UN partners," leading to inefficiencies, incoherence, and missing opportunities to apply IOM's expertise.[49] Second, "there is a growing call from many quarters for a stronger UN involvement in policy debate and international cooperation on migration," leading to the risk of overlapping efforts and a need for increased integration.[50] Third, the administration argued that access to UN administrative arrangements, particularly being able to travel on the UN laissez-passer, would increase cost-effectiveness and staff security, particularly for those working on humanitarian operations.[51]

IOM's members again decided against major changes. Forced to continue to try to improve the status quo, in July 2007 McKinley wrote to Ban, newly in office as UN secretary-general, to propose two "steps we could take right now" to deepen cooperation.[52] Building on IOM's participation in the IASC, he advocated adding IOM to the UN Development Group (UNDG), the consortium of UN agencies established in 1997 to advance development planning and effectiveness, and inviting IOM to meetings of the Chief Executives Board for Coordination (CEB), the highest-level coordination forum in the UN system, chaired by the secretary-general. McKinley argued that:

> The advantages of these two steps are apparent. For us, it would mean membership in bodies where important discussions are held and decisions taken regarding global priorities for multilateral action. The access thus gained would deepen mutual understanding and encourage cooperation. For you, it would help fill a gap in policy and operational coverage by bringing closer the leading multilateral migration agency and allowing you to know about, call upon and collaborate with us more directly and more easily than is presently possible.[53]

Ban was unpersuaded. In his October 2007 response to McKinley, Ban cut through the ambiguity in IOM's status, categorically distinguishing between IOM and organizations in the UN system. He wrote,

> We do not yet have a body like the IASC which brings together the UNDG members with the IGO and NGO partners. Similarly, CEB membership is restricted to Specialized Agencies with formal relationship agreements with the United Nations, as well as to the Funds and Programmes of the United Nations. It would, therefore, not be possible for IOM to be a formal member of either of these bodies.[54]

In fact, the International Atomic Energy Agency (IAEA) and the World Trade Organization (WTO), as related organizations, are members of the CEB, and IOM joined the CEB when it became a related organization in 2016. Ban's indication that CEB membership is necessarily restricted to specialized agencies

The UN migration agency? IOM–un relations **109**

was thus inaccurate. Nonetheless, Ban's denial delayed and imposed distinct perceived limits on the degree of integration that IOM could achieve in the UN system without formally changing its status.

Renewed negotiations, new arrangements: 2014–2016

Following Swing's installation as director general in 2008, debates on the IOM–UN relationship entered a comparatively dormant period until 2014, when the discussions in the Working Group on IOM-UN Relations were re-energized. In the meantime, Swing invested considerably in repairing and building up new relationships with UN partners at the senior level, ameliorating tensions and trying to (re)position IOM as a team player in the international system.[55] IOM–UN relations are broadly seen to have improved in this period. Despite some continued difficulties (unsurprising, given the pronounced tensions between and within many UN agencies), eventually some senior leaders in IOM concluded, "There is nothing more we can improve. . . . We have reached the limit" of the arrangement.[56]

As the Working Group resumed, a perceived global refugee and migration "crisis" was unfolding, uprooting millions within their own countries and across borders. This brought new urgency to the question of ensuring a reliable, robust, and effective international response to human mobility, and particularly to displacement in emergency settings – recognizing the limits of the UNHCR mandate and that many of those in need of protection and assistance would not qualify as refugees under international law. It also fueled debates on what such a reliable, robust, and effective response might entail – facilitated mobility and protection of migrants' rights? Restrictions on movement? Some uneasy combination of these approaches? Many member states saw IOM as a key partner in this balancing act, and concluded that as migration issues became increasingly high-profile, the UN's patchwork of engagement on migration was no longer tenable. Instead, momentum was building to have a migration-focused agency within the UN system, raising the question of whether the IOM would be this agency, or if another outfit would be created.

Loath to establish a new IO, and positively predisposed to IOM's approach under Swing's leadership, IOM's member states passed Council resolution 1309 on November 24, 2015, requesting Swing to formally approach the UN to "develop with it a way in which the legal basis of the relationship between IOM and the United Nations could be improved." In April 2016, in resolution 70/263, the General Assembly responded to this development by "Recognizing the *need* to establish a closer relationship between the United Nations and the International Organization for Migration" (emphasis added), and inviting the secretary-general to engage in developing a new IOM–UN agreement, to be taken up for approval at the next General Assembly session – making the arrangement a key, pre-cooked "deliverable" for the impending September 2016 Summit on Refugees and Migration. In this way, years of tensions, rapprochement, and debate gave way to a rapid negotiation process, culminating in IOM becoming not a specialized agency but a related organization in the UN system.

Is IOM *really* in the UN system? On the status of related organizations

IOM has concertedly rebranded as the "UN Migration Agency," yet some suggest that as a related organization, IOM is still not *really* part of the UN system, and that the 2016 Agreement merely delays a meaningful decision on the IOM–UN relationship. For instance, Guy Goodwin-Gill contends that "Although banners and leaflets may suggest otherwise, [IOM] is not a United Nations agency, and neither has it 'entered' or 'joined' the UN. It remains an inter-governmental organization, still outside the system, but in a 'closer relationship'" with it.[57] Similarly, Pécoud argues that IOM is still "situated outside the UN system," and dismisses the notion that IOM could, as a related agency, be part of the UN system as a misperception.[58] Others recognize that IOM is indeed in the UN system but that the degree of integration reached in 2016 is insufficient, contending that IOM should have been made a specialized agency.[59] In this section I explain the status of related agencies in the UN system, clarifying that IOM is now part of the UN *system*, as understood by the UN itself. I also briefly trace shifts in thinking within the IOM administration on the viability and desirability of related agency status.

What are related organizations? How do they compare with other organizations in the UN system, such as specialized agencies? The UN Charter envisions the establishment of specialized agencies, brought into relationship with the UN under Article 57, which provides that "various specialized agencies, established by intergovernmental agreement and having wide international responsibilities, as defined in their basic instruments, in economic, social, cultural, educational, health, and related fields, shall be brought into relationship with the United Nations in accordance with the provisions of Article 63."[60] Article 63 indicates that the UN Economic and Social Council (ECOSOC) may pursue agreements to bring specialized agencies into the UN fold, subject to General Assembly approval. In contrast, according to the CEB, the "related organization" term

> has to be understood as a default expression, describing organizations whose cooperation agreement with the United Nations has many points in common with that of Specialized Agencies, but does not refer to Article 57 and 63 of the United Nations Charter, relevant to Specialized Agencies. Nonetheless, these organizations are part and parcel of the work of CEB.[61]

The relationship agreements for related agencies go through the General Assembly directly, rather than first through ECOSOC.[62]

The UN's related agencies are a motley crew. They include large and influential organizations such as the IAEA, the WTO, and the International Criminal Court, as well as the secretariats of various international treaties, such as the Preparatory Commission for the Comprehensive Nuclear Test Ban Treaty Organization (CTBTO PrepCom), and the Organization for the Prohibition of Chemical Weapons. The UN Convention on the Law of the Sea established the

International Seabed Authority and the International Tribunal for the Law of the Sea as related agencies.[63] The Secretariat of the UN Framework Convention on Climate Change, self-christened "UN Climate Change," is also a related agency, described by the UN Secretariat as "the United Nations entity tasked with supporting the global response to the threat of climate change."[64] These organizations present their relationship to the UN system in different ways. Some, such as the WTO, do not generally emphasize their UN connection, while for others such as UN Climate Change, this is integral to their identity and posture in the international system. Some of these agencies, such as the IAEA and now IOM, have relationship agreements with the UN that are strikingly similar to those establishing specialized agencies, which are also governed and funded independently of the UN's principal organs. In all their diversity, the related agencies are explicitly recognized by the UN Secretariat as part of the United Nations system, as approved by the UN's member states. Accordingly, the largest and most influential related organizations – including IOM – appear on the United Nations' own map of the UN system.[65]

Related organizations are thus clearly in the UN *system*, but is there a difference between being in the UN system and being a UN agency? This is where some ambiguity remains. The answer depends on whether one privileges legal explanations, or the political realities created by the ways in which IOs position and present themselves, with their member states' acquiescence if not blessing. As a legal matter, related organizations *and* specialized agencies are separate organizations from the United Nations, with independent legal personalities. From this perspective, "neither specialized agencies nor related organizations are part of 'the UN,' but they are part of 'the UN system.' In contrast, the funds and programmes are subsidiary bodies of the UN and do not have separate legal personality."[66] Does the legal distinction between being part of "the UN" and part of "the UN system" translate into practical political consequences? The UN General Assembly and ECOSOC have less of a coordination and oversight role vis-à-vis the related organizations than they do with the specialized agencies, and the related organizations are generally not obliged to report on their budgets and activities to the General Assembly or to the Secretariat.[67] However, several related organizations voluntarily report to the General Assembly, and are highly entwined with UN funding systems. In some cases, arguing about whether a related organization is part of the UN is simply splitting hairs. To a significant extent, this is not so much about legalities as it is about how organizations position and portray themselves, and the consequences for the relationships they build, the turf they occupy, and the influence they exert. As noted, there is significant variation in the ways in which related organizations conceive of and leverage their relationship with the UN. Some present themselves as part and parcel of the UN system; others keep their distance. The same is true of the specialized agencies: it seems a stretch to suggest that UNESCO is not a "real" UN entity, while the IMF seems in many ways to be a different creature – although they are both specialized agencies and thus legally part of "the UN system" rather than "the UN itself."

112 The UN migration agency? IOM–un relations

In its own analysis of related organizations and specialized agencies, IOM suggests that security-focused organizations such as the IAEA, OPCW, and CTBTO did not become specialized agencies because their work is outside the parameters of Article 57 of the UN Charter, with its focus on organizations active in "economic, social, cultural, educational, health and related fields."[68] By this logic, the WTO and IOM would be specialized agencies; their designation as related agencies underscores that this decision is more than a simple classification exercise. Why would an organization be a related agency in the UN system, rather than, for example, a UN fund, program, or specialized agency? What are the plusses and minuses of related agency status? There are no straightforward answers to these questions. Rather, this depends on the organization's history, structure, mandate, and culture, and the specificities and sensitivities of the substantive issue that is the focus of the organization's work. It is also a matter of perspective – the merits of related agency status will vary when considered from the vantage point of, for example, member states (in all their diversity), the organization's bureaucracy, or the populations affected by the organization's activities. Generally, states have avoided creating funds or programs when they want to more directly govern an organization's work without the intermediary influence of the UN Secretariat, or avoid direct funding obligations. Related agency status may help states achieve these goals – but from the perspective of the bureaucracy, it may be desirable to have more robust funding commitments, or a closer formal relationship with the UN Secretariat. Related agency status may be simpler and faster to arrange bureaucratically, as agreements between the UN and prospective related organizations go through the General Assembly directly, rather than first being debated in ECOSOC. The status of related agencies is often somewhat confusing, but this can be both a blessing and a curse, again depending on perspective. Occupying a liminal space – in the system, but not of the system – may curtail an organization's influence or prestige, if being part of the UN does indeed help an agency secure these benefits. But given that UN itself is met with skepticism and critique in many quarters, it may be helpful for some related agencies to be able to portray themselves as, in some ways, independent.

As discussed previously, in early debates on its relationship with the UN, IOM avoided taking an explicit stance on the desirability of different institutional configurations, but tacitly conveyed the view that specialized agency status was preferable to becoming a related organization. In 2003, in response to a request from its member states for more information on the "related agency" option, the administration pooh-poohed this possibility, stating that this "is not a realistic option insofar as it is granted only to agencies whose mandate does not fall within the terms of reference of ECOSOC. Seeking a related agency status whose contours are still ill defined would be more confusing than helpful."[69] In 2006, reporting to its member states on discussions with UN agencies on "possible modalities for a more comprehensive agreement between the two organizations," the IOM administration indicated that, according to its UN counterparts, the "sole viable option would be specialized agency status."[70] Over the next decade, however, conceptions of the viability and implications of related organization status shifted. Just one year after dismissing the possibility of becoming a related agency as "more confusing than helpful," the administration gave a somewhat more positive assessment of the related agency option, expressing interest in the related agency arrangement between the UN and the WTO, which enabled the WTO to become a member of the CEB, and use the UN laissez-passer. Yet the UN Secretariat insisted that the agreement with the WTO was unique and could not be a precedent for IOM.[71] Ten years later, migration dynamics, member states' demands, and the institutional calculus had shifted, such that an arrangement that had been dismissed by both IOM and the UN became the means through which IOM joined the "UN family." While some hope that IOM could still be transformed into a specialized agency, it is unlikely the issue will be reopened in the near future. The related organization status suits IOM's powerful member states well, and has enabled the IOM administration to achieve its primary goals vis-à-vis its relationship with the UN. Although some ambiguity remains around what it really means to be a related agency, its practical effects are clear: "IOM is part of the system. Period."[72]

Joining the UN system: drivers, process, and misgivings

As authorized by IOM Council resolution 1309, on February 5, 2016, Swing sent a letter to Ban conveying IOM member states' desire to recast the organizations' relationship. Swing suggested three options: IOM could become a specialized agency, a related agency, or negotiate a *sui generis* agreement that would allow it to join key coordination mechanisms and resolve formal obstacles to cooperation.[73] From this point the process unfolded rapidly: on April 26, 2016, the General Assembly approved resolution 70/263 authorizing the negotiation of a new agreement, and on June 30, 2016, the IOM Council approved the draft agreement, making IOM a related agency. The agreement was approved by the General Assembly through resolution 70/976 in July 2016, and entered into force when it was signed by the secretary-general and IOM director general at the Summit on Refugees and Migration on September 19, 2016.

In his speech at the signing ceremony, Swing argued that IOM's entry into the UN system was enabled by three main factors. First, the dynamics of migration as a "mega-trend" demanded a strong international response – the implication being that this could be achieved only with IOM joining the UN system. Swing's account of migration trends focused significantly on displacement and humanitarian crises. The director general observed that "a record number of people are uprooted" in "unprecedented simultaneous, complex and protracted crises and humanitarian emergencies in an 'arc of instability' that stretches from the Western bulge of Africa to the Himalayas."[74] Second and relatedly, the timing was right. 2015 saw the emergence of a perceived migration and refugee crisis in Europe, and the conclusion of a series of agreements and negotiations in which migration and displacement figured prominently, including the UN Sustainable Development Goals, the Paris Agreement on climate change, the Sendai Disaster Risk Reduction Framework, and the World Humanitarian Summit. The New

114 The UN migration agency? IOM–un relations

York Summit – the first meeting to bring heads of state together from around the world to discuss migration and refugees – provided an opportune moment, in Swing's view, to strengthen the international architecture for implementing these agreements and addressing migration challenges by bringing IOM more clearly into the UN fold. Third, Swing suggested that the agreement was largely a matter of "formalizing an old relationship."[75] In his rose-tinted assessment, "We've done everything together, we cooperate with all agencies, and we've built up a level of trust that made the negotiations fairly straightforward. . . . We were born, after all, together with our traditional partner UNHCR in 1951," and "since then we have collaborated so closely that we have continued to think of ourselves as UN in many ways."[76]

The reasons for IOM's entry into the UN system, and perspectives on this development, were of course more complex than Swing's speech allows. Swing's three drivers were indeed a significant part of the story, but they influenced the process in ways unacknowledged in this moment of diplomatic niceties. Many of the considerations that prompted Purcell and McKinley to broach reforming the IOM–UN relationship remained salient. In 2016, one of the most obvious but largely unspoken factors influencing the decision was the drive to claim and protect turf. Given migration's increased significance as a governance challenge, by 2016 it was glaringly clear that the UN needed a focused migration "shop." IOM wanted to preclude a new agency encroaching on "its" issue area. At the same time, the majority of member states – particularly donors – did not want to create a new agency that would overlap with IOM. IOM also wanted clear recognition as the leading IO on migration. Some 28 entities in the UN system address migration in varying ways. However, none of them concentrated first and foremost on migration, there was no clear focal point or hierarchy among them, and many had only a handful of staff explicitly focused on migration.[77] Existing UN agencies were therefore poorly positioned to take a primary role on migration, particularly operationally, making it a seemingly logical step to bring IOM into the UN system as the lead migration agency. Some fought this conclusion. In particular, UN DESA, which is involved in migration research and statistics, vehemently resisted IOM's designation as the leading migration IO.[78] Consequently, the 2016 agreement awkwardly states that the UN recognizes IOM as "*an* organization with *a* global role in the field of migration," while also conceding that IOM's member states regard IOM "as *the* global lead agency on migration."[79] IOM's need to sustainably resolve its turf claims had been heightened by a memo from the UN Development Operations Coordination Office, the secretariat of the UNDG, that hampered IOM's ability to work in the field as part of UN country teams, on the basis of IOM's lack of formal legal standing in the UN system. Although bureaucratically arcane, this memo reinforced the view that the "enhanced status quo" idea had reached its limits, further simulating interest in IOM in entering the UN system.[80] The misgivings of some UN officials were outweighed by member states' support.

In terms of the timing, the occasion of the New York Summit proved critical, particularly to the decision to make IOM a related organization instead

The UN migration agency? IOM–un relations **115**

of a specialized agency. Senior IOM officials who played important roles in the process suggest that the rapid conclusion of the agreement was in part a response to the "need for some low-hanging fruit" to show progress from the Summit.[81] When it became clear that the Summit would kick off a multi-year process leading to the Global Compact on Migration, the drive to bring IOM into the UN system intensified. IOM was well equipped to play a major role in supporting this process, building on its long experience convening conferences, forums, and dialogues on migration. However, as the Summit and subsequent compact negotiations were a UN initiative, the perception was that they should be serviced by actors within the UN system, fueling the push to quickly conclude the new relationship agreement. This shaped the decision to make IOM a related organization rather than a specialized agency. Going through ECOSOC would have prolonged the process and raised new bureaucratic hurdles, perhaps making it impossible to meet the September Summit deadline, and raising concerns that the window to bring IOM into the UN system might close without an agreement.

Beyond turf battles and timing issues, the decades-long process of expanding IOM's membership was pivotal to the quick conclusion of the negotiations. At earlier points, discussions on recasting the IOM–UN relationship struggled to gain traction as IOM had relatively few members, but by 2016 almost all UN members were also part of IOM.[82] Over many years IOM concertedly cultivated champions for its work among different member state blocs, such that it had vocal supporters among donor states, and major migrant-sending countries, which were particularly supportive of IOM joining the UN system. These long-term efforts meant that once the issue was decided among IOM member states, the only real obstacles came from within the UN bureaucracy, rather than from governments. And given that powerful states, particularly the United States, backed IOM's entrance, the resistance the UN could mount was limited. It was, however, enough to make the negotiations at times tense and quarrelsome.[83]

This is not to say that there was unity among the member states and donor agencies on whether IOM should join the UN system when Swing revived the question. Some were surprisingly indifferent. For example, at the 2015 IOM Council session, the US representative publicly asked the director of operations from ECHO (the leading European Union humanitarian donor, and a major contributor to IOM) for the agency's views on IOM's status inside or outside the UN. ECHO's representative responded that as long as IOM could deliver with its characteristic speed and efficiency, it was largely unconcerned with whether IOM was formally part of the UN system. Persuading member states took time because, as noted in Chapter 1, many manage their relationship with IOM through their interior ministries, rather than through their ministries of foreign affairs, which typically oversee IO relations. In comparison to diplomats predisposed to value multilateralism, many interior ministry officials are more skeptical of the UN, viewing it as bureaucratically bloated, meddlesome, and impractical.[84] Consequently, many member states were concerned that entering the UN system

116 The UN migration agency? IOM–un relations

would "ruin" IOM, undercutting its prized flexibility, responsiveness, and efficiency with little to show for it. For member states frustrated with UN agencies perceived as wasteful and out of touch, bringing IOM into the UN system was not so much a chance to enhance IOM as it was an opportunity to improve the UN itself.[85] Given member states' concern that IOM risked "contamination" from the UN bureaucracy, they gave IOM a short leash in negotiating with the UN.[86] Member states backed IOM's desire to ensure that it could not be excluded from key planning and coordination bodies or field operations on the basis of its legal status, but insisted that IOM preserve certain characteristics valued by its member states.[87]

With this mandate, the tension became "how to square the circle."[88] IOM officials were themselves divided on whether this was possible, and desirable. As I have discussed, IOM's recent directors general have promoted IOM's entry into the UN system, suggesting that this would protect IOM's migration mandate, avoid overlap, enhance coordination, ensure migration issues are consistently integrated into relevant global governance debates and initiatives, facilitate access to funding, expedite operations by allowing IOM staff to travel on the UN laissez passer, raise IOM's institutional profile, and enable it to influence strategic planning and policy processes at the UN, thereby strengthening both the UN and IOM.[89] This positive disposition was shared by many staff members who saw joining the UN system as part of IOM's maturation, as a way to gain increased influence and status. But many saw clear, concerning costs in joining the UN system, and expressed ambivalence about the prospect, suggesting that "If IOM is unique and needs to be preserved, then probably the UN is not the best road for it."[90] Particularly among IOM's humanitarian staff, there was concern that membership in the UN system could draw the agency away from its traditional, operational focus. Several stressed that there are advantages, especially at the country level, to being outside the UN system, but recognized that these advantages diminished as IOM became dependent on the UN: "We now abide by the system's rules, without having some of the advantages of the system. . . . IOM's rules mirror the UN system rules, but without the advantages."[91] A common concern among IOM's highly operationally oriented staff was that "being in the UN will turn us into bureaucrats."[92] According to one senior official, because IOM has expanded so dramatically, and is part of a humanitarian system that is driven by the UN, further integration is "an unavoidable part of growing up," but

> from a business perspective – you're not supposed to talk about it this way but everyone does – there are aspects of our work that we would lose . . . so it's not just a win-win game. . . . The last thing the world needs is another agency that [just] organizes meetings. If we lose the operations, then we're really screwed.[93]

As this comment underscores, perceptions of the potential costs and benefits of joining the UN system vary depending on different positions, interests, and normative commitments within the organization.

What's new? Analysis of the agreement concerning the relationship between the United Nations and the International Organization for Migration

What was perhaps most conspicuously absent from discussions on the IOM–UN relationship is explicit analysis of whether IOM entering the UN system would be good for migrants themselves. Given IOM's lack of a formal protection mandate and concerns about its involvement in migration management activities that sit in tension with human rights standards, one might have anticipated some pushback from advocacy organizations. And yet serious opposition never materialized. This may be a sign of increasing acceptance of IOM, or optimism that entering the UN system would encourage greater adherence to key norms and standards. It may also or alternatively be an indication that in an era of widespread abuses against migrants, advocates simply have bigger worries. After little direct engagement with the question of migrants' interests and well-being in debates on the IOM–UN relationship, the 2016 agreement nods towards this issue. Article 1 indicates that the purpose of bringing the UN and IOM into a new, formal relationship with each other is to strengthen "cooperation and enhance their ability to fulfill their respective mandates in the interest of migrants and their Member States."[94]

Whether IOM's entry into the UN system will actually benefit migrants remains to be seen, and is admittedly impossible to conclusively determine. What then has the agreement concretely achieved? Very little, some suggest. Micinski and Weiss, for example, argue that while IOM "joining the UN system was meant to be a major outcome of the September meeting, the agreed text basically extends the previous IOM-UN relationship."[95] Superseding and replacing the 1996 Cooperation Agreement, the 2016 agreement promotes cooperation, including in exchanging expert advice, information, research, and assistance; and in the statistical field. The signatories pledge to avoid duplication in their activities and services, and to collaboratively promote efficient organizational administration. The agreement allows for reciprocal representation and participation (without a vote) in one another's deliberation and governance bodies; enables IOM staff to travel on the UN laissez-passer; makes IOM a full, formal member of key coordination mechanisms including the UNDG and the CEB; and confirms IOM's full participation in UN country and regional teams. At face value these changes do seem modest, as IOM was already highly integrated in the UN system. However, the agreement is highly significant for IOM, as it gives the agency the recognition it has long craved, secures its place as the primary IO in the migration field, and removes bureaucratic and legal barriers to its continued expansion. It may additionally have the effect of hemming in work that is undertaken by other agencies in the UN system, and limit activities that sit uncomfortably with international migration, refugee, and human rights law, as IOM undertakes in the agreement to work in accordance with these standards, and the Purposes and Principles of the UN Charter.[96]

The agreement is notable as much for what it preserves as what it creates. As Swing's negotiating mandate was premised on the "explicit condition" that the new arrangement protect the "essential elements" of IOM's identity laid out in IOM Council resolution 1309, the agreement can only be meaningfully interpreted alongside a careful reading of this resolution.[97] Article 2(a) of Council resolution 1309 conveys the member states' view that IOM is a "non-normative organization with its own constitution and governance system, featuring a predominantly projectized budgetary model and a decentralized organizational structure," with key traits including "responsiveness, efficiency, cost-effectiveness and independence." In recognizing these attributes and explicitly reiterating much of this language – including, as discussed next, the controversial "non-normative" designation – the agreement conveys a strong sense that IOM and its member states want to have their cake and eat it too. That is, they want IOM to have the stature and influence associated with the UN; many member states and staffers also want to see IOM step up more consistently to promote the protection of migrants' rights, and the agreement strengthens the foundations for this. But they want to enjoy these gains without sacrificing qualities that have at some points led IOM to engage in disreputable behavior. In this sense, the agreement carries forward the tensions and contradictions that have colored the IOM–UN relationship since its inception.

The "non-normative" designation

IOM's member states insisted on including the "non-normative" label in Council resolution 1309, and subsequently in the 2016 agreement.[98] This term was not previously prominent in the lexicon of terms used to characterize IOM and its role in the international system, and its inclusion in the 2016 agreement has raised the concern that it may excuse behavior incompatible with the norms underpinning the UN system.[99] Guild, Grant, and Groenendijk, for example, argue that "The UN is a fundamentally normative organization," and ask,

> Is it possible to define the term 'non-normative' in a manner which is consistent with the human rights objectives of the UN? We do not see exactly how this would be possible, bearing in mind the normal meaning of the term non-normative.[100]

"Non-normative" is not a legal term of art, nor is it common in the discourse surrounding IOs. On a certain level it is nonsensical to describe any IO as non-normative in that they are all, in one way or another, informed by and implicated in spreading norms. Beyond human rights and humanitarian principles, IOs may be influenced by and help to promote norms ranging from respect for state sovereignty and non-intervention, to principles on the collaborative management of environmental resources. They are also influenced by legal norms on the status, immunities, and obligations of IOs, and by more informal norms on the professional culture of international bureaucracies. It is particularly nonsensical to describe IOM as non-normative, as the agency has assertively promulgated and encouraged states to accept migration management norms.[101]

Others suggest that over the past 20 years, IOM has been the "biggest driver" of important new norm-setting efforts to facilitate increased international cooperation on migration, based on the view that "migration is good for everyone, if it is safe and orderly."[102] A case in point: on the same day that Ban and Swing signed the 2016 agreement characterizing IOM as a non-normative organization, states initiated the Global Compact on Migration process, which IOM was tapped to service in cooperation with the UN Secretariat.[103] What then are we to make of this designation, and the inconsistencies it seems to entail? When the 2016 agreement was negotiated, the term "non-normative" took on a specific meaning, commonly understood among the IOM administration and its member states: that IOM would not be a venue for setting binding international norms on migration, in the way that, for example, the ILO does on labor standards. Understood from this perspective, IOM's role in, for instance, servicing the Global Compact on Migration process is appropriate, as the compact is not binding.

In some ways, IOM's non-normative characterization is analogous to UNHCR's depiction as "non-political" in its Statute.[104] These words have important consequences. UNHCR has at times used its "non-political" character as an excuse to avoid forthright challenges to powerful, refugee-abusing governments on whom the agency depends, and IOM could, in the future, hide behind the non-normative label. But part of the power of these words is that they enable useful fictions. UNHCR is obviously political, in that identifying, protecting, and assisting refugees are inherently political tasks: they require political savvy, and depend on laws and systems that reflect the political preferences of powerful states. UNHCR is non-political in a narrower sense, reflecting the principle that humanitarian actors should not engage in partisan politics, or take sides in war. And yet in conflicts in which certain parties engage in ethnic cleansing or purposefully violate refugees' rights, UNHCR's mandate effectively requires it to take a stand against such acts and, by extension, the groups undertaking them. Notwithstanding the contractions it entails, designating UNHCR as non-political was essential to enabling the creation of the high commissioner's office in the context of highly charged Cold War rivalries, and positioned the office to walk a fine, shifting line to execute its mandate. Some similar dynamics apply to IOM, as recast by the 2016 agreement. Calling IOM "non-normative" seems incompatible with its recognized role in the agreement as an "essential contributor . . . in the protection of migrants," and its work has inherently normative dimensions, just as UNHCR's work has inherently political dimensions.[105] A narrower sense of what it means to be "non-normative" informed the 2016 negotiations (that IOM would not set binding standards), just as a narrower sense of "non-political" is at play in the UNHCR Statute, and this arrangement made it possible to overcome state objections to IOM entering the UN system. Of course, shared understandings of the non-normative designation, and its ramifications, may change over time and require close evaluation. This comparison suggests, however, that the significance of the term should not be overstated, and must be understood in temporal and political context.

120 The UN migration agency? IOM–un relations

Conclusion: uncertain implications

It is still too soon to map out the main implications, risks, and rewards of IOM's entry into the UN system. Early indications suggest that, three years on, it is in many ways business as usual for IOM, with the agency continuing to cultivate its niche areas of work while entrepreneurially seeking out new opportunities. This is in part a reflection of the extent to which IOM was already integrated into the UN system. But the continuation of business as usual is more significant than it may seem, as IOM's usual business over the past 20 years has been one of major growth and increased influence. At a time when new obstacles threatened this continued growth and informal avenues to improve the IOM–UN relationship seemed to have reached their limit (at least from IOM's perspective), IOM's entry into the UN system has paved the way for the agency to guard its ground and sustain further expansion. The differences will likely be most keenly felt in terms of IOM's involvement in development activities, as the agency was already extensively engaged in the UN's humanitarian country teams. Indeed, as I have argued, cooperation between the UN and IOM in the humanitarian sector provided the foundation for the development of this institutional relationship.

Importantly, this shift means that IOM's continued expansion will take place *within* the UN system, which may constrain some of its more contentious lines of work. Such pruning may help other parts of the organization to grow; officials in the Department of Operations and Emergencies, for example, suggest that IOM's humanitarian work has been hampered by its involvement in controversial migration management work. Alternatively, others warn that IOM's membership in the UN system may in fact enable and normalize or "blue wash" morally questionable migration management interventions.[106] These possibilities merit careful, continued examination.

Being part of the UN system presents new challenges for IOM. The agency will have to prove to its member states that being part of the UN system has not eroded its prized attributes. Differences in working cultures will need to be navigated, and staff across the system will need to learn more about one another's mandates and approaches. The agency has taken on significant coordination roles, including as the secretariat for the new UN Network on Migration – a role likely to further heighten IOM's visibility and influence on the direction of debates and activities on migration in the UN system. Working more firmly within the UN system necessitates ensuring that staff across IOM are better aware of the organization's rights but also its obligations, recognizing that in the assessment of IOM's own legal office, the agency is now bound by the general laws and principles applicable to UN entities, including in relation to human rights due diligence assessments.[107] Staff must also be trained to operate in an environment in which "partnership is higher in the modus operandi" than it has been in the past.[108] Some strengthened collaborative approaches are already evident. For example, for the first time in their histories, UNHCR and IOM have deployed a joint envoy. In September 2018, the high commissioner and IOM director general named former Guatemalan Vice President Eduardo Stein as their joint special representative for Venezuelan

The UN migration agency? IOM–un relations **121**

refugees and migrants, tasked with supporting governments' responses to the departure of more than 3.4 million Venezuelans from their country since 2016.[109] And yet stark differences and mandate struggles persist, including in relation to other high-profile crises such as the Rohingya refugee situation in Bangladesh, where the government tapped IOM to serve in a leading role, despite UNHCR's clear remit.

Prospects for coordination and cooperation between the UN and IOM were buoyed with the election of António Vitorino as IOM director general in October 2018. A former Portuguese politician, Vitorino's official IOM biography underscores his service as defense minister and deputy prime minister in the government of António Guterres, the current UN secretary-general.[110] These links bode well for more harmonious relationships between the organizations, at least at the highest levels. Challenges and tensions certainly remain in the IOM–UN relationship, as they do within and between all UN agencies. Yet these leadership developments and IOM's entry into the UN system suggest that the trend of rapprochement and integration, alongside ongoing contestation, will continue to be a defining feature of the IOM–UN relationship in the near future.

Notes

1 Statement of IOM Director General William Lacy Swing at the September Summit and Signing of the IOM-UN Agreement, 19 September 2016.
2 Interview, member state official 1, November 2015. On the pre-2016 IOM-UN relationship, see Susan Martin, *International Migration: Evolving Trends from the Early Twentieth Century to the Present* (Cambridge: Cambridge University Press, 2014), 145–153.
3 Report of the Special Representative of the Secretary-General on Migration (General Assembly document A/71/728), 3 February 2017, para 9.
4 Ishan Ashutosh and Allison Mountz, "Migration Management for the Benefit of Whom? Interrogating the Work of the International Organization for Migration," *Citizenship Studies* 15, no. 1 (2011): 26; Guy Goodwin-Gill, *A Brief and Somewhat Sceptical Perspective on the International Organization for Migration*, 7 April 2019, www.kaldorcentre.unsw.edu.au/publication/brief-and-somewhat-sceptical-perspective-international-organization-migration; Elspeth Guild, Stefanie Grant and Kees Groenendijk, "IOM and the UN: Unfinished Business," *Queen Mary University of London School of Law Legal Studies Research Papers*, no. 255 (2017).
5 Elizabeth Ferris and Katharine Donato, *Refugees, Migration and Global Governance: Negotiating the Global Compacts* (London: Routledge, 2019), chapter 3.
6 Interview, humanitarian actor 1 (UN), November 2015.
7 The consequences for migrants themselves demand focused analysis, but this is outside the scope of this initial discussion.
8 IOM, *World Migration Report 2011* (Geneva: IOM, 2012), 102.
9 Megan Bradley, "The International Organization for Migration (IOM): Gaining Power in the Forced Migration Regime," *Refuge* 33, no. 1 (2017); Jerome Elie, "The Historical Roots of Cooperation between the UN High Commissioner for Refugees and the International Organization for Migration," *Global Governance* 16 (2010): 345–360; and Anne Koch, "The Politics and Discourse of Migrant Return: The Role of UNHCR and IOM in the Governance of Return," *Journal of Ethnic and Migration Studies* 40, no. 6 (2014): 905–923.
10 Interview, member state official 2, December 2016.

122 The UN migration agency? IOM–un relations

11 Jérôme Elie, "IOM from 1951–1953: The Creation of PICMME/ICEM," Presentation for 2011 World Migration Report Seminar Series, Geneva, 9 December 2010. "Surplus population" refers to the perceived imbalance between individuals in need of work, and labor needs in European economies. This amorphous idea was not applicable or influential in all post-WWI European states, but shaped policies in countries including the Netherlands, Italy and Greece.

12 Elie, "Historical Roots"; IOM, *World Migration Report 2011*, 94; Rieko Karatani, "How History Separated Refugee and Migrant Regimes: In Search of Their Institutional Origins," *International Journal of Refugee Law* 17, no. 3 (2005): 517–541.

13 Elie, *IOM from 1951–1953*.

14 IOM, *Annual Report 1991* (Geneva: IOM, 1992), 36.

15 Ibid.

16 UNGA A/RES/47/4, 16 October 1992.

17 Ibid.

18 Interview, humanitarian actor 5 (NGO), November 2015.

19 IOM, "IOM accesses CERF," *IOM News*, no. 1/1994, 1.

20 Interview, IOM official 1, November 2015.

21 IOM, *IOM Strategic Planning: Toward the Twenty-First Century*, 71st session of IOM Council, MC/1842, 9 May 1995, para 20.

22 Ibid., para 35. Staff working with humanitarian agencies would and do still contest IOM's claim that it respects other agencies' mandated roles. See Tim Morris, "IOM: Trespassing on Others' Humanitarian Space?" *Forced Migration Review* 22 (2005): 43.

23 Cooperation Agreement between the United Nations and the International Organization for Migration, 18 July 1996, E/1996/90.

24 Ibid., Article 1(1).

25 IOM, *IOM News*, June/July 1996, 1, 7.

26 Ibid.

27 IOM, *IOM News*, November/December 1996, 1.

28 Ibid.

29 Cooperation Agreement between the United Nations and the International Organization for Migration, Article V(1).

30 *Strengthening the United Nations: An Agenda for Further Change, Report of the Secretary-General* (General Assembly document A/57/387), September 2002.

31 *IOM-UN Relationship: Summary Report of the Working Group on Institutional Arrangements*, IOM Council, 86th Session, 10 November 2003, MC/INF/263, Annex III, paras 4–7.

32 *IOM-UN Relationship*, MC/INF/263, para. 1.

33 *IOM-UN Relationship*, MC/INF/263, Annex III, para 7.

34 Statement by the Director General, Mr. Brunson McKinley, at the Eighty-fourth Session of the Council (MICEM/7/2002), 2–4 December 2002.

35 *IOM-UN Relationship*, MC/INF/263, Annex I, para 22.

36 *IOM-UN Relationship*, MC/INF/263, para 7.

37 *IOM-UN Relationship*, MC/INF/263, Annex I, para 6.

38 *IOM-UN Relationship*, MC/INF/263, Annex I, para 38.

39 *IOM-UN Relationship*, MC/INF/263, Annex I, para 22.

40 *IOM-UN Relationship*, MC/INF/263, Annex I, para 3.

41 *IOM-UN Relationship*, MC/INF/263, Annex III, para 33.

42 *IOM-UN Relationship*, MC/INF/263, paras 4, 9, 10.

43 *IOM-UN Relationship*, MC/INF/263, para 3.

44 Letter from Amina Mohamed, Ambassador and Permanent Representative of Kenya to the UN in Geneva and Chair of the IOM Council to Kofi Annan (KMUNG/IOM/10A), 28 May 2003.

45 *IOM-UN Relationship*, MC/INF/263, para 11. See also *IOM-UN Relationship*, IOM Council, 92nd session, 14 November 2006, MC/INF/285, para 11.

The UN migration agency? IOM–un relations **123**

46 *Options for the IOM-UN Relationship: Additional Analysis of Costs and Benefits*, IOM Council, 94th session, 9 November 2007, MC/INF/290, para 4.
47 *Options for the IOM-UN Relationship*, MC/INF/290, paras 6–24.
48 *Options for the IOM-UN Relationship*, MC/INF/290, para 65.
49 *Options for the IOM-UN Relationship*, MC/INF/290, para 66.
50 *Options for the IOM-UN Relationship*, MC/INF/290, para 67.
51 *Options for the IOM-UN Relationship*, MC/INF/290, para 68.
52 Letter from IOM Director General Brunson McKinley to UN Secretary-General Ban Ki-moon, 10 July 2007.
53 Ibid.
54 Letter from UN Secretary-General Ban Ki-moon to IOM Director General Brunson McKinley, 8 October 2007.
55 Interviews, independent expert 3 and humanitarian actor 8 (NGO), December 2016; Interview, independent expert 6, October 2019.
56 Interview, IOM official 14, December 2016.
57 Guy Goodwin-Gill, *A Brief and Somewhat Sceptical Perspective on the International Organization for Migration*, 7 April 2019, www.kaldorcentre.unsw.edu.au/publication/brief-and-somewhat-sceptical-perspective-international-organization-migration.
58 Antoine Pécoud, "What Do We Know About the International Organization for Migration?" *Journal of Ethnic and Migration* Studies 44, no. 10 (2018): 1632, 1622. Pécoud goes on to argue that "IOM's exteriority towards the UN does make for certain key differences, especially in terms of its normative mandate. . . . IOM is indeed not bound by the human rights framework that forms the basis of the UN's work." See Pécoud, "What Do We Know," 1665. As discussed in Chapter 2, while IOM lacks a formal legal protection mandate (like other humanitarian agencies such as WFP), it is incorrect to suggest that it is not bound by human rights obligations. These are incumbent on IOM both in virtue of its own institutional commitments, and under international law pertaining to IOs and the accountability of these institutions. On this issue, see the extensive scholarship of Jan Klabbers. See also Carla Ferstman, *International Organizations and the Fight for Accountability: The Remedies and Reparations Gap* (Oxford: Oxford University Press, 2017).
59 Nicholas Micinski and Thomas Weiss, "International Organization for Migration and the UN System: A Missed Opportunity," *Future UN Development System Briefings* 42 (2016): 1–4. Micinski and Weiss offer a helpful discussion of the merits of specialized agency status in comparison to related organization status.
60 Charter of the United Nations, Article 57.
61 United Nations Chief Executives Board for Coordination, *Directory of United Nations System Organizations: Related Organizations*, www.unsystem.org/members/related-organizations.
62 Peter Szasz, "The Complexification of the United Nations System," *Max Planck Yearbook of United Nations Law* 3 (1999), cited in *IOM-UN Relationship*, MC/INF/263, Annex I.
63 Ibid. For descriptions of the roles of these bodies, see United Nations, *Funds, Programmes, Specialized Agencies and Others*, www.un.org/en/sections/about-un/funds-programmes-specialized-agencies-and-others/index.html.
64 United Nations, *Funds, Programmes, Specialized Agencies and Others*.
65 United Nations, *The United Nations System*, 2019, www.un.org/en/pdfs/18-00159e_un_system_chart_17x11_4c_en_web.pdf.
66 Personal communication from the Office of the Legal Adviser, US State Department, on the status of related organizations including IOM vis-à-vis the UN, 20 December 2016.
67 Ibid.
68 UN Charter, Article 57; *IOM-UN Relationship*, MC/INF/263, Annex I, paras 40–42.
69 *IOM-UN Relationship*, MC/INF/263, Annex III, para 25.
70 *IOM-UN Relationship*, MC/INF/285, para 9.

124 The UN migration agency? IOM–un relations

71 *Options for the IOM-UN Relationship*, MC/INF/290, paras 8–11.
72 Interview, IOM official 14.
73 Guild, Grant and Groenendijk, "IOM and the UN: Unfinished Business," 7.
74 Statement of IOM Director General William Lacy Swing at the September Summit and Signing of the IOM-UN Agreement, 19 September 2016.
75 Ibid.
76 Ibid.
77 Micinski and Weiss, "Missed Opportunity," 2. On competition between the UN agencies involved in migration and the implications for global migration governance, see Nicholas Micinski and Thomas Weiss, "Global Migration Governance: Beyond Coordination and Crises," in *The Global Community: Yearbook of International Law and Jurisprudence*, ed. Giuliana Ziccardi Capaldo (Oxford: Oxford University Press, 2018), 175–193.
78 Interviews, independent expert 2 and member state official 4, December 2016.
79 Agreement Concerning the Relationship between the United Nations and the International Organization for Migration, Article 2(1) (emphasis added).
80 Interviews, IOM officials 1 and 14.
81 Interview, IOM official 14.
82 In 2003, IOM explicitly recognized that its own small membership base was an impediment to entering the UN system, particularly as a specialized agency. At the time, IOM had 98 member states; few of these members were from the Middle East, and five of the world's largest countries – including India, China, Indonesia, the Russian Federation and Brazil – were observers rather than members of IOM. In contrast, most specialized agencies had 140–185 member states, covering all geographical areas. See *IOM-UN Relationship*, MC/INF/263, Annex 1, para 59.
83 Interview, independent expert 2.
84 Interview, IOM official 2, November 2015.
85 Interview, independent expert 3.
86 Interview, IOM official 2.
87 Interview, IOM official 14. See also IOM Council Resolution 1309, 24 November 2015.
88 Interview, IOM official 1.
89 See e.g. *IOM-UN Relationship*, MC/INF/263, Annex 1, paras 52–56.
90 Interview, IOM official 13, November 2015.
91 Interview, IOM official 2.
92 Interview, IOM official 11, November 2015.
93 Interview, IOM official 9, November 2015.
94 Agreement Concerning the Relationship between the United Nations and the International Organization for Migration, Article 1.
95 Micinski and Weiss, "Missed Opportunity," 2.
96 Agreement Concerning the Relationship between the United Nations and the International Organization for Migration, Article 2.5.
97 See also the discussion of these characteristics in chapter 1.
98 Interview, IOM official 2; Interview, member state official 1.
99 See Guild, Grant and Groenendijk, "IOM and the UN: Unfinished Business," for an analysis of the 2016 agreement from an international law perspective, with a focus on human rights obligations.
100 Guild, Grant and Groenendijk, "Unfinished Business," 14.
101 See e.g. Rutvica Andrijasevic and William Walters, "The International Organization for Migration and the International Government of Borders," *Environment and Planning D: Society and Space* 28, no. 6 (2010): 977–999; Inken Bartels, "'We Must Do It Gently'. The Contested Implementation of the IOM's Migration Management in Morocco," *Migration Studies* 5, no. 3 (2017): 315–336.
102 Ferris and Donato, *Negotiating the Global Compacts*.

The UN migration agency? IOM–un relations **125**

103 UN General Assembly Resolution 71/280 on "Modalities for the intergovernmental negotiations of the global compact for safe, orderly and regular migration" reaffirms in Article 11 that "the Secretariat of the United Nations and the International Organization for Migration would jointly service the negotiations, the former providing capacity and support and the latter extending the technical and policy expertise required, and decides that such joint servicing shall apply to the entire preparatory process to develop the global compact." For IOM's summary of its activities in support of the compact, see IOM, *IOM Activities in Support of the Global Compact for Safe, Orderly and Regular Migration*, www.iom.int/sites/default/files/our_work/ODG/GCM/TPs-on-IOM-GCM-Related-Efforts.pdf.

104 The UNHCR Statute states that the "work of the High Commissioner shall be of an entirely non-political character." (Chapter 1.2) On UNHCR as a "non-political" actor, see David Forsythe, "UNHCR's Mandate: The Politics of Being Non-Political," *UNHCR New Issues in Refugee Research* 33 (2001): 1–34.

105 Agreement Concerning the Relationship between the United Nations and the International Organization for Migration, Article 2.2.

106 Asher Lazarus Hirsch and Cameron Doig, "Outsourcing Control: The International Organization for Migration in Indonesia," *International Journal of Human Rights* 22, no. 5 (2018): 681–708.

107 Interview, IOM official 17, December 2019.

108 Interview, IOM official 14.

109 UNHCR and IOM, *Joint Statement by UNHCR and IOM on the Appointment of Mr. Eduardo Stein, as a Joint Special Representative for Venezuelan Refugees and Migrants in the Region*, 19 September 2018, www.unhcr.org/news/press/2018/9/5ba262454/joint-statement-unhcr-iom-appointment-mr-eduardo-stein-joint-special-representative.html; Manuel Rueda, "Colombia and UN Test First Border Camps for Venezuelans," *The New Humanitarian*, 2 April 2019.

110 IOM, *António Vitorino*, 2019, www.iom.int/director-general.

5
CONCLUSION

- *Limitations, consequences, and future challenges*
- *Areas for future research*
- *Implications for policy and practice*
- *On pleasing no one*

In his inaugural speech as director general of IOM, António Vitorino emphasized IOM's "commitment to be simultaneously at the service of migrants and our member states alike," and stressed "our key roles to guarantee their [migrants'] human rights, their human dignity, [and] their wellbeing, irrespective of their legal status."[1] This was a striking start for the new director general, given IOM's reputation for prioritizing deferential service to its member states, its lack of a formal protection mandate, and its historical reluctance to speak up about migrants' rights. Vitorino's speech reflects some of the myriad ways in which IOM has changed since its inception in 1951. The significance of these changes is of course open to interpretation: some may applaud Vitorino's conceptualization of IOM's commitments and constituents, while others may react skeptically, dismissing such discourse as only a superficial change underneath which the organization continues to advance states' interests in controlling mobility at the expense of migrants' rights and well-being.

This book cannot aspire to resolve such different interpretations, but has more modestly attempted to provide a foundation for exploring them. I have attempted to offer a brief, empirically grounded, critically engaged but even-handed introduction to IOM, focusing on its activities in the humanitarian sector and with forced migrants – work that now comprises the bulk of IOM's budget and field presence, but which remains remarkably under-examined. In Chapter 1, I examined IOM's evolving structure, composition, mandate, and culture, demonstrating how it has grown and gradually accrued increased institutional autonomy and influence, despite its continued dependence on states. In probing IOM's humanitarian entrepreneurialism in Chapter 2, I showed how the organization has served as a jack-of-all-trades, filling in gaps in the humanitarian system, while also cultivating particular niches and populations of concern. I also explored IOM's development as a humanitarian actor through analysis of a series of important internal policies and frameworks on key issues, including humanitarian principles and human rights protection. This is of course still a work in progress – as demonstrated in Chapter 3 through analysis of IOM's operations in Haiti and Libya. These cases reveal the tensions in IOM's nature as a multi-mandate agency that undertakes migration management work that sometimes sits uncomfortably alongside, or is at odds with, humanitarian principles and human rights protection. In Chapter 4, I discussed the evolution of the IOM–UN relationship, the process that led to IOM joining the UN system in 2016, and the still uncertain implications of this change. In this short conclusion, I reflect on the limitations and consequences of this analysis, areas for future research, and implications for policy and practice.

Limitations, consequences, and future challenges

As this book has not sought to provide a comprehensive overview of IOM, there are inevitably issues that I have not explored in depth, despite their significance. For example, I have not engaged in a detailed discussion of the organization's early history, or IOM's activities in relation to migration policy and research, international dialogues and negotiations, anti-trafficking, information campaigns, border management, migrant health, migration and climate change, or migration and development. This may appear to be a strange choice from the perspective of predominant assumptions about what IOM is all about, and the existing literature on IOM, which focuses primarily on these activities, particularly as they relate to movements from the global South to the North. In centering IOM's work in the global South, particularly as it relates to humanitarian emergencies, I am driven by the conviction that this work and its consequences are critical issues in their own right. Further, I have been motivated by the recognition that IOM's ability to engage in the migration management activities for which it is more well known "has become highly dependent on its capacity to expand its operations into emergencies that receive more public attention and larger government resources."[2] Humanitarian work is therefore essential to understanding IOM itself and its influence on global governance. As I have stressed, although IOM's headquarters is divided into two main operational divisions, the Department of Operations and Emergencies (primarily responsible for humanitarian response) and the Department of Migration Management, humanitarian aid and migration management are not separate endeavors. By concentrating on IOM's involvement in humanitarian emergencies and "post-crisis" situations, I hope to have troubled the tendency to overlook this work as peripheral to or a foil for IOM's "real" business of managing international migration. Indeed, this analysis points to the need to reconsider the assumption that economic migrants moving

128 Conclusion

internationally are IOM's "bread-and-butter," and devote more attention to the organization's engagements with IDPs, who now comprise the majority of people on the receiving end of IOM interventions.[3]

IOM is often portrayed as a rather strange creation, neither fish nor fowl. Some stress its similarities to NGOs or for-profit companies, and its differences from organizations like UNHCR that have formal protection mandates. In contrast, this analysis has suggested that while aspects of IOM are indeed distinctive, it has much more in common with other IOs than is often assumed. This is true even in the humanitarian sphere, where IOM faces dilemmas and tradeoffs similar to those encountered by many other agencies who also have to juggle multiple mandates and member state relations, and deal with the classic "dirty hands" problems that arise from having to decide between bad options. IOM's own decisions, institutional culture, and turf-hungry *modus operandi* can heighten these concerns, but this is again a familiar problem across humanitarian agencies who are both partners and competitors.

IOM is shaped by sometimes stark tensions – between its discourse and operational practices; between the roles it aspires to play and its structural constraints; between the notion that managed migration can be for the "benefit of all," and the reality that existing migration governance efforts reliably reinforce the privilege of powerful states and elites. This book has drawn out some of these tensions and inconsistencies, and probed some of their implications. While some of these tensions are inherent to IOM's mandate and its place in the international system, others may be reconciled or reduced. For example, a major future challenge for IOM will be to resolve some of the inconsistences associated with its decentralization. As discussed in Chapter 2 and demonstrated in Chapter 3 through the cases of Haiti and Libya, IOM has dramatically different incarnations depending on the context. IOM's member states insist that decentralization, flexibility, and an operationally informed approach must remain defining qualities of the organization; the challenge is to preserve these attributes while reining in the "cowboy" approach and ensuring more consistent adherence to principles and standards. Achieving greater coherence depends not only on choices made by IOM administration and staff, but also by its member states. A more consistent approach requires more systematic donor support so that IOM can reliably respond to populations for whom it is now a key interlocutor, such as migrant workers in emergencies, and IDPs in disasters. Different branches of IOM's member states pull it in different directions; for instance, some of IOM's humanitarian donors have urged and applauded the development of policies that more explicitly anchor the agency to human rights and humanitarian principles, while other departments within the same member states want IOM to remain available to undertake activities that may be incongruous with these commitments. Coherence is an elusive goal in any large organization, but resolving or at least reducing some of IOM's most obvious inconsistences is essential to its continued maturation, particularly now that it has entered the UN system. Other major future challenges highlighted by this analysis, and discussed in the next section, include IOM's continued

Conclusion **129**

integration into the UN system; the further clarification of its protection commitments; and the effective implementation of the policies and frameworks discussed in Chapter 2.

Areas for future research

While the organization has changed dramatically since 1951, research on IOM remains limited, and too much of the existing work presents the agency in static, monolithic terms.[4] This book points to the value of considering the ways in which IOM has evolved, and the consequences of these shifts. IOM's new policies, practices, and discourses should not simply be taken at face value, but they should be taken seriously as a window into how the organization positions itself in crowded global governance fields. They should also be interrogated to better understand the commitments to which IOM can and should be held accountable. Future research on IOM may helpfully question assumptions about IOM and its work, including the idea that cross-border economic migrants are IOM's primary and natural focus. As this analysis has emphasized, IOM has a remarkably broad mandate, including international *and* internal migration undertaken for complex, intertwined reasons. Instead of myopically focusing on IOM's impacts on the minority of migrants trying to travel from the global South to the global North, more attention should be devoted to the consequences of IOM's work for the majority of migrants moving within the global South, particularly overlooked populations such as IDPs. Devoting more attention to internal movements may prompt reconsideration of which of IOM's many activities are directly connected to migration, and which represent mission creep. For example, some question IOM's involvement in post-disaster reconstruction as unrelated to migration, but this view is plausible only if internal displacement following disasters is discounted as a form of migration.[5]

Research on IOM has been dominated by migration studies scholars, with migration management serving as the primary analytical lens. Building on this work, the application of broader conceptual apparatuses may deepen understanding of IOM from different disciplinary perspectives. IR perspectives may productively trouble assumptions about IOM as *sui generis* by placing and comparatively analyzing IOM within broader constellations of IOs – including but not limited to those focused on migration. There is a clear need for more work on the politics of IOM's member states, including the relationship between the agency and particular member states, and how the members govern IOM and interact through the IOM Council.[6] Studies on IOM's leadership could also helpfully show how different directors general have shaped the organization over time, contributing to the broader literature on the influence of IO heads on global governance. But IOM cannot be understood only from the top down. The vast majority of IOM employees are national staff working in their own countries, but there are few if any serious analyses of how the organization shapes and is shaped by its national staff. Approaches from organizational sociology and institutional ethnographies could help illuminate this issue, and deepen understanding of IOM's institutional

130 Conclusion

culture, at headquarters and field levels. IOM's internal decision-making processes merit further exploration, particularly in relation to when, why, and how the organization declines requests from its member states; this would shed light on IOM's continued cultivation of institutional autonomy, and evolving conceptions of its obligations and interests. Perhaps most importantly, there is a need to explore the perspectives, experiences, and influence of migrants themselves on IOM, considering how displaced persons and other migrants are not simply on the receiving end of IOM interventions, but also shape perceptions and possibilities for action.

Understanding IOM's contemporary dynamics demands looking more closely at its history, building on important work from scholars such as Venturas and Elie.[7] Independent historical research on IOM is hampered by the fact that it does not have a formally organized, publicly accessible archive, as the UN and most of its major agencies do. Establishing such an archive would be a critical step not only for independent researchers, but for IOM's own continued development into a more serious, orderly, and transparent organization with systems in place to ensure that it can preserve, learn from, and share its own history.

Finally, much of the existing independent research on IOM reflects implicit ideas about what an international organization concerned with migration *should* be doing – legally, ethically, and politically. Drawing out and explicitly contending with normative questions raised by the study of IOM will be an essential step for future research. For example, what are the moral purposes and obligations of IOs generally, and of IOM in particular? How do these relate to IOM's legal obligations? As an organization created and governed by states, should IOM first and foremost serve its members, or migrants themselves – or both? What would this mean, given the diversity and deep divisions within and between states, communities, and individuals on migration policy and ethics, even in the context of humanitarian crises? In the Trump era, plugging the idea that well-managed migration is broadly beneficial seems like more of a political stance than it once did – although authoritarian and populist, anti-migrant governments may be particularly attracted to the idea of migration management as the best way to keep unwanted foreigners out. Should IOM move beyond appeals to states' self-interest based on the benefits of migration to promote freedom of movement within and across borders as a matter of principle? Would this be a smart move strategically, for IOM itself and for the migrants it now claims to serve? Recognizing that IOM is not merely a servant of states but an actor in its own right brings such normative questions to the fore. If IOM is autonomous, at least in part, then it can be subject to moral obligations, in addition to its legal responsibilities. Explicitly grappling with such questions may also help move scholarship on IOM from a position of detached critique to more pointed and constructive engagement, with a view to seeing IOM improve and reform. Of course, some scholars are uninterested in such practical engagements, and doubt the possibility of meaningful reform – but even for those working from such perspectives, it cannot be assumed that the answers to these questions are simple or unimportant.

Implications for policy and practice

This brief introduction raises a host of questions – empirical, normative, and strategic – about the future of IOM. Should IOM seek out a formal mandate to protect migrants' rights? Would this likely translate into strengthened protections for migrants in practice? Should IOM's decentralization and project-based model be revised? If so, in what ways? Should IOM continue to play its jack-of-all-trades role, or transform into a more precisely honed agency? What will be the implications of IOM joining the UN system? I cannot hope to answer these questions here, but in closing I will briefly highlight some of the implications of this analysis for policy and practice, particularly in terms of IOM's structure and governance, potential constitutional changes, implementing internal policies, strengthening policy analysis and evaluation capacities, and promoting accountability.

First, in terms of IOM's structure and governance: Given IOM's dramatic expansion and increasing influence, it needs a better-funded, fully-staffed headquarters that can support the ambitious and important roles IOM now plays in humanitarian governance and migration, including in relation to the Global Compact on Migration. Top-heavy organizations present problems of their own, but there is little risk of this for IOM. As it stands, IOM's headquarters operates on an unsustainable shoe string, reliant on meager assessed contributions and project overheads. As much as IOM prides itself on its leanness and operational focus, a stronger headquarters is needed in order to help overcome some of the problems associated with IOM's decentralization. A stronger headquarters could help ensure more thorough training on key human rights and humanitarian standards throughout IOM; promote more consistent interpretations of and adherence to normative standards and obligations; and help refine or reject involvement in projects with potentially detrimental implications for migrants' rights and well-being. With a more adequately staffed headquarters, IOM could also participate more actively in inter-agency coordination efforts. All this would of course require changes in how states fund IOM. Although these changes are unlikely in the near future, they are necessary if IOM is to effectively execute its manifold roles.

Changes to the IOM Constitution are also highly unlikely in the near future, and are risky in the current political climate of widespread antipathy towards migrants. However, constitutional changes should be considered in order to clarify IOM's protection commitments. Some have suggested that a more fully-fledged protection role for IOM would necessitate the organization taking on responsibility for overseeing a particular convention, such as the Migrant Workers Convention. Given the diverse populations IOM engages, including IDPs, reducing the scope of its protection activities in this way is inadvisable. Rather, a "change to IOM's Constitution to include a clear commitment to promoting and respecting UN human rights standards would be very valuable," grounding the protection-related provisions in the 2016 Agreement between the UN and IOM, and key internal frameworks and policies such as the MCOF, MiGOF, and the

132 Conclusion

2015 Humanitarian Policy.[8] Changing the IOM Constitution would not be a panacea for ensuring that IOM consistently and effectively supports the protection of migrants' rights in practice. Organizations with clear, formal legal protection mandates often fail to uphold them, and wrangling over formal mandates can be a way of sidestepping or deferring practical action to improve protection. Even in the absence of formal constitutional changes, IOM's existing protection commitments and obligations can and should be more forthrightly acknowledged inside and outside the organization, moving past the simplistic and erroneous suggestion that IOM has no protection responsibilities simply because they are not formally enshrined in its Constitution. IOM's designation as a "non-normative" organization, particularly in the 2016 Agreement between the UN and IOM, has raised concerns about how this relates to IOM's protection roles and obligations, and may perpetuate the view that IOM has no protection responsibilities. The IOM Council should formally and explicitly clarify what "non-normative" means, foreclosing the possibility that this designation may be used to undercut IOM's protection responsibilities, including as reflected in frameworks and policies the Council has already approved.

Absent formal constitutional changes clarifying IOM's protection commitments, the internal policies and frameworks related to human rights and humanitarian principles discussed in this book are all the more important. From IOM's perspective, these documents are primarily for internal use, but they are critical to understanding the organization and its obligations, and so should be widely available to and read by those working with organizations that have important stakes in IOM's activities. IOM should make its key frameworks and policies available on a prominent centralized site, so that IOM staff and external actors alike can easily access and work with them. IOM and its member states invested significantly in the development of some of these policies, particularly the MCOF, MiGOF, and the 2015 Humanitarian Policy. IOM's member states should match this initial investment with longer-term support for more systematic, ongoing training for IOM staff across headquarters and field offices on these tools, and the international laws related to them. At the same time, clearer strategies are needed to ensure that IOM's raft of recent policies are effectively implemented and regularly reviewed, and translate into improved practice. The implementation process should be clearly tied to performance reviews and promotions, ensuring that the metric for managerial success in IOM is not merely the capacity to bring in money and execute logistically complex projects, but to uphold the organization's principled commitments. More systematic, high-level, publicly available analyses and evaluations of IOM's programs and policies are also needed, as part and parcel of the implementation process. Many of IOM's projects are externally evaluated, but these reports are not necessarily public, and the focus on discrete projects can deflect attention from broader organizational challenges. To help address this limitation, IOM's member states should support the creation of a unit modeled on UNHCR's former Evaluation and Policy Analysis Unit. This unit could report to the IOM director general on questions of high-level policy analysis and evaluation, moving beyond compendiums listing

Conclusion **133**

the hundreds of activities IOM undertakes in different issue areas to produce more rigorous analyses of defining institutional challenges, with practical recommendations for improvement.[9]

Finally, increased civil society engagement, including with advocacy organizations, is critical to IOM's continued development. IOM's civil society consultations have been growing, but room remains for more open and extensive engagement with NGOs, especially from the global South and the advocacy community. IOM has a somewhat paradoxical reputation of being highly sensitive to criticism but also inured to it. Compared to other major IOs like UNHCR, IOM has generally not engaged as openly with leading advocacy organizations such as Amnesty International, Human Rights Watch, and Refugees International. The agency has often been reluctant to openly discuss its own operations, and has in some cases also been reticent or refused to share data with advocacy organizations if this would reflect badly on governments with whom IOM wants to maintain congenial relationships. In contrast, international organizations like UNHCR and ILO are reportedly less likely to position themselves as protectors of state interests, and are more inclined to provide data to major human rights advocacy organizations, seeing these actors as useful amplifiers of shared human rights concerns who may broach issues that would be sensitive for an IO to raise directly.[10]

And yet engagement between IOM and advocacy NGOs is a two-way street. Most major advocacy NGOs concerned with refugees, IDPs, and other migrants devote remarkably little attention to IOM, even in reports on situations in which IOM plays active and sometimes controversial roles. For example, 27.8 percent of Human Rights Watch reports on displacement and migration from 1998–2017 referenced IOM, but only 14.2 percent analyzed IOM's role even in passing, and a mere 9.1 percent addressed IOM in their recommendations. Amnesty International devoted even less attention to IOM: in the same period, IOM is mentioned in 13.3 percent of Amnesty reports on migration and displacement and its role is analyzed in 10.1 percent of these reports. Only 2.2 percent of Amnesty reports on migration and displacement issue recommendations to IOM. In contrast, UNHCR was a sustained focus of Human Rights Watch and Amnesty advocacy, despite its much smaller target population: 47.7 percent of Human Rights Watch reports on displacement and migration analyze UNHCR's role and 44.9 percent address recommendations to UNHCR; 29.5 percent of Amnesty reports concertedly analyze UNHCR's role, and 21.9 percent make recommendations to UNHCR.[11] This disengagement is striking given IOM's extensive field presence, and concerns about its approach to protection. With the clearer articulation of commitments to human rights and humanitarian principles in its recent frameworks and policies, and in the 2016 Agreement, IOM has set the table for increased accountability efforts. The challenge is for advocacy organizations, as well as scholars concerned about human rights protection, to leverage these commitments to promote increased accountability from IOM, moving beyond reiteration of the fact that IOM does not have a formal protection mandate to instead pursue accountability on the grounds of the policies and frameworks it

134 Conclusion

has adopted. Accountability efforts should not only target IOM as a bureaucracy, but also its member states, calling out those states that contract IOM to roll out programs that restrict migrants' ability to access their rights, and pushing IOM's members to ensure that the organization behaves appropriately. Some have suggested that IOM's entrance into the UN system may have a "blue washing" effect, normalizing interventions with troubling human rights implications. Advocacy NGOs and critically engaged scholars can help limit this possibility by using the increased visibility associated with IOM's membership in the UN system as an opportunity to promote stronger and more systematic protection interventions. IOM is poised to keep growing and accruing influence; external scrutiny and openness to critique are essential to shaping the contours of this growth.

On pleasing no one

The arguments and analysis I have offered in this brief introduction to IOM may please no one. For supporters of the organization, this book may seem to dwell too much on IOM's shortcomings and its failures, downplaying its considerable contributions and the striking ways in which it has developed as an institution, particularly in terms of its extensive involvement with forced migrants and humanitarian response. For advocates and researchers working in the critical tradition that has dominated scholarship and activism on IOM, my analysis may appear to concede too much, and give more benefit of the doubt in assessing IOM's evolution than is deserved. If I have made no one happy, I may well have achieved my goal in troubling assumptions about IOM and highlighting the tensions that shape its work. In a time of reinforced restrictionism, xenophobia, and staggering levels of displacement and migrant abuse, IOM has central if contentious roles to play. My hope is that this work provides a foundation for the continued study of IOM and its influence on these critical challenges, in all their complexity.

Notes

1 António Vitorino, Message to IOM Staff, Geneva, 1 October 2018.
2 Susan Martin, *International Migration: Evolving Trends from the Early Twentieth Century to the Present* (Cambridge: Cambridge University Press, 2014), 145.
3 Nicholas Micinski and Thomas Weiss, "International Organization for Migration and the UN System: A Missed Opportunity," *Future UN Development System Briefings* 42 (2016): 1–4.
4 For further discussion of gaps in research on IOM, see Antoine Pécoud, "What Do We Know About the International Organization for Migration?" *Journal of Ethnic and Migration Studies* 44, no. 10 (2018): 1621–1638.
5 Pécoud, "What Do We Know," 1622.
6 Ibid., 1623, 1628. For one of the few existing studies of IOM's relationship with a particular member state, see Martin Geiger, "Ideal Partnership or Marriage of Convenience? Canada's Ambivalent Relationship with the International Organization for Migration" *Journal of Ethnic and Migration Studies* 44, no. 10 (2018): 1639–1655.
7 Line Venturas, ed., *International "Migration Management" in the Early Cold War: The Intergovernmental Committee for European Migration* (Corinth: University of the

Peloponnese, 2015); Jerome Elie, "The Historical Roots of Cooperation between the UN High Commissioner for Refugees and the International Organization for Migration," *Global Governance* 16 (2010): 345–360.

8 Elspeth Guild, Stefanie Grant and Kees Groenendijk, "IOM and the UN: Unfinished Business," *Queen Mary University of London School of Law Legal Studies Research Papers*, no. 255 (2017): 20.

9 On policy and analysis capacity within IOM, see also Martin, *International Migration*, 139–140.

10 This observation is supported by my interviews with staff members from several major human rights advocacy NGOs.

11 Megan Bradley and Merve Erdilmen, "Speaking of Rights: Protection Norms, Rights-Talk and the International Organization for Migration," Paper presented at International Studies Association Conference, Toronto, March 2019.

SELECTED BIBLIOGRAPHY

Andrijasevic, Rutvica and William Walters, "The International Organization for Migration and the International Government of Borders," *Environment and Planning D: Society and Space* 28, no. 6 (2010): 977–999.

Ashutosh, Ishan and Allison Mountz, "Migration Management for the Benefit of Whom? Interrogating the Work of the International Organization for Migration," *Citizenship Studies* 15, no. 1 (2011): 21–38.

Brachet, Julien, "Policing the Desert: The IOM in Libya Beyond War and Peace," *Antipode* 48, no. 2 (2016): 272–292.

Bradley, Megan, "The International Organization for Migration (IOM): Gaining Power in the Forced Migration Regime," *Refuge* 33, no. 1 (2017): 97–106.

Ducasse-Rogier, Michelle, *The International Organization for Migration: 1951–2001* (Geneva: IOM, 2001).

Elie, Jerome, "The Historical Roots of Cooperation between the UN High Commissioner for Refugees and the International Organization for Migration," *Global Governance* 16 (2010): 345–360.

Frowd, Philippe, "Developmental Borderwork and the International Organization for Migration," *Journal of Ethnic and Migration Studies* 44, no. 10 (2018): 1656–1672.

Geiger, Martin and Antoine Pécoud, eds., *The Politics of International Migration Management* (Basingstoke: Palgrave, 2010).

Georgi, Fabian, "For the Benefit of Some: The International Organization for Migration and its Global Migration Management," in *The Politics of International Migration Management*, eds. Martin Geiger and Antoine Pécoud (Basingstoke: Palgrave, 2010): 45–72.

Guild, Elspeth, Stefanie Grant and Kees Groenendijk, "IOM and the UN: Unfinished Business," *Queen Mary University of London School of Law Legal Studies Research Papers*, no. 255 (2017): 1–24.

Hall, Nina, *Displacement, Development, and Climate Change* (London: Routledge, 2016).

IOM, "The International Organization for Migration: Renewal and Growth Since the End of the Cold War," in *World Migration Report 2011*, ed. IOM (Geneva: IOM, 2011), 93–121.

Selected bibliography **137**

Koch, Anne, "The Politics and Discourse of Migrant Return: The Role of UNHCR and IOM in the Governance of Return," *Journal of Ethnic and Migration Studies* 40, no. 6 (2014): 905–923.

Lazarus, Asher Hirsch and Cameron Doig, "Outsourcing Control: The International Organization for Migration in Indonesia," *International Journal of Human Rights* 22, no. 5 (2018): 681–708.

Martin, Susan, *International Migration: Evolving Trends from the Early Twentieth Century to the Present* (Cambridge: Cambridge University Press, 2014).

Olin, Anders, Lars Florin and Björn Bengtsson, "Study of the International Organization for Migration and its Humanitarian Assistance," *Sida Evaluations* 40 (2008): 1–96.

Pécoud, Antoine, "What Do We Know About the International Organization for Migration?" *Journal of Ethnic and Migration Studies* 44, no. 10 (2018): 1621–1638.

Perruchoud, Richard, "From the Intergovernmental Committee for European Migration to the International Organization for Migration," *International Journal of Refugee Law* 1, no. 4 (1989): 501–517.

Webber, Frances, "How Voluntary Are Voluntary Returns?" *Race and Class* 52, no. 4 (2011): 98–107.

Venturas, Line, ed., *International "Migration Management" in the Early Cold War: The Intergovernmental Committee for European Migration* (Corinth: University of the Peloponnese, 2015).

INDEX

Addis Ababa 31; *see also* IOM, special liaison offices
Afghanistan 47, 53
Africa 7, 8, *31,* 35, 51, 83, 87, 113; *see also* Central African Republic (CAR)
African Union 31
Agreement Concerning the Relationship between the United Nations and the International Organization for Migration 15n39, 22, 99, 117, 124n79, 124n94, 124n96, 125n105; *see also* IOM, UN relations with
Algeria 83, 84
Amnesty International 13n18, 70, 88, 94n37, 97n86, 133
Aristide, Jean-Bertrand 77–8
assisted voluntary return (AVR) 10, 32–3, 35, 45n73, 54, 57, 62, 67, 69, 83, 88; *see also* voluntary humanitarian return (VHR)
authority 12, 48, 58–60, 85; *see also* IOM, moral authority of

Ban Ki-moon 99, 123n52, 123n54
Barnett, Michael 12, 13n16, 16n58, 16nn62–3, 21, 42n1, 42n3, 43n17, 44n40, 48, 58, 71n3, 73nn63–64
border management 26, 34, 60, 65, 77, 83, 84, 127; as border control 11, 32; and humanitarianism 65
Boutros-Ghali, Boutros 103–4
Brachet, Julien 83, 90, 95nn44–5, 96n60, 96n66, 98n99

camp coordination and camp management (CCCM) 56, 60, 80, 90, 94n24, 95n38
camp management agency (CMA) 80; *see also* Haiti
camps *see* camp coordination and camp management (CCCM); camp management agency (CMA)
Canada *28,* 78, 134n6
Carlin, James 25, *34,* 71n7
Castles, Stephen 3
Central African Republic (CAR) 52, 54
Central Emergency Response Fund (CERF) 101, 102, 103
Chief Executives Board for Coordination (CEB) 108, 110, 113, 117, 123n6
children *see* migrant detention; populations of concern; UNICEF
China 20, 25, 124n82
climate change 7, 8, 32, 56, 72n36, 111, 113, 127; Paris Agreement on 113; *see also* disasters; Sendai Disaster Risk Reduction Framework; World Humanitarian Summit
Cold War 20, 35, 54, 102, 105, 119
Colombia 26, *28,* 60
combatants *see* disarmament, demobilization, and reintegration (DRR)
Comfort (US Navy ship) 77
complex emergencies *see* humanitarian emergencies
Comprehensive Nuclear-Test-Ban Treaty Organization (CTBTO) 110

Index **139**

data 9, 31–3, 36, 47–8, 57–9, 61, 77, 80–1, 87–8, 90; *see also* Displacement Tracking Matrix
Democratic Republic of Congo (DRC) 35, 36, 47
Department of Migration Management (DMM) 6, 11, 18, 31–4, 59, 68, 88, 127; *see also* Department of Operations and Emergencies (DOE)
Department of Operations and Emergencies (DOE) 6, 7, 18, 31–4, 37, 45n71, 67–8, 88, 120, 127
deportation 3, 83, 85
detention *see* migrant detention
development 57, 62, 64–7, 69–70, 76, 78–9, 82, 84, 92, 99–100, 102, 108–9, 114, 120, 127–8, 130, 132–3; *see also* humanitarian emergencies; UN Development Group (UNDG); United Nations Development Programme (UNDP)
diaspora 65
directors general of IOM 3, 25, 28, 30, 34, *34*, 77, 116, 129
disarmament, demobilization, and reintegration (DRR) 8, 47, 52, 69
disaster risk reduction 7, 8, 55, 65, 82
disasters 12, 15n42, 21, 47, 54–6, 58, 69, 80–1, 104; *see also* earthquakes; humanitarian emergencies
displacement 5, 7–8, 18, 20, 25, 32, 40–1, 47, 52, 57–8, 65, 77, 79, 101, 109, 113, 133, 134; internal 55–6, 69, 81, 129; *see also* disarmament, demobilization, and reintegration; Displacement Tracking Matrix; internally displaced persons
Displacement Tracking Matrix (DTM) 40, 57–9, 80–2, 87, 92
Directorate for Combatting Illegal Migration (Libya) (DCIM) 87–9
Doctors Without Borders *see* Médecins Sans Frontières
Dominican Republic 77, 78, 82
Doyle, Michael 104–5
durable solutions to displacement 67, 81–2; IASC Framework on 81, 94n34
DynCorp 78

earthquake 1, 47, 55; *see also* Haiti
Ebola 8, 51, 71
economic migrants 2, 127, 129
Elie, Jérôme 5
emergency evacuations *see* humanitarian emergencies

Emergency Response Unit (ERU) 50
ethnic cleansing 86, 119
EU Migration Partnership Framework 86; *see also* Valletta Action Plan
European Union *28*, 53, 83, 115

family reunification 4, 101
Finnemore, Martha 12, 21
foreign workers *see* migrant workers
freedom of movement 5, 20, 101, 130

Gaddafi, Muammar 83–5, 87, 92; *see also* Libya
gender equality 65
Germany *28*, 57
Global Compact on Migration 29, 31, 61, 115, 119, 131
Global Migration Data Analysis Centre (GMDAC) 31, 57
Global Protection Cluster 64
Grandi, Filippo 85
Guantanamo Bay 77
Guiding Principles on Internal Displacement (1998) 55, 80, 94n31; *see also* internally displaced persons (IDPs)
Guild, Elspeth 118
Gulf War 8, 50, 54, 61
Guterres, António 121

Haiti 9, 12; camp closures in 80–2; Cité Soleil 78, 80; cholera outbreak in 79; and colonialism 93n4; Department of Civil Protection 80; earthquake (2010) 12, 55, 79–83, 93n22; housing shortage in 81; National Police 77–8; Port-au-Prince 79–82, 91; rental subsidy cash grants in 82, 90–1; *see also* camp coordination and camp management (CCCM); internally displaced persons (IDPs)
Haiti Stabilization Initiative (HSI) *see* Haiti Transition Initiative (HTI)
Haiti Transition Initiative (HTI) 78–9
Hezbollah 54
housing, land, and property (HLP) 38, 60
human dignity 55, 69, 126
humanitarian emergencies 9, 32, 34, 36, 47, 69; assistance with 2, 7, 49, 65, 67, 87; defined 3; and emergency evacuations 53, 54, 65, 71, 84, 103; post-conflict 7, 9, 14n25, 78; and post-disaster reconstruction 28, 59, 129; response gaps in 8, 21, 38, 40, 50, 52, 69, 80, 127, 134n4; *see also*

140 Index

earthquakes; Ebola; Haiti; internally displaced persons (IDPs); Libya
Humanitarian Evacuation Cell 84
humanitarianism 3, 9, 11, 13n16, 48, 50, 58, 62, 90
humanitarian law 21; *see also* International Committee of the Red Cross (ICRC)
human rights 3, 6–7, 48–9; law 10, 25, 117; obligations 7, 26, 123n58, 124n99; *see also* internally displaced persons; non-normative; protection; United Nations High Commissioner for Human Rights
Human Rights Watch 13n18, 62, 70, 133
human trafficking 3, 6, 45n73, 57, 83; anti- 4, 127

Inter-Agency Standing Committee (IASC) 7, 20, 36–7, 50, 54, 64, 81, 101–2, 108
Intergovernmental Committee for European Migration (ICEM) 4–5, 8, 18, 20, 77, 101–2; *see also* Provisional Intergovernmental Committee for the Movement of Migrants from Europe (PICMME)
Intergovernmental Committee for Migration (ICM) *see* Intergovernmental Committee for European Migration (ICEM)
internally displaced persons (IDPs) 4–5, 7–9, 12, 32, 48, 50, 52, 54–8, 60, 67, 80–4, 86; "cluster system" 9, 56, 80, 94n24; conflation with camp residents in Haiti 81–2; defined 14n32, 80; key IOM policies relating to 65–6; *see also* durable solutions to displacement; humanitarian emergencies; Haiti
International Atomic Energy Agency (IAEA) 108, 110–12
International Committee of the Red Cross (ICRC) 1, 21, 101
International Convention on the Protection of the Rights of Migrant Workers and Members of their Families *see* migrant workers
international human rights law 23, 24, 43n31
International Labor Organization (ILO) 63, 101, 106, 119, 133; *see also* migrant workers
International Organization for Migration (IOM): and accountability 12, 24, 68, 80; asylum policies 43n31, 49, 51, 53–5, 68, 77, 84–8; and borderwork 14n23; and Communist countries 5–6, 20,

101; Constitution of 5–6, 8, 11, 18–21, 24, 35, 55, 60, 68, 131, 132; Council 6, 11, 19, 20, 22, 25, 30, 37, 50, 51, 65, 70, 102, 105, 106, 113, 115, 118, 129, 132; Council resolution 1309 30, 109, 113, 118; decentralization of 18, 40, 66, 131; Development Fund 32, 33, 37, 69; donors 15n42, 26, *28*, 35, 70, 79, 91, 128; Emergency Fund 39; and expert authority 48; funding 12, 32, 33, 37, 39, 52, 69, 107, 131; gender equality in 65, 67; generational differences within 18, 37–9; and Global Compact on Migration 14n23, 29, 31, 57, 61, 115, 119, 131; as humanitarian entrepreneur 12, 48–50, 62, 69, 127; humanitarian policy of 7, 22, 27, 65, 67–9, 85, 92, 132; and human rights 7, 26, 27, 33, 62, 70, 117, 123n58, 128, 131; and immigration 20, 60, 77; insignia of 1; institutional culture of 11, 18, 37, 92, 128; institutional identity of 33; inter-agency reputation of 3, 12, 25, 36, 37, 40, 64, 66, 89, 126; intra-organizational competition 30–4; major humanitarian operations of 47; mission creep 79, 91, 129; moral authority of 58, 60; as multi-mandate agency 77, 91, 107, 127; observer states 25, 102; origins of 1, 4–9, 101; populations of concern 9, 25, 48, 60, 61, 127; projectization system 35; protection 2, 5–6, 11–12, 18, 20–5, 36–9, 48, 61, 62–4, 68, 76, 92, 117, 131–2; regional offices 31, 32, 40, 41, 50; staff 2, 22, 30, 38, 40, 51–2, 56, 58, 62–3, 66, 68, 91, 100, 116–17, 132; special liaison offices of 31; UN relations with 12, 27, 29, 30, 100–2, 104–5, 107, 109–10, 114–15, 117–21, 127; US influence on 3, 9, 11, 18, 28–9, 112, 118; *see also* border management; Department of Migration Management (DMM); Department of Operations and Emergencies (DOE); directors general of IOM; Displacement Tracking Matrix (DTM); housing, land, and property (HLP); humanitarian emergencies; Inter-Agency Standing Committee (IASC); internally displaced persons (IDPs); mandate of IOM; member states of IOM; migrants; Migration Data Portal; non-normative; refugees
international refugee law 61

Index **141**

International Refugee Organization (IRO) 5, 19, 101
International Seabed Authority *see* UN Convention on the Law of the Sea
International Tribunal for the Law of the Sea *see* UN Convention on the Law of the Sea
Iraq 25, 47, 53, 58; invasion of Kuwait 8, 54; US invasion of 58
irregular migration 6, 57, 79, 83–4, 86; *see also* human trafficking
Isaacs, Ken 29

Jordan 53

Kosovo 50

labor migrants 4–5, 8, 12, 32, 47, 50, 54, 61, 84, 128; evacuation of 50, 84; and Migrant Workers Convention 131; *see also* surplus population
Lampedusa 84
Lebanon 25, 53–4
Liberia 35
Libya: 5+5 Ministerial Conference 83, 95n49; IOM–EU Strategic Cooperation Frame-work 86; and IOM membership 84; Joint Operational Framework for Humanitarian Response in 85; and Mediterranean migration 85–6; post-Gaddafi 85–90, 95n56, 98n105; *see also* Libyan Directorate for Combatting Illegal Migration (DCIM); migrant detention; UN Support Mission in Libya (UNSMIL)
Libyan Directorate for Combatting Illegal Migration (DCIM) 87–9
local integration 81; *see also* durable solutions to displacement; refugees

Malawi 47
Malta Declaration (2017) 87
management *see* migration management
mandate of IOM 2–6, 10–12, 18–25, 68, 116, 128–9, 131
Martin, Susan 3
McKinley, Brunson 25, *34*, 35–6, 39, 40, 50, 51, 77, 102, 105–6, 108, 114
Médecins Sans Frontières 1, 88
member states of IOM 1–3, 5–6, 11, 18, 20–1, 23, 25–32, 35, 50–1, 54, 67–8, 70, 102–3, 106, 109, 113–15, 118, 124n82, 128–9, 132; *see also* non-normative

Mercy Corps 38
Micinski, Nicholas 117
Middle East 25, *31*, 60, 124n82; *see also* International Organization for Migration; member states of IOM
migrant detention 3, 39, 84; and slave markets 86; *see also* Libya; repatriation
migrants 4; in post-9/11 context 104–9; *see also* internally displaced persons (IDPs); refugees
migrants in crisis *see* populations of concern
migrant workers *see* labor migrants
Migration Crisis Operational Framework (MCOF) 21–2, 27, 33, 51, 65, 68, 74n91, 85, 92, 131–2
Migration Data Portal 57
Migration Governance Framework (MiGOF) 21–2, 27, 65, 68, 74n91, 131–2
migration management 2, 3, 10, 13n9, 14n25, 33–4, 45n82, 49, 53–4, 59, 62–5, 69, 74n84, 77, 82–3, 88–9, 91, 98n101, 117–18, 120, 127, 129–30; *see also* Department of Migration Management (DMM)
missing migrants *see* Displacement Tracking Matrix
Mohamed, Amina 106

natural disasters *see* disasters
non-normative 23, 26, 30, 118–19, 132
non-refoulement *see* refoulement
North Atlantic Treaty Organization (NATO) 85, 95n56

Office for the Coordination of Humanitarian Affairs (OCHA) 70, 75n111
Office of the United Nations High Commissioner for Refugees (UNHCR) 1, 3, 5, 7–8, 12, 13n18, 15n55, 17, 20–1, 24, 27, 30, 36, 38, 40, 43n14, 44n40, 44n62, 46n108, 48, 52–6, 60–2, 68–9, 72n31, 75n111, 83–9, 92, 96n65, 97n78, 97n92, 100–2, 105, 109, 114, 119–21, 125n108, 128, 132–3
Office of US Foreign Disaster Assistance 51
Operation Mare Nostrum 86
Operation Uphold Democracy 78
Organization for the Prohibition of Chemical Weapons 110

Pécoud, Antoine 110, 123n58
Perruchoud, Richard 5, 20

142 Index

Peru 26, *28*
Port-au-Prince *see* Haiti
Programme de Revitalisation et de
 Promotion de l'Entente et de la Paix
 (PREPEP) 78
projectization 35, 39–41, 51, 91
protection 20–4, 62–8, 101, 109, 117–19,
 126–9, 131–4; *see also* IOM, protection
Provisional Intergovernmental Committee
 for the Movement of Migrants from
 Europe (PICMME) 1, 4–5, 18, 20,
 101–2, 121n11
Purcell Jr., James (Jim) N. 25, *34*, 35, 50,
 102–4, 114

reconstruction 28, 55, 81–2, 129; *see also*
 humanitarian emergency
refoulement 84, 88
Refugee Convention (1951) 86
refugee regime 17
refugees: defined 14n32, 61; Eritrean 83;
 Ethiopian 83; Haitian 77; Iraqi 13n18;
 Palestinian 23–4; repatriation of 19,
 54, 85, 87–90; Rohingya 15n55, 121;
 see also assisted voluntary return
 (AVR); international refugee law;
 refoulement; resettlement
reintegration *see* disarmament,
 demobilization, and reintegration (DRR);
 internally displaced persons (IDPs);
 refugees
related organization 1, 6, 12, 22, 27,
 29, 49, 65, 99–101, 105, 108–15,
 123n59
repatriation *see* assisted voluntary
 return (AVR); refugees; voluntary
 humanitarian return (VHR)
resettlement 1, 15n42, 28, 30, 32, 52–4,
 57, 102–3
restitution 47, 60, 73n61
return migration 3–4, 55, 86, 88, 89;
 see also assisted voluntary return
 (AVR); internally displaced persons
 (IDPs); refugees; Tawergha; voluntary
 humanitarian return (VHR)
Russia 25, 124n82

Sendai Disaster Risk Reduction
 Framework 113
sexual violence 36, 80
Sida (Swedish donor agency) 7, 67;
 see also IOM, donors
specialized agencies 104–13, 115

Stein, Eduardo 120
surplus population 8, 50, 101, 121n11
Sutherland, Peter 99–17
Swing, William (Bill) Lacy 25, 29, 34–7,
 34, 69–70, 77, 89, 99, 102, 109, 113–15,
 117, 119, 121n1, 123n74
Syria 25, 38, 47, 54

Tawergha 86, 96n71
trafficking *see* human trafficking
Trump, Donald 29, 37, 130

United Nations (UN): Charter 110, 112,
 117; Consolidated Appeals Process 101;
 General Assembly Resolutions 23, 102,
 124n103; General Assembly Summit
 for Refugees and Migrants (2016) 109;
 Staff Rules and Regulations 101; *see*
 also IOM, UN relations
United Nations Children's Fund
 (UNICEF) 36, 48, 60, 100
United Nations Convention on the Law of
 the Sea 110
United Nations Department of Economic
 and Social Affairs (DESA) 100, 114
United Nations Department of
 Humanitarian Affairs (DHA) 103
United Nations Development Group
 (UNDG) 108, 114, 117
United Nations Development Programme
 (UNDP) 100
United Nations Economic and Social
 Council (ECOSOC) 110–12, 115
United Nations Educational, Scientific
 and Cultural Organization (UNESCO)
 106, 111
United Nations High Commissioner for
 Human Rights 86, 88
United Nations High Commissioner for
 Refugees, Office of (UNHCR) *see*
 Office of the United Nations High
 Commissioner for Refugees
United Nations Humanitarian Country
 Teams 64
United Nations laissez-passer 108, 113,
 117; *see also* IOM, staff
United Nations Network on Migration
 100, 120
United Nations Relief and Rehabilitation
 Agency 101
United Nations Relief and Works Agency
 for Palestine Refugees in the Near East
 (UNRWA) 23–4

Index **143**

United Nations Stabilization Mission
in Haiti (MINUSTAH) 78; *see also*
Haiti
United Nations Support Mission in Libya
(UNSMIL) 88
United States 5, 7, 11, 18, 25, 28, 29, 67,
77, 115

Valletta Action Plan 86
Venezuela 47, 120
Vitorino, António 10, *34*, 49, 121, 126

voluntary humanitarian return (VHR)
55, 88; *see also* assisted voluntary
return (AVR)

World Bank 106
World Food Programme (WFP) 23, 123n58
World Humanitarian Summit 61, 113
World Migration Report 57
World Trade Organization (WTO) 108,
110–13
World War II 5, 25, 50, 52, 60, 101

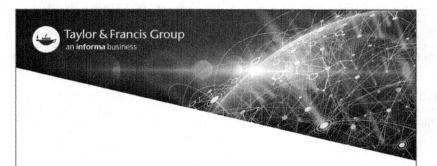